Harold Evensky (Author of *Wealth Management: The Financial Advisor's Guide to Investing and Managing Your Client's Assets*):

"Great ideas, great practice initiatives and a glimpse into the future. *The Cutting Edge* is a terrific collection of wisdom, from one of our profession's preeminent journalists. Bob has done it once again."

"Bob continues to teach, educate and challenge our profession. To quote my nephew, '*The Cutting Edge* rules.' I've read it and will re-read it; if you're in this business, you should too."

Bill Glasgall (Editorial Director, *Investment Advisor* magazine):

"Bob Veres has produced a masterful review of the evolution of the financial planning industry, and has coupled this with a study of the issues, tools and techniques advisors need to be aware of to make their practices thrive in this challenging time."

Richard Koreto (Executive Editor, *Financial Planning* magazine):

"No writer today has studied so intently or thought so deeply about where the planning profession is, or where it is going. Planners may agree with Bob Veres or disagree with him, but they're making a big mistake if they don't read him."

Bob Casey (Editor, Bloomberg *Wealth Manager* magazine):

"Every profession needs a Bob Veres. But only one — financial planning — has him. His new book is the all-you'll-want-to-know introduction to the new, new thing in financial advice: life planning."

David Drucker (Co-author of *Virtual-Office Tools for a High-Margin Practice: How Client-Centered Financial Advisors Can Cut Paperwork, Overhead, and Wasted Hours*):

> "Bob Veres expertly chronicles our profession's evolution, and then shares his insights gleaned over 20 years of listening to the industry's best thinkers."

Joel Bruckenstein (Co-author of *Virtual-Office Tools for a High-Margin Practice: How Client-Centered Financial Advisors Cut Paperwork, Overhead, and Wasted Hours*):

> "Thought-provoking, practical and entertaining. Bob Veres has distilled the best practice management ideas from the industry's leading thinkers into a blueprint for the financial services firm of the future. Highly recommended!"

BY BOB VERES

The CUTTING EDGE
In Financial Services

The
NATIONAL
UNDERWRITER
Company
PROFESSIONAL PUBLISHING GROUP

P.O. Box 14367 • Cincinnati, Ohio 45250-0367
1-800-543-0874 • www.nationalunderwriter.com

ISBN: 0-87218-622-9

Library of Congress Control Number: 2002116488

TABLE OF CONTENTS

DEDICATION

This book is dedicated to all of you in the financial services world who have demonstrated the courage to question what you were told, and the even greater courage to put your clients' interests ahead of all the other agendas that you're routinely presented with. May you prosper, and may the future come to you.

ACKNOWLEDGEMENTS

We might as well start with April Caudill, because I would never have written this book if she hadn't brought up the idea four or five times, and finally found the words to convince me to write it. And Sonya King did a great job of editing my sometimes clumsy prose, and of turning a raw manuscript into a book.

Wherever possible, I have tried to recognize the people who donated their insights by putting their names directly in the text of the book. You will soon see that they represent many excellent, thoughtful practitioners from all over the financial services world.

But credit must also be given to the people who have taken the time to share their thoughts and ideas, and whose thoughts and ideas became part of my own. My writing technique is to attempt (as much as possible) to suspend my own understanding and let people fill my mind with their perspectives, and then let the most compelling (best?) of these perspectives "win" without imposing my own prejudices on them.

Over the years, it seems that an uncommon number of the most persuasive ideas and best thinking have come from the following individuals, whose voices appear invisibly throughout this book and my writings at large: Roger Gibson, Ross Levin, Roy Diliberto, Linda Lubitz, Elissa Buie, John Henry McDonald, Jack Blankinship, Larry Carroll, Mike Ryan, Phil Johnson, Stan Hargrave, Margie Welder, Nancy Langdon Jones, Eric Bruck, Eileen Sharkey, Bob Willard, Andy Hudick, Alex Armstrong, Dave Polstra, Margie Mullen, Cynthia Meyers, Norm Boone, Marilyn Capelli Dimitroff, Elaine Bedel, Mark Tibergien, Henry Montgomery, Greg Sullivan, Bill Carter, Dave and Deena Diesslin, Deena Katz, Judy Shine, Rick Adkins, Mary Malgoire, Johnne Syverson, Barry and Mark Freedman, Glen Buco, John

Brown, Charlie Haines, Isabel Smith, Ray Ferrara, Curt Weil, Jon Guyton, Katharine McGee, Diane MacPhee, Steve Hample, Dave Drucker, Joe Kopczynski, Judy Lau, Cicily Maton, Myra Salzer, Brian Grodman, Lew and Karen Altfest, Peggy Ruhlin, Bart Francis, Brent Hicks, Ron Roge, Michael Zmistowski, Chris Cooper, Lou Stanasolovich, Rick Kahler, Lynn Hopewell, Paul Fain, Bob Wacker, Bill Morrissey, Tom Grzymala, Bill Bengen, Don Phillips, Warren Mackensen, Guy Cumbie, Henrietta Humphreys, Bob Maloney, Peg Downey, Alan Brown, Bill Glasgall, Bert Whitehead, Bob Dreizler, Joel Bruckenstein, Ron and Suzette Rutherford, Bart Boyer, Dave Foster, Cheryl Holland, Bill Prewitt, Janet Briaud, Lloyd LeVine, Steve Morris, Marilyn Falls, Greg Galecki, Jim Johnson, Troy Jones, Scott Kahan, Ginger Applegarth, Ed Olsen, Diahann Lassus, Jeannie Robinson, Jack McCord, Bob Casey, Steve Leimberg, Karin Stifler, David Brand, Carol Nowka, Richard Koreto, David Yeske, Mimi Lord, Graham Rich, Judi Martindale, Liz Pulliam Weston, Kathleen Day, Neal Solomon, Paula Kennedy, Mary Sullivan, Geoff Davey, Harv Ames, Jason Zweig, Dave Bohannon, Laurie McClain, Andy Gluck, Sydney LeBlanc, Phyllis Bernstein, Mike Haubrich, Dave Foster, David Williams, Mark Nickell, Marv Tuttle, Mike Chasnoff, Steve Johnson, Dave Strege, Karen Ramsey, Bob and Peg Eddy, Elizabeth Jetton, Al Barnes, Jay Lewis, Scott Neal, Jean Sinclair, Marcee Yager, Greg Friedman, Chuck Jaffe, Tom Connelly, Janet McCallen, Ed Shobe, Deborah Thomas, Steve Weinstein, Susan Bradley, George Kinder, Barbara Culver, Bill Howard, Don Trone, Mary Rowland, Dick Vodra, Bruce Berno, Skip Schweiss, John Lame, Eric Flett, Tracy Beckes, Ted Roman, George Gay, Kathleen Cotton, Bob Barry, Rick Volpe, Stephen Barnes, Rick Kagawa, John Cammack, Harry Kasanow, Joe Piellucci, Dennis Stearns, Bob Clark, Kate Campbell, Robert Levitt, Lincoln Pain, Iris Dayoub, Laura Schoenborn, Ken Ziesenheim, Bob Thompson, Dan Moisand, Krista Lindberg, Bruce Heling, Gretchen Hollstein, Brent Kessel, Kathleen Rehl, Scott Leonard, Richard Sincere, Tom Wirtshafter, Don Rembert, Olivia Mellan, Nancy Nelson, George Taylor, Bill Ramsay, Bobbie

Munroe, Chip Roame, Harold Holcombe, Glenn Kautt, Vern Hayden, Wendy Conlin, Cindy Conger, Bill Jahnke and Eleanor Blayney.

I am grateful to their contributions, not just to this book, but to my thought processes themselves. Nobody could have interacted in any significant way with this group of people and not come away much smarter and wiser than he or she was before.

Finally, I'm grateful to the subscribers of my *Inside Information* service, who have made it possible for me to stop and sit and think without wondering where my next meal was going to come from.

INTRODUCTION

Thee's an old, old story – I'm sure you've heard it – about two woodcutters who live near each other in (where else?) the woods. They make their living by cutting down trees and sawing the wood into lumber, and (economics being what it is) the more they cut and saw, the more money they earn.

In this sense, their business is a lot like those of us in the financial services world. Productivity and effectiveness are the key variables to generating income.

In the beginning of this story, both of the woodcutters are earning roughly the same income and enjoying roughly the same productivity. But gradually, one of the woodcutters begins to outpace the other one. After a few years, he is producing nearly twice as much lumber as the slower woodcutter – and, surprisingly, he is also working fewer hours and enjoying more leisure time with his family.

His secret is that he takes some time, each and every day, to sharpen his saw.

The interesting part of the story is that the other woodcutter knows this secret. But he still continues to work with the dull blade, for many additional hours every day.

Why? He's trying to catch up, and because he is so far behind, he doesn't feel like he can afford to take the time to stop and sharpen his saw.

The Raw Ingredients of Success

I'm a writer in the financial planning world, and I see this simple story played out every day in thousands of offices around the country. Most financial advisors I know work very hard and are focused on helping their clients solve their problems. Some are financially successful and their business growth seems effortless. Others keep their noses to the grindstone and never seem to rise above the piles of work on their desks.

The difference between the two is that the successful advisors never forget to take the time to sharpen their professional tools. They stay aware of new ideas and innovations. They anticipate change, rather than getting blindsided by it. They attend conferences and talk with their professional peers.

By these simple habits, they reenergize themselves and remain aware of why they got into the business in the first place.

Sharpening the saw is also, as we'll see later in this book, about creating systems and procedures that automate things that don't absolutely require the advisor's work time. It is amazing how many financial planners will bill themselves out at the equivalent of $200 an hour, and spend hours a day on the kind of work that they could easily delegate to an employee who is happy to earn $10 or $15 an hour.

This book is not *about* sharpening your saw; by reading it, you *are* sharpening your saw. It is a collection of thoughts, ideas and wisdom from planning practitioners around the country. I guarantee that if you read it, you will find not one, or two, or three good ideas, but dozens that will help you provide better service to your clients, to become better-known in your community, and to do more with less work.

More importantly, this book will offer you a guide to the future of your profession. When change comes, you'll see it coming from afar, and you'll be ready for its challenges and opportunities.

These thoughts, ideas, innovations and wisdom are the raw ingredients of success – not only of financial and personal success, but also the ability to successfully effect positive changes in your clients' lives.

The two, of course, are related. If you are very good at help-ing people make changes for the better, you will tend to be very successful financially. There's another feedback mechanism at work as well: practitioners who can watch their clients grow and blossom and make progress tend to earn very high psychic rewards, and tend to glow with fulfillment and confidence. This too attracts clients and customers, who sense the aura of success and personal satisfaction of many jobs well done.

The Fatal Flaws of Journalism

In my 20 years of talking with financial advisors, I have learned something very powerful: that the financial services pro-fession is a living laboratory that produces great, practical ideas and innovations every day in thousands of different practices around the country.

The question is: how do you find out about these successful innovations?

One way, as I said earlier, is to go to conferences, which gen-erally attract the most active, flexible, innovative people in any profession. I personally attend 20 conferences a year, and my constant technique is to get groups of people together in the hall-ways, ask a question and let the people in the group talk.

But this is really not a very efficient process – especially for the professional who only goes to one or two conferences a year.

A New System

Is there a better way?

I think there is. This book is a product of that "better way."

Let me explain.

As a financial writer, I've always been extremely dissatisfied with the way my own profession delivers information. You can see it yourself: magazine and newspaper writers are very seldom as knowledgeable as the professionals they cover, and they usually have certain biases in the things they write.

Am I right?

What's worse is the way journalists deliver their information. Like gods, they throw informational thunderbolts down from Mount Journalistic Olympus to a passive audience. There is very little interaction with the readers, and no real accountability except the very short letters-to-the-editor section that hardly anybody reads.

And of course, the writers of our trade magazines very seldom get at the information that people like you could really benefit from: real world reports from real world professionals on how their experiments are going in the laboratory that we call the financial services profession. When trade writers do run across a terrific client services idea, or a way to outsource rote chores in the office, they don't always understand the concept, because they don't practice financial planning themselves.

It seemed to me that, in the age of the Internet, we could create a much better system of collecting and using information. So I started experimenting with the (quite radical) idea of being truly accountable to my professional audience, and interacting with them directly on a daily basis.

The idea was to create the equivalent of those hallway conversations at conferences, using the communications power of the Internet.

It works like this: I have roughly 1,500 paid members to an information service that I call *Inside Information*, and for a modest fee ($179 a year, if you must know), they receive synopses of any relevant articles in the financial press, and also (this is the innovative part) weekly messages.

Often, a financial advisor suggests the topic of these messages, who will say (for example):

"I'm in the process of hiring a coach to help me improve my practice and my life. But I don't have any idea where to start looking for one. Could you ask the group where they find a business coach or personal business trainer? And what their experiences were when they were being coached?"

Or: "I'm worried that with improvements in health care and the possibility of dramatically increasing longevity, my retirement plans are going to blow up. I have clients who are retiring at age 55, who might live to age 120. Their retirement assets might have to last them 65 years. Has anybody done any thinking on this subject? And if so, what have they come up with? What is a safe amount to take out in distributions, and how do they structure the distribution planning?"

Or: "I've been working in this business for 10 years, and I consider myself to be a starving idealist. I have never achieved financial success because I am constantly trying to give to my clients more benefit than I receive in compensation. How can I get out of this professional rut?"

Wisdom Collection

Being a journalist, I have no idea what the answer is to these questions. If I were a *traditional* journalist, I would talk to a couple of people who have been quoted before on the subject, misunderstand a lot of what they said and dismiss some of their really important points, and finish the article in a week or two.

Now I do it differently. Now, I send out a discussion of the subject to the members of the *Inside Information* community, in an e-column that they get in their e-mailbox.

I ask for feedback. What is it that I don't know about this subject?

The members of my readership are the sorts of people who go to one or two conferences a year, and are generally among the most thoughtful people in the profession. Yet on any given topic, 90% of them won't have an answer at their fingertips. They read the topic, realize that they are not alone in not knowing the answer, and get on with their practices. Just knowing that others are asking the same questions that they are, or just seeing a good question posed well is, to many thoughtful people in this business, a valuable service all by itself.

The other 10% will have already thought about this question in some depth.

These people will share with me, in more or less detailed e-mail responses, what they've learned. In a typical week, I'll receive 200 responses from advisors all over the country, who will offer information, advice and ideas that I, frankly, would never have thought of.

These will take the discussion in entirely new directions. And in the next e-column, I'll report what they said. The feedback loop is quick, very powerful, and (by design) it doesn't take long for the members of the community to stay on top of what we're learning.

I have learned that the very best, most useful responses are those that show how I, personally, was wrong in my initial assumptions and conclusions. Generally, my opinions tend to run with the conventional wisdom (I think that's true of all of us), and so, when thoughtful practitioners show me that this conventional wisdom is incorrect or outmoded, we learn something outside of our collective box.

The entire profession moves forward in interesting and useful ways.

Week in, week out, we learn incredibly interesting, profound lessons from the laboratory that is the financial services profession. And sometimes the answer to the first question will lead to a better question. We learn how to find a coach, but the next issue is: how do we, ourselves, become more coachable? How do we prepare ourselves to make the changes that we have decided we want to make, given all the clutter of our daily lives?

Then: how can we learn to effect positive changes in the lives of our clients? As we become coached, as we uncover ways to improve our lives, how can we add some of what we've learned to our professional services?

I think this is what journalism was meant to be. I think someday, all writers will interact with their audiences directly, and will draw on the collective wisdom of their readership to create a far more useful service than anything the journalistic profession has ever offered before. The Internet is making this possible; the only thing holding my profession back is its own inertia.

The Tool to Sharpen the Saw

This book is a collection of those messages that I've received, and the wisdom that has come out of them. It was created with the direct involvement of a cast of thousands, of many of the best and most thoughtful people in the financial services profession. Even those insights and ideas and suggestions that seem to come from me (the first part of the opening chapter, which gives an overview of future changes, for example) is really a synthesis of the best thinking of professional advisors out there in the real world – thoughtful people who have found ways to sharpen their saws and were willing to share what they learned with the rest of us.

My role was to create a system where the insights could come together in one place, where they could be harvested and then passed back out to the community. Through my e-columns, I have helped the financial services profession recapture its collective wisdom, and to give it back to the individuals who make it up.

In addition, I have helped people to see the future, because the future is what works. If somebody has come up with an insight or innovation that is working well for her, then you are going to see a lot more of it.

As we identify great ideas and great practice innovations, we are looking at the future of the profession.

This book is another outlet for those insights, for that wisdom. It is a collection of what we've talked about in those e-conversations, and what we've learned over two years of creating a better, sharper tool for gathering relevant information.

As I said earlier, my career in the financial planning world goes back more than 20 years. I have never seen a time where there was more change, more opportunity, more demand for your services than there is today. It is a time when those who take a few minutes to sharpen their professional saws can make a profound difference in the world, and enrich their lives and the lives of their clients.

Your practice is the saw, and this book is the tool to sharpen it with.

Let's get started.

Bob Veres
Inside Information
bobveres@yahoo.com
http://www.bobveres.com

1 OUTLINING THE FUTURE

I f you review the history of the planning profession, you'll find that the profession has moved in boom and bust cycles that look an awful lot like the well-discussed cycles of the U.S. economy. Planners have experienced powerful expansion periods like the mid-1960s, the early 1980s and, of course, the very mellow business climate of the 1990s. And there were times (e.g., the late 1960s, early 1970s, the last four years of the 1980s, and the first two years of the new millennium) when a lot of people got caught up in the boom, recommended too much of the wrong stuff, and either got sued out of the business or lost their credibility in their communities.

Not surprisingly, financial planners boom and bust, too – just like the economy.

The financial services profession is about to enter a new professional cycle. If you can understand what that cycle will look like, and the services that will be offered by leading-edge professionals, and the practice management issues that will be addressed there, then you will be able to move into the future with a clear vision. You will be able to anticipate the changes that are coming, instead of (as people have done in past cycles) reacting to them by making abrupt, painful changes, and by constantly feeling blindsided.

I think this may be the first time that the financial planning profession has had a chance to see what's coming in the *next* 10 years. This could be important because, if I'm right, these next 10 years will see more change coming faster and harder than any comparable time in the history of the profession.

Put another way, there could be dangerous times ahead. However, there also might be fantastic opportunities for those advisors who see the outlines of the profession-wrenching changes the planning world is about to go through, and who can gradually adapt to it, while others are buried in the work on their desk just waiting to be blindsided.

The Professional Cycle of the 1980s: Tax Planning

To understand the changes that are coming our way, we need to take a quick look backward and see what we've learned from the professional cycles that have come before.

Let's start with the professional cycle that ran its course back in the 1980s.

If you have a little gray hair on your head, you may remember that during the very early 1980s, the entire financial services profession was really struggling. We were coming off of a bust cycle that was characterized by low returns on equities for the previous *17 years!* Think of it – during the period from the end of 1964 to the end of 1981, the U.S. gross national product (now known as the gross domestic product) rose a total of 373%, yet the Dow Jones Industrial Average closed the end of 1964 at 874.12, and finished calendar year 1981 at 875.00.

No wonder *Business Week* wrote a 1982 cover story entitled "The Death of Equities."

For financial salespeople (who *were* the financial services profession at the time), this was not a great environment to be recommending stocks. Today there is a great deal of commission bashing in the press and around the profession, but it is helpful to remember that commissions are a great way to compensate people operating in that kind of climate. With commissions, you only get paid after you have gotten the client to take action. Those commission-compensated advisors who managed to convince their clients to take action and invest in stocks or mutual funds – at a time when every bit of recent history argued powerfully against it – gave advice that was worth much more than whatever commissions they earned. Over the next 17 years (1981-1998) the Dow rose from 875 to 9,181.43.

People who were lucky enough to run across a persuasive commission-compensated advisor in those dark days were the ones who were able to pay for their children's educations and fund a prosperous retirement.

But in the early days of that 1980s cycle, professionals were struggling to make a living. So, as the usual last resort during periods of professional darkness, a few brave practitioners asked their clients what services *they* wanted from their advisors.

And their clients said, "Well, you know, I've noticed that the top marginal tax bracket is around 90%, and it would be great if some of that money I'm paying the government could be invested on my behalf instead."

The advisors who listened to their clients went out and created a new service for which there was no business model – tax planning. Their early efforts spawned the great age of tax shelter investments. And as we climbed out of the previous professional bottom toward the top of that cycle, there were many well-structured investments and some very sophisticated tax work offered to planning clients.

And then the cycle turned downwards, and thousands of tax shelter products were born – and (this is an important point) over the course of the next 10 years, tax planning became the dominant, top-of-the-menu service in the planning profession.

Tax planning and the commissions earned from limited partnership sales paid for the rest of the financial planning services that were offered to consumers during the professional cycle of the 1980s.

Here's a very important thing to notice about that cycle: people gradually began to *specialize* in tax planning, and gave up the much harder work of full-service financial planning.

This specialization made good business sense because tax planning and earning generous 8% to 10% commissions on investment programs that practically sold themselves, combined with due diligence trips to exotic locations, was much more profitable than the difficult job of full-service financial planning.

My guess is that you know what happened next. The tax laws changed in 1986, making it much more difficult to deduct the pass-through losses arising from limited partnership programs. In the summer of 1986, before the Tax Reform Act had been signed by then-President Reagan, I wrote an article for *Financial Planning* magazine. The cover art showed a giant wrecking ball falling onto the unsuspecting tax shelter investors and planners who sold these programs. In the article, I talked about whether it made sense to make the next staged pay-in investment into investments with greatly reduced tax benefits. (In many cases, it didn't.)

What was obvious to me became obvious to everybody else over the course of the next two years. The limited partnership products all blew up, their promoters went out of business, and thousands of financial advisors tumbled into the bust part of the professional cycle.

One of the important lessons we learned from that cycle is that abandoning the full-service, diversified financial planning relationship is not a good long-term business strategy, no matter how attractive it looks in the short-term.

Everybody who had specialized in tax planning suddenly didn't have a business any more. Many of the specialists who had abandoned full-service financial planning were driven out of the profession altogether. Roughly one out of every four planners was gone within two years. That is not a good survival rate. It is about the same percentage of fatalities as Europe experienced during the Black Death plague in the 14th century.

Who were the survivors? The people who had continued to practice full-service financial planning, even though it wasn't the most efficient or lucrative way to run their businesses.

And here's another lesson that we learned from the 1980s: If you want to understand the next cycle, look for the "visionaries" who have turned to their clients and asked for guidance, and then used that information to begin pioneering new services with no business model or clear idea where the money is going to come from.

The "visionaries" in the profession at the beginning of the tax planning cycle were the early tax planners, who began to delve into the complex nuances of the tax code and find solutions for their clients. The next cycle was defined by a small niche group of practitioners who turned their backs on the lucrative tax shelter business and, instead, pioneered a new service called "assets under management." They managed primarily mutual fund portfolios for their clients, even though there were no back office solutions available to them until the Schwab organization began accepting institutional accounts half a decade later.

The Professional Cycle of the 1990s: Assets Under Management

Today we are at the end of that assets under management cycle, and the beginning of a new one. Let's say, for the sake of this book, that the assets under management cycle ended yesterday.

In many ways, this last cycle was the same story all over again. For the last 12 years or so, assets under management has paid for most of the financial planning services offered to clients. Asset management replaced tax planning as the top-of-the-menu service offered by financial advisors. And as the cycle reached its height and consumers began clamoring for the new service, many planners realized that they could be a lot more profitable if they abandoned the hard, messy planning activities, and simply specialized in managing client assets.

And then, as I'm sure you've noticed, the markets went down and kept going down until, suddenly, we found ourselves in the middle of the worst bear market since 1973-74 (some say the worst since the 1930s). As you read this, a lot of people in the financial services business are being shaken out of the profession. Not nearly as many as the last cycle, but the purge still has a way to go before it's finished.

Once again, the specialists are being shaken out, and the full service planners have not only survived the bust phase of the cycle, but (as we'll see later) have even prospered a bit. But it is the "visionaries" – the ones who seem to have no business sense – who will define the new mainstream service of the planning profession.

Asset Management in the Background

This is the creative destruction and rebirth of the profession. The interesting thing to me is that in every cycle, financial planning looks a lot different than it did in the last one.

Once we were primarily tax planners; then, just a very few short years afterwards, tax planning was at most a background part of the financial planner's service menu, and asset management became the dominant service.

Now let's look at the future. The first thing we know about these professional cycles is that whatever paid for financial planning in the last cycle won't be a good source of revenues for the next one. (If you don't believe this, then let's have a show of hands among all the readers of this book. How many of you earned a substantial part of your income from the sales of tax shelters in any year since 1990?)

I have every reason to believe that a change of this magnitude will happen again – very soon. In fact, as you'll see in a minute, the change has already begun. I also have every reason to believe that within two or three years, asset management services will be a background service, and that it will not pay for your financial planning services. Now how could this be? What could possibly cause that to happen? Let me give you one quick piece of evidence.

The Incredible Shrinking Risk Premium

Last December, twelve financial advisors and I attended a briefing in New York City at the invitation of TIAA-CREF executives Marty Leibowitz and Brett Hammond, who told us about a summit meeting of the leading academics who study equities returns. These academics, some with considerable real world experience, had gathered to talk about the risk premium on equities – which is another way of saying the expected future return, after inflation, above a riskless return, on equities going forward. The attendees included:

- Stephen Ross of MIT's Sloan School of Management;

- Roger Ibbotson of Yale;

- Campbell Harvey and Ravi Bansal of Duke University's Fuqua School of Business;

- John Campbell of Harvard;

- Robert Shiller of Yale;

- Richard Thaler and Rajneesh Mehra of the University of Chicago;

- Clifford Asness, Managing Principal of AQR Capital Management;

- Jeremy Siegel at Wharton;

- Robert Arnott, Managing Partner (with Peter Bernstein) of 1st Quadrant Corp.;

- Brad Cornell of the Anderson School at UCLA; and

- Bill Reichenstein of Baylor University.

At the end of the meeting, Leibowitz and Hammond took a poll of what these people thought the risk premium was today – which means what they think the after-inflation, above risk-free return on stocks will be over the next 10-15 years. Their answer: 0% to 4% a year. Jeremy Siegel, the raging bull of the group, set the risk premium at 4% a year.

At our summary meeting a month later, Roger Gibson and Harold Evensky (both prominent trade authors and investment thinkers) reconstructed these numbers into the language of consumers. If inflation averages 2% a year, and inflation-protected Treasuries (TIPS) are delivering a risk-free 3% a year, then these academics are talking about nominal returns of 5% to 9% a year – with an emphasis on the lower side of the scale.

This consensus becomes even more significant when you realize that the academics at this meeting approach the risk premium question from many different angles. Some look at the capacity for economic growth in the economy, and project the possible boundaries on the future expansion of corporate earnings. Some look at trends in the corporate world itself. Others look at historical numbers and averages. Still others are evaluating investor and market psychology.

And they all, perhaps for the first time in history, are in rough agreement that the returns achieved over the last 17 years are unlikely to be repeated in the near future.

What happens if this strange academic consensus is right? One consequence is that the industry standard 1% management fee is going to be much more noticeable than it was in the past. It is going to be much harder to charge 1% of assets when the assets are generating 2% a year real returns, than it was when clients were earning 15% or 20% or more, year-in and year-out.

Second, planners typically communicate the planning progress of their clients with what document? With the quarterly report on their investment performance – which, by the way, communicates implicitly (although not verbally) that the financial advisor's primary value lies in helping clients achieve a high rate of return in the equities markets.

If the markets make it impossible for you to achieve a high rate of return for your clients, and clients are receiving that implied message from you, then clients will probably begin to grow dissatisfied that you aren't doing what they expect and pay you to do. That will force advisors to begin offering and communicating other services.

When you see that, the next cycle will be under way.

Conclusion: The Question of the New Cycle

So the question before us today is: what will financial advisors *be* and *do* over the next ten years? If history is any guide at all, the profession is going to transform itself with sudden, shocking speed into something else altogether different once again.

If I can tell you what that is (with the help of thoughtful members of the planning community), then you will be among the few who can make the transition with your eyes open.

As it happens, the nature of this transformation is not as difficult to discern as you might expect. In fact, from our discussions, it appears that more than a few members of the *Inside Information* community are already beginning to practice in the next professional cycle.

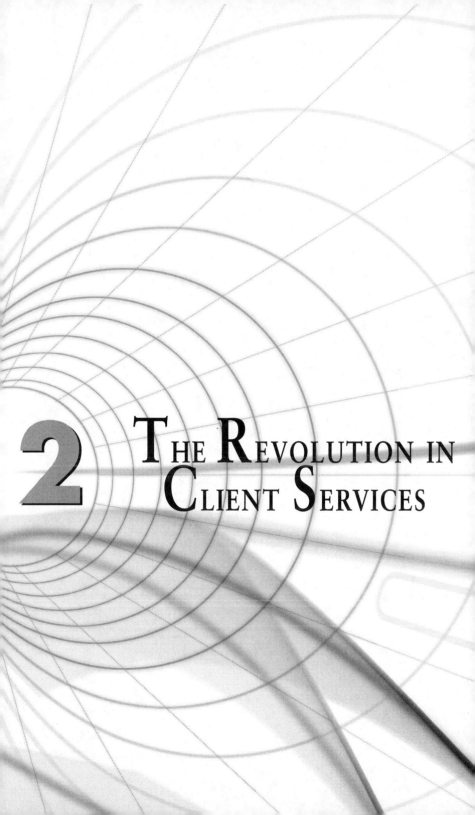

2 THE REVOLUTION IN CLIENT SERVICES

I f you look back over the previous professional cycles, you will notice that the only really major change, cycle to cycle, has been the top-of-the-menu service. This is an enormously important change, to be sure, but it tends to obscure the fact that in each cycle financial services clients will always need a full range of services, and the full range won't change very much.

So let's nail down one of the things we already know about the future: it will be just as important as it has always been for the planner (or firm) to have a solid grounding in retirement planning, estate planning, and tax planning. Furthermore, the planner must be able to handle the risk management and investment services that have always been important components of a full-service financial planning engagement. The ability to handle the nuts and bolts of planning, and to bring in focused specialists as needed, will be crucial to success in the future, cycle after cycle after cycle.

In the past, clients would seek out a professional to handle their tax planning, and if they were lucky, they got a financial plan plus a broad range of advice on all their personal finances. Then, in the new cycle, clients would seek out a professional to handle their investments, and if they were lucky, they received service and advice in every financial area they needed it. Now, going forward, they are going to come to you for something else altogether. But your service will still include the broad range of planning activities that you (hopefully) offer today.

I think this is great news for financial advisors who are nervous about their ability to adapt to the new cycle. As we talk about the new top-of-the-menu service, it will be easy to lose sight of the fact that the top-of-the-menu service tends to be a facade for all the rest of the financial planning services.

It will also be easy to become intimidated by focusing on what is different, when, in fact, much of the engagement will be very similar to what you do today for your clients.

The Service of the Future

To find the dominant new service that defines the next cycle, we do what we did in the last cycle and the one before it – we look for the "visionaries." We look for people who have asked their clients (as the usual last resort) what services they want from their professional advisor, and have listened to the answers without any preconceived boundaries.

How do we identify today's visionaries, those persons who will define the *new* business cycle in financial services? These people asked their clients what they wanted from a professional advisor. And their clients said, in one way or another, something new, something we haven't heard before: *I want a better life.* These are the persons who, today, are pioneering "life" planning services.

Post-Affluent Issues

Interestingly, the planning profession itself may be responsible for this yearning for a better life that seems to be emerging from every direction all at once. The planning profession was born with an important and powerful mission – to fight poverty at some of its most persistent root causes. For the last 30 years, financial planners have helped thousands (and perhaps millions) of people to spend less than they earn, invest in an organized (rather than haphazard) way, avoid short-term trading and hot stocks or funds, and control the risks of death and disability in the family.

And, perhaps not totally as a coincidence, in the past 30 years, people have created and accumulated more wealth than in all the rest of history combined.

And what now? There has been a muted rumbling in the consumer press about people suffering from a kind of "post-affluence syndrome," where people suddenly realize that successfully accumulating more money didn't really address their happiness in any direct way. The old saw that "money can't buy happiness" was never before directly experienced by as many people (perhaps millions), more or less simultaneously, until now.

Now, for these people, a quiet, still-unconscious consensus has emerged that something is missing in all the retirement and investment and tax planning – and this missing element is only clearly visible after the retirement, investment and tax planning have been successful.

Listen carefully; you can hear this background murmur rippling through society. *What do I do now? I should be happy, but I'm still doing the same things I did before I had these financial resources. I'm still the same person.*

How can my financial advisor help me address these post-affluent issues of my life?

Name Games

The service that addresses the issue of "how to have a better life" has been labeled "life" planning as a quick way to distinguish this emerging service from "tax" planning, "estate" planning or "retirement" planning. The name has attracted some controversy. For technicians (i.e., professionals who are well grounded in the technical aspects of financial planning), the term "life" planning implies an open-ended engagement that has virtually no limits and no definitions. "It sounds like the ultimate triumph of form over substance," as one advisor told me in one of our e-mail discussions. "What, exactly, are we doing? Implementing peoples' dreams? Fulfilling their fantasies? How can I get my arms around a service that doesn't seem to have any clear objectives?"

Others are concerned that the term "life" planning will replace the term "financial" planning, rather than taking its place alongside "retirement" planning, "tax" planning, and "estate" planning as one of the subsets of the total client engagement.

Several competing terms are emerging, but none of them seems to be a significant improvement. Rick Kahler, who practices in Rapid City, South Dakota, prefers the term "goals clarification," but acknowledges that this term really describes the first step in what should be a lifelong ongoing service. Dick Wagner, who practices in Denver, is a strong advocate of "integral" planning since the service, in its ideal form, integrates life and money, goals and relationships, and exterior (physical) and interior (psychological) needs. Marcee Yager calls the service "interior" planning to distinguish the psychological components and psychware tools (more on that in a minute) from the procedural work that planners have traditionally done.

The subject of what to call the new service is an important one that deserves more attention than we can give it here. At this point, let's stipulate that "life" planning (we're going to drop the quotation marks for the rest of the book) is defined for the purposes of this book as a subset of financial planning (like retirement, estate and tax planning). And we'll further stipulate that it may not be the right name for the service.

Unlimited Demand

Is life planning a viable service? Advisors in the *Inside Information* community who are exploring the life planning service have been startled by how quickly and eagerly some clients have embraced it. They are beginning to believe that the emerging service is leading the profession to a much more important place in the community than it has ever been before.

Why? First, because they've found most people have never actually explored their personal goals. In fact, most of them have no idea that they have power and control over the circumstances of their lives.

Incredible as this may sound, the average person feels like a prisoner to circumstances beyond his or her control, and is moving unhappily through a life dominated by the agendas of others.

After going through the goal-setting exercises and recognizing what they want out of life, and that these things may be achievable, there is an actual difference in the clarity of the client's vision and in his or her awareness of the world around them. It is like an awakening!

When people begin to recognize that they can change their circumstances and achieve fulfillment and happiness, rather than just earn money and retire early, then the demand for the "helping achieve a better life" service will be virtually universal. After all, who in this world *doesn't* want a better life?

"Unlimited demand" is an impressive place to be from a marketing standpoint. And it is certainly a step up from the traditional lament that most people don't value the financial planning service enough to pay for it.

Looking around, some planners realized that there is (astonishingly) no mechanism for addressing these fundamentally crucial issues in the personal lives of world citizens. No profession is devoted to it; no service platform exists to address it.

Is that really true? Look around you. Who else is working to help people achieve better and more fulfilling lives? Lawyers? (That suggestion should at least bring an amused smile to your face.) Doctors? (This isn't what they're trained to do.) Accountants?

Four Qualifications

In our discussions within the *Inside Information* community, advisors have identified four factors that make the readers of this book the logical professionals to help people achieve better lives:

1. The planning profession is trained to deal with the procedural issues of navigating through the very complicated financial landscape, which may be the biggest obstacle for most people in achieving the desired outcome in their lives. We live in the most complicated tax, financial, investment, regulatory environment ever created by the human mind, and most people simply don't have the knowledge or experience to move through it with clear bearing and confidence.

2. Financial services professionals are already experienced in the basics of helping clients set their goals; it is already a part of their engagement. As one advisor said to me in a recent e-mail, "I'm the only person who knows when my clients are going through financial trauma, when they want to have a baby or take care of their elderly parents, or when they make plans to send their children to a private school. I'm the first person they call when something changes in their lives."

3. Perhaps the most overlooked resource that many financial services professionals have today is their accumulated experience of dealing with the most successful people in their communities, day-in and day-out. What other professional group routinely works and interacts with successful professionals, business executives, philanthropists and entrepreneurs? The accumulated wisdom from seeing how successful people behave in their daily lives is going to become a powerful asset that financial planners have – and which very few others can claim to have.

4. Thirty years of retirement planning work has given financial advisors mastery of a very powerful secret

that may be the key to successful achievement of any goal. The secret to retirement planning is that one can take a seemingly insurmountable goal (e.g., the accumulation of $2.5 million in an investment account over a 30-year period), and break it down into manageable steps (e.g., invest $1,075 a month in the first year and increase your investment amount by 10% a year). Suddenly, you realize that any goal can be achieved!

Nobody understands better than financial planners one of the fundamental secrets of success: that even seemingly insurmountable goals can be achieved by breaking them down into achievable steps and focusing on the accomplishment of each individual step. Savvy financial advisors will be able to apply this powerful secret to a much broader array of personal goals.

For the four reasons listed above, financial planners are uniquely qualified to pioneer and ultimately deliver this new service (and perhaps begin to play a central role in the lives of people), in addition to occupying a most coveted place in the professional/business landscape – offering "the service that everybody wants."

Structuring the Engagement

So, how do you start offering life planning services in your practice? Leading-edge professionals are developing two essential standardizing components. First, a framework for how the service should be offered. And second, a tool kit, which – like the products and software used in a traditional planning engagement – can be applied to the new service.

Brent Kessel, who practices in Santa Monica, California, has done a nice job of defining the framework of the expanded "better life" planning engagement. "I see life planning," he says, "as the process by which a highly-trained comprehensive financial planner helps an individual (or couple, or family)."

This process follows several distinct steps.

a. describe in detail the most highly fulfilling vision of life the client can imagine, including the financial, time-management, and environmental attributes of that life;

b. identify the strategies by which the client can most easily transition from today's life to that "fulfilled" life;

c. coordinate and hold parties accountable for the implementation of those strategies; and

d. periodically review and report on the client's progress towards that life.

The alert reader will notice immediately that "a," "b," "c," and "d" mirror the traditional financial services engagement – goal setting, the development of a plan, the implementation of the plan, and the ongoing review that monitors progress and allows new goals to be introduced into the process. So, in its broadest terms, the structure of the life planning engagement is likely to be very familiar to the experienced planning practitioner.

Where the structure differs is in scope. Start, for example, with Kessel's "a" component, which mirrors the traditional goal setting process but makes it a full step broader. "I think the primary way in which life planning's goal setting differs from conventional financial planning is that it doesn't rely on some widely held premises," Kessel explains.

Meaning what? Well, it appears that the traditional "goals and objectives" client meeting has been dominated by predetermined boundaries. (*How much net worth do you want to achieve? When do you want to retire?*)

Therefore, the first step in offering life planning services is to open up the boundaries (*What do you want to do with the rest of your life? If you knew you were going to die in three years, in what ways might you change the way you are living now?*), and allow clients to make the professional (technical) services much more relevant to their lives than they ever were before.

"It started off with 'here's a checklist,' says Roy Diliberto, who practices in Philadelphia. "We'd say, 'tell me which of these are important to you, and prioritize on this list that I've already prepared for you.' Now for us at least, getting to know your client requires us to know the client's relationship with money, what their history was around money, what their fears are around money, and how money distracts from what they want to accomplish in their life."

"Then," he says, "you focus on the client's 'true' goals and objectives." By "true" goals, Diliberto simply means what the client wants *to do* and *to be*, as opposed to the purely procedural answers that were once accepted by financial professionals. (*I want my money to grow* or *I want to beat the S&P 500.*) Those are not goals," he says. "To really get inside someone, to truly understand what they're all about, is what we do."

As Kessel sees it, planners are going to have to start rethinking their basic underlying assumptions about what's "right" and "wrong" in the planning process.

"Take the idea that more money/time is necessarily better," he says. "For many, the excess time created by early retirement is depressing. I believe a great life planner really needs to investigate what fulfillment means to this particular client, rather than relying on old assumptions. (*Retire early and you'll be happy! Don't you want that second home? Spend more, you'll be happier!*) This allows a truly customized plan to be developed, one that needs to deal with more than just money; it must address time, skills, relationships, peace of mind, forms of play and joy, and meaning."

From Software to Psychware

So how does an advisor get into these issues from a procedural standpoint? The profession is developing a set of tools that may collectively become known as "psychware" – analogous to the "software" tools that are routinely used in retirement planning, estate planning, tax planning and risk management today. There is, as yet, no definitive set of tools, but one book whose tools are being used by many advisors is *The Seven Stages of Money Maturity* by George Kinder (Delacorte Press, 1999).

Some examples of psychware in the goal-setting arena may include questions that take clients out of current circumstances into the realm of the hypothetical, and then allow them to reflect the answers back on the life they're currently leading.

The advisor might begin with a question like, "if you were certain that you were going to die in five years, and knew that you would be in perfect health right up until your death five years from today, what would you do differently?" This may prompt the client to outline significant changes she would make in her life, brought about by the tangible immediacy of death. But of course, there are no guarantees that any of us will live ten more minutes, much less five additional years. This question helps clients to recognize that they are in a condition of immediacy right now.

Here's another example of psychware. You ask the client, "what if you suddenly had all the money in the world, how would you live differently than you live now?"

When advisors ask this question, many clients fantasize about a life that, in fact, they can afford now. They've been saving and investing with no clear goal in mind when, in fact, they can already afford their most personal goals, today.

Other advisors are beginning to ask the "R-Factor" question, which was co-developed by Dan Sullivan of the Strategic Coach program in Toronto and Dick Zalack of Focus Four in Cleveland. The question takes many forms, but it goes something like this: "Suppose you were to come back here to this room three years from today. What must have happened over that three-year period for you to feel good about your progress?"

Another way to ask the same question is to ask the client to envision his or her perfect day three years in the future. Who is there with them? Where are they? What are they doing?

Interestingly, advisors who ask this question of their clients discover that most of us are doing literally nothing on a daily basis to achieve the goals that we've identified as important to us.

Why? We're too busy! However, once clients realize this (a true "aha!" moment), they begin setting aside a little bit of time every day toward achieving their own treasured goals.

Hypothetical Shopping

Are you ready for a slightly more complicated (and versatile) psychware tool?

Susan Bradley, of the Sudden Money Institute (http://www.suddenmoney.com/) has noted that many thousands of people are dealing with instant wealth and windfalls from a variety of sources, including inheritances, stock options, lump sum retirement payouts, sports contracts, insurance settlements, divorce agreements and lottery winnings.

For these people, the problem is that (for a variety of interesting psychological reasons that will not be explored here) they tend to fritter away the money in a couple of years.

This could become an incredibly widespread problem in the very near future. American society is finally entering that long-awaited period when trillions of dollars of wealth will pass from those who earned it to those who are destined to receive it through inheritance and estate planning.

How can advisors prevent those assets from being lost before they can have a meaningful, positive impact on the lives of the recipients? To address this issue, Bradley has created a deceptively simple tool that she uses with clients – and that people who subscribe to her Sudden Money network learn to use early in their training.

The tool can be called the "hypothetical shopping trip." Suppose, for example, that you have clients who have been living on an income measured in tens of thousands of dollars, and then, suddenly, $2 million comes into their lives (it doesn't matter how). You, the planner, know from your retirement planning experience that this is not an unlimited sum of money, but to them it feels like they can now buy everything they want for the rest of their lives.

And so, unless you find an effective way to intervene, these people will probably buy a new house, and perhaps a second home, and a new car or two. They may also promise large sums of money to relatives and friends, take an expensive trip, upgrade their furniture and wardrobes – and within two or three years at most, they're back at their employer's door asking for their old job back.

The "hypothetical shopping trip" is a psychware tool that lets clients make these mistakes on paper and see the consequences before they make them irrevocably in their lives. When the money comes into their hands, Bradley asks her clients to take a little time and write on a sheet of paper all the things they want to buy with their newfound wealth. The clients list the house, cars, and the money for friends and relatives. Bradley also suggests that they "buy" a lifetime yearly income in an amount that they list on the sheet. (The "cost" of the lifetime income can be determined by the cost of an immediate annuity whose yearly distributions would equal the income on the sheet of paper.)

The result? People take their shopping trip on paper, add up the expenditures and discover that they've spent three times the money that came in the door. And most of the early money went out for purchases that really weren't at the top of their priority list.

Through the use of the psychware tool, they quickly realize that the sudden windfall is not only *not* unlimited, but that unless they prioritize fairly quickly it will be gone without having made a positive impact on their lives.

It leads them to take a second look at the list, to prioritize, and then delete – *before* they've made a series of financially fatal mistakes.

Unlocking Estate Planning

Interestingly enough, the same psychware tool can be used by the experienced estate planner, to handle issues which the profession's traditional poverty tools will do nothing to address.

Scott Fithian, of the Legacy Companies (http://www.legacy-boston.com), offers a marvelous (and unintentionally funny) definition of tax-effective wealth transfer as "the separation of your clients and their money as soon as possible forever."

No wonder people hesitate to follow even the best estate planning advice!

To help clients unblock their resistance to implementing an estate plan, Fithian uses the hypothetical shopping trip tool in a somewhat different way than Bradley does. He encourages them to write down everything they would spend their existing money on in their lifetime, and offers no judgment at all on what they put on their list. They "buy" a lifetime of income. They may want a $200,000 second home or a $2 million primary residence; it doesn't matter to him. They may want to create a yearly travel budget, and spend the first year's on paper to see how realistic it is.

In many cases, they discover, in the process, that there's money in the portfolio that simply won't get spent, no matter how hard they try.

Presto! Suddenly it becomes possible to move forward with estate planning.

To demonstrate the versatility of this simple tool, Fithian may take the process to a second level, and have the parents create a list of the things their heirs might buy with the money they are leaving them. They may discover that they're leaving so much that the children will never have to work a day in their lives —which is not necessarily a bad thing, but which will certainly lead them to recognize, perhaps for the first time, the potential impact of their legacy. Do they want their children to inherit so much money that they (the children) cannot have a significant impact on their own financial existence with their own labor?

If not, then charitable planning is suddenly on the table.

Today I am Nothing

Planners who are on the cutting edge of this service readily admit that the profession has developed many more tools for the goal-setting part of the service than for the plan creation and follow-through parts of it (i.e., parts "b" and "c" of Kessel's four-stage life planning structure). Indeed, there is some debate about exactly how to move from goal setting to planning to implementation.

One of the most productive parts of this debate involves a complete transformation of traditional retirement planning.

To understand what is wrong with traditional retirement planning, from the perspective of a life-planning practitioner, consider the story told to a spellbound audience by Scott Neal, who practices in Lexington, Kentucky. Neal told the story of a doctor who had lived virtually his entire life "on call" (as they say in medical circles) and wanted his financial advisor to put him on an aggressive investment program so he could retire early.

The advisor did the work, and the bull market did even more, and the short version of the story is that the doctor was finally able to take himself off call and work on his golf game – five years earlier than he expected.

Then, one day, about six months after he had left the medical profession, this ex-doctor got up one morning, made himself a cup of coffee, washed the dishes, drove his pickup truck out into the country, pulled off the road and shot himself in the head.

About three days later, a suicide note arrived in the mailbox of a relative. The note said, simply: "Yesterday, I was Doctor Smith. Today I am nothing."

"Now understand that from a conventional standpoint, this was a very successful retirement planning engagement," Neal told the stunned audience. "This man had plenty of money to live the rest of his life, a house in the country, and his stated wish to leave his profession had been achieved earlier than expected. But from a more holistic viewpoint, the outcome would have to be termed a failure."

Indeed. Neal's message was that financial planners are often the only people in a position to monitor their clients for post-retirement depression – a common malady that seems to strike hard-working men especially hard. His conclusion is that advisors need to cultivate the ability to recognize the symptoms of depression, and also to ask pertinent questions about what the clients expect to *do* when they leave the workforce. Do they have hobbies? Passions? Can they envision spending all day, every day, on these things that they devote so little time to today?

If the emergent answer is "no," then there are several possibilities.

From Retirement Planning to Career Planning

One possibility can be found in the "new retirement."

The "new retirement" is one of those extremely fuzzy concepts that is invoked more often than defined, but the idea seems to be that people will work, at least part-time, during the traditional retirement years. It is interesting to note that *there really never have been traditional retirement years.* In the generation when Social Security was introduced (late 1930s) actuarial studies showed that the average retiree quit work at age 65 and typically lived to collect benefits for two more years. (No wonder today's Social Security system is such a mess!) So people who grew up expecting to stop work altogether at age 65 are suddenly looking at 35 (or more) years of essentially unproductive life. As one retiree said to his financial planner: "I can only play so much golf."

The other side of the equation is driving people to the same conclusion. In a later chapter on investment planning, we'll look at the stress that can be put on a retirement portfolio when a retiree quits work at age 55 and lives to age 105. But if the "new retiree" is working, at least part-time, for some of those years, then suddenly the numbers begin making sense again.

In the hands of future financial planners, the concept of a "new retirement" seems to abolish the traditional definitions of retirement planning. The reasoning goes something like this: *My clients will want to keep earning income both for the meaningfulness it provides in their lives, and also so they can afford the costs of living longer. So how can I help them find a kind of work that they really, really enjoy doing?*

From there, it's a small step to realizing that many people in their 30s and 40s and 50s are working at jobs they dislike. Why not take them through the same search for a terrific, meaningful, enjoyable occupation?

Presto! Suddenly the traditional retirement planning service (i.e., running the numbers to see how much needs to be set aside, at what rate of return, at what inflation rate, and at what retirement date) becomes something else altogether – career counseling and planning.

Jim Johnson, who practices in Sacramento, probably does the best job of articulating this transition. Johnson thinks he has a better definition of the "new retirement": find something you really like to do, and work at – on your own terms– for the rest of your life. It may be part-time consulting; it may be starting your own business, it may be almost anything. As Johnson points out, that is the function of the goal-setting process.

Interestingly, the planner may (and often will) be called on to do the same kind of goal-oriented planning that the traditional retirement planning called for. Why? Because the more meaningful/enjoyable work, which may be done on a part-time basis, may not offer as much income as the job that the client is escaping from. Thus, it is necessary to use the same savings habits, the same investment assumptions, and the same calculations, to free up the capital to train the client in a new career, or allow the client to set up a new business, or – often – simply to replace the lost income.

"I'm seeing more and more people doing what I call 'trading a great-paying, crappy job for a crappy–paying, great job,'" says Johnson. "They are able to accept reduced income for more meaningful work. I see people who look at that issue and say that in the right type of job, they may be interested in working many, many more years," he continues. "Before, it was "how quickly can I afford to retire and quit this damn job?"

In his e-mail discussion with the *Inside Information* group, Johnson went on to list some examples from his own practice: The retired Air Force officer working full time as a manager who quits that to work for reduced pay at an aircraft museum at a former base – and who plans to never retire. The former telecom worker, who took the golden handshake, invested the money and works for a charity. The burned out teacher who now works half-time and plans to work until at least 75.

"What makes this work," Johnson says, "is what they have saved for retirement gets to grow for a longer period of time before distributions begin, which leaves less time to draw on the funds." If the client has a life expectancy of 99 years, and he's working until age 75, the portfolio has 10 more years to compound and then 10 fewer years to make distributions than it would under a more traditional retirement.

Permission to Succeed

With the "new retirement" in mind, advisors suddenly find themselves making different kinds of recommendations than they might have a few years ago, before the life planning concept had entered the picture. Jim Helba, who practices in Bridgeville, Pennsylvania, tells the story of a surgeon client of his who was agonizing over whether to renew the lease on her medical office or create an office in her home. She really didn't want to work out of her home just yet. But she wanted to have a post-retirement place where she could continue working.

What was Helba's "outside the box" advice to her? "Do both!" "I told her you're going to need an office for work and recreation and your hobbies after you retire, and that is a very important space," he says. "If you spend the money to create it now, you'll be better able to plan what you want to do in there when you finally retire." She has interest in music and art, and this workspace will encourage her to be active.

"Her reaction was immediate gratitude," says Helba. "Creating the home office space was no longer a frivolous expenditure." Helba gave her client a solid rationale for spending the money in an area that she knew intuitively would be important to her, and the income that is generated in that office will exceed the amount that would have been saved in the investment portfolio if the renovations were deferred or canceled.

This may be advice that fits many pre-retirees, who might have plans to continue earning an income after they leave their current job, but may not have thought about where their work – and their hobby activities – will take place.

The Other Side of Drudgery

The central insight of the "new retirement" also happens to be a central insight of life planning: no matter what stage of life you're at, you want to find ways to make work less drudgery and more enjoyable.

Another important insight of life planning is that practitioners need to focus this same attention on their own lives. In order to have credibility in offering this new service, you (the advisor) have to start your own journey toward a better, more fulfilling life. In order to help people identify their personal talents, dreams and desires, and achieve them; you have to identify your personal talents, dreams and desires and show measurable progress toward them – first.

One of the most interesting stories to come out of our *Inside Information* community discussions was sent to me by Alice Bullwinkle, a respected advisor who practices in Denver. Bullwinkle had become successful in her business life, but was dissatisfied with the long hours and drudgery that her financial services business was demanding. (Sound familiar?)

So she sat down with fellow practitioner Eileen Sharkey and asked for advice.

"Eileen suggested that I not plan to retire at a set time," says Bullwinkle, "but that I take my retirement as I went along, taking longer vacations etc. Since the laptop computer and telephone enabled me to keep in touch with the information and clients quite easily wherever I was, this was a great solution. I followed through with her suggestion, taking about eight weeks a year away from the office, two to four of them without working much, and four to six other weeks keeping up with projects while away from home. All in all," she continues, "this enabled me to avoid burnout and, in addition, to serve on the board of trustees of my college, and still avoid working on nights and weekends. In those years I built the firm to our current $55 million assets under management, kept doing financial planning for clients, and helped clients weather the last two years in a way that has earned praise from them, not defections."

Bullwinkle now stands on the other side of drudgery, and is in a much better position to help her clients achieve the same thing. She is living her version of the "new retirement," which happens to be synonymous with the life that can be achieved with the help of life planning services.

How does it feel? "Most days I stand in the middle of the office and say, "Isn't this a great business to be in?" she says. "This business is working for me."

I think this is an example of the financial planner of the future. Your own goals may differ from Bullwinkle's. But if you want to participate fully in that future, then sooner, rather than later, you should begin applying the goal-setting psychware tools to yourself and your own situation, and spend the next five years working on the goals you identify – perhaps with the help of an outside professional.

The goal is to achieve the same degree of success (however you define it) as Bullwinkle has. With that will come life planning insights that a busy workaholic with too much work on his or her desk simply could not offer.

Four Years to Achieve the Impossible

We will revisit the investment planning implications of the "new retirement" in more detail in a separate chapter; for now, it may help to see how another retirement plan was created by a pioneering life planner.

Mary Sullivan, who practices in San Francisco, tells the story of a local nurse who came to her under what might politely be described as interesting circumstances. Although she had set aside no money for retirement, she wanted to quit the workplace in four years. She wanted an investment program that would accomplish her goal. "This," the woman told Sullivan, "is your chance to become a legend in your profession."

Most advisors, grounded in the realities of past profession-al cycles, would reject this arrangement out-of-hand, but Sullivan decided to apply her psychware tools to the problem. "What," she asked, "does retirement mean to you? Help me to envision your retirement."

As it happened, this woman wanted to retire because she had a mother who had recently been diagnosed with early-stage

Alzheimers, and she wanted to quit her nursing job in four years so she would be able to stay home with her mother. Sullivan went to work, and almost immediately identified an asset that had been overlooked – the equity in the woman's home. She was living in San Francisco, where houses were far more expensive than comparable properties elsewhere.

Her first recommendation: sell the house, move to a less expensive (but still pleasant) home in another location, and invest the freed-up capital.

Sullivan's next recommendation: get certified as a home health care provider.

After the woman had moved to the other location, and gotten her certification, Sullivan had a third recommendation: start a home health care business in your new location. As it happened, she was the *only* such professional practicing in her market, and was able to hire other nurses as the business grew. This business brought in more income than the nursing job almost from day one.

And the nurse's mother became her first customer.

Isn't that powerful? The seemingly impossible was achieved within four years, simply because the financial planner was able to think outside of the normal boundaries of retirement planning.

Off the Treadmill

Sullivan offers the broader theme of step A and step B life planning, and how it differs from traditional goal setting and plan writing. "The first financial plans I did for people had to do totally with their money and material objects," she says. "But gradually, I realized that what people want more than anything else is to get off the treadmill. Everybody is on the treadmill.

They have to work harder to make more money to pay more taxes to pay higher bills."

And traditional financial planning, she says, is confined to the treadmill and just doing it better and faster. Meanwhile, most people have a real disconnect between what they're doing on a daily basis and what they say (when they finally get to the core of it) that they want to accomplish in their lives.

It is, in fact, a broader form of exactly the same disconnect that financial planners have dealt with for years: people put together a portfolio that will achieve maximum wealth (and take on enormous market risk), when in fact what they really want is a portfolio that will get them safely to a destination.

"One thing we do is look at where they're spending their money," says Sullivan. "In our culture, people are searching for something, and they don't know what it is, but I think we can call it 'fulfillment.' They're searching, they don't know what's missing, and so they go out and buy material things that they think will make them happy, that will fill up the empty place that they can't seem to get at. Once they can look at that empty place inside, and see what they need to fill it, then they can be just as happy buying curtains at Wal Mart instead of top-of-the-line and be just as happy, because the money is going to something else."

Such as? Sullivan tells the story of a physician who, in the expanded goal-setting exercise, discovered that what she really wanted was to cut back on her work hours and spend more time with her teenagers, because she felt that they needed more of her attention at this stage of their lives. The physician was able to reduce her expenditures, and reduce her work hours (and income) and accomplish a goal she didn't realize she had before she walked in.

Another woman had two friends die of cancer in the same year. "She came to me two weeks after September 11, and said,

'I'm at an age where I could die any time,'" Sullivan reports. "We ran some numbers for her, and discovered that she has enough money that she can rent a recreational vehicle and travel around the country. I haven't heard from her in four months."

Expenditure Planning

At the risk of being repetitious, let me point out, again, that running the numbers and finding out how far this person could cut back without endangering her financial life were traditional financial planning tasks. In this sense, the casewriting tasks of a life planner are not very different from the traditional activities that you are probably doing now: you pull out a piece of software (spreadsheet or retirement planner) and determine whether a goal can be achieved based on current assets, the current savings rate and some assumptions about what the markets will do between now and some defined point in the future.

The difference is that the life planning goal tends to arrive sooner than the traditional retirement age and (especially if the goal is to change careers). The numbers will reflect lowered income in the future, rather than a cutoff of income and total dependence on a retirement portfolio.

Another difference is that life planning has begun to put a new emphasis on budgeting. In the traditional engagement, the planner's focus tends to be almost exclusively on the investing side of the client's life. But increasingly, life planning practitioners are discovering that their clients' expenditures are out of synch with the goals they uncover in the first interview.

This has led a small group of financial advisors to begin helping their clients get a better handle on their spending habits.

One of the early proponents of this expenditure planning service is Pamela Christensen, who practices in Sacramento, California. "I see a lot of people who are bringing in $10,000 a month in income and they have no idea where the money goes," she says. "Cash flow planning is the cornerstone of meeting their future goals."

How, exactly, does this work? The process begins with an unusually frank first meeting, where Christensen asks her clients if they are willing to put some effort into making their lives better. "I ask them point blank, 'are you serious about financial organization?'" she says. If they say they are, they have to prove it. Christensen asks them to bring in the last four months of checkbook registers and bank statements, plus last year's tax return and the latest check stubs.

Then she gives her clients an assignment sheet, which includes a daunting task. "They are assigned to track their expenses for 30 days," says Christensen. "They write down every penny that goes out of their pocket. Yes," she adds, answering the obvious question: "90% of them will do it, because they know they're going to see me in 30 days."

The results are routinely surprising. "People seem to have a natural tendency to underestimate what they spend in every category," says Christensen. "They go through this process and find that they spent $600 in groceries, when they estimated $200. One couple was taking care of their daughter's pets, and it was costing them $150 a month. They couldn't afford it, but until we went through this exercise, they didn't even realize it was costing them money."

With a better handle on expenses, Christensen finds that her financial planning advice acquires unusual depth and power. "We'll talk about their goals and objectives," she says, "and you can see that they're not on track to be able to afford their priorities," she says. "Then I can say, you have your children in private school, and you're paying for karate lessons, and you have season tickets to the basketball games, and you buy a new car every couple of years. Those may be important to them, but once we know where the money is going, we can start to prioritize today's expenses against future goals."

Most financial planners, Christensen says, will tend to shy away from budget planning, in part because it's very labor-intensive work, and in part because there is some risk to bringing up sensitive budget issues early in the client relationship. "Other planners tell me that it would be hard to talk about these things without being judgmental," she shrugs. "But if you're confident in your business and your advice, you can say things like, "if you can drive this car as long as it lasts, then it will help achieve this other goal."

Saving the Difference

Sherry Hazan-Cohen, of Dream Achieve in Plano, Texas, has also been offering budgeting services for her clients as part of a life planning engagement. "If I can get them focused on their goals, and then we discover that they're not spending their money on their priorities, then I've helped them make progress already," she says. "I'll say, how is $1,000 a month for a Jaguar in line with saving for your child's education? What would your life look like if you bought a less expensive car and saved the difference?"

Unlike Christensen, Hazan-Cohen will do the budget evaluation work for her clients – or, more precisely, her firm will. She has her clients bring in six months of bank statements, cancelled checks and credit card statements, and then turns the whole thing over to a company called Financial Outsource Solutions (OutsourcePro@ev1.net). FOS will input everything into a Quicken file that Hazan-Cohen can evaluate. Hazan-Cohen will give her clients the information on CD-ROM, so they can continue to track their expenses.

What categories does she divide the expenses into? Mortgage and costs of maintaining a household (including lawn mowing, home repairs, housewares, light bulbs, a cleaning service, lawn and garden expenses and pest control); real estate taxes and insurance; entertainment (including eating out, golf, dancing lessons); personal growth (books and classes); food (groceries); child-related expenses (gymnastics, soccer, music lessons); child care; medical; clothing; gifts; and of course utilities like cable TV, telephone, electricity, gas and water. And gifts to friends and family. "That's an item that can get out of control fast," says Hazan-Cohen.

The household expenses tend to be an eye-opener, which helps Hazan-Cohen talk about how, if clients could move to a smaller house, the savings would be much higher than just the lower mortgage payment. "I haven't had anybody downsize yet," she says. "But we always talk about it."

Another eye-opening expense is entertainment. "It's not unusual to see people spending $1,200 a month in this category," she says. "Most people are surprised at how much it's costing them to eat out." And even if they're not eating out a lot, some interesting expenses can sneak into this category. "Somebody goes to Starbucks every morning, and it's costing them $3 a day," says Hazan-Cohen. "That comes to $20 a week; $960 a year."

For one client, Hazan-Cohen created a separate category entitled "boat," which tracked the gas, maintenance, insurance and storage of the family's most visible toy. Another client had dog expenses tracked individually. "People have no idea what their pets are costing them," she says.

The budget also has to include a category called "transfers;" otherwise checks that pay credit card bills or car loans are double-counted. And most clients have a miscellaneous cash category to cover ATM withdrawals. "I'm very anti-ATM because it makes it hard to know where the money goes," Hazan-Cohen admits. "But they're a fact of life and you have to account for them."

Lower Income, Higher Savings

Christensen will go so far as to quantify the yearly expenses – which are often left out of short-term budgets. For example, everybody has car repair expenses; they just don't know when they'll have to pay for them. "If we set aside $50 a month for this expense, as part of the budget, then the money is there in the bank. It's not an unexpected expense and an excuse to go into debt," she says. Vacation and holiday expenses are not always budgeted for.

Both advisors have noticed that their higher-income clients tend to be saving less, as a percentage of income and in real terms, than many of their lower-income clients. "If we have a lot of money coming in, we sometimes don't spend a lot of time thinking about it," says Christensen. "If money is tight, people will be more aware of it." Her favorite stories come when low-income clients are able to save more, in real dollars, than higher-income neighbors – and reach their goals more quickly.

The Accountability Service

Sullivan has found that, by offering detailed budget work, she makes it possible for clients to define their expenditures in such a way that they can get off the treadmill tomorrow, rather than in 20 or 30 years. And at the same time, they can eliminate what may be the foundation of our consumerist society: spending, and buying, in an effort to fill the inner void that life planning addresses directly.

So if budget planning will be a new component of the planning process in this next professional cycle, helping clients spend less (according to the plan) will be a new service in the implementation phase of helping clients achieve a better life.

And, of course, there are the usual services: helping clients create investment portfolios and monitoring those investments and keeping an eye on taxes and, at year end, offsetting gains with losses, and identifying the right life insurance coverage – the things that really don't change from cycle to cycle.

The Power of Nagging

The implementation phase of life planning may also include one of the simplest services of all: holding clients accountable for their progress. Or, to put it another way, a service that falls equally between nagging and encouragement.

Interestingly, a number of advisors who have participated in various discussions have reported that, for most people, the hardest barriers to success and personal fulfillment are self-created. That is, something in their own mind and heart is stopping them from having the life they dream about. True, they need the outside expertise of a seasoned advisor. But they also need somebody to hold them accountable for making progress in a world that demands that we all spend our time and attention on everything but our own goals. They need somebody they trust to remind them that they really are capable of achieving their dreams.

And even more important than this accountability service, they need somebody they trust to reassure them, at difficult times, that they are capable of achieving their life goals.

With this in mind, it becomes clear that the life planning engagement will be more hands-on than the traditional planning service has been, and will require more work on the part of the client. Instead of simply delegating their financial affairs to their planners, clients in the new cycle will take on new responsibilities that they, themselves, have defined. And advisors will be responsible for holding them accountable to these responsibilities.

Interestingly enough, there is an actual, well-structured practice model for providing exactly this component of the life planning service. It is called (appropriately enough) "coaching," and coaching classes are readily available to professionals of all stripes.

Planner as Coach

"Coaching" is a service that has been formally pioneered by an ex-financial planner named Thomas Leonard, who founded something called Coach University (www.coachu.com), and whose basic concept has been further adapted by Fredric Hudson of the Hudson Institute.

One of the leading proponents of the financial planner as coach is Judi Martindale, who practices in San Luis Obispo, California. "The problem with life planning," she says, "is that it can get into the psychological areas that are beyond our competency."

Coaching, says Martindale, happens when both you and the client look at the client's problem together, and in many cases you will see what they don't see themselves.

There are three distinct steps to the process. The client describes a dissatisfaction – which could be anything. Then the coach intervenes and looks for new ways for the client to see the problem. Is it really about not enough time? What can we give up, temporarily or permanently, to give us more of it? Money? The same questions apply. Is there something else you need to accomplish first?

Then, in step three, the client and coach design new ways of behaving, and as the engagement continues, the client and coach assess progress and refine the new behaviors – so, Martindale says, "new ways of being can come into existence and continue."

"We need to know that making progress isn't only a matter of making up our mind to change," says Martindale. "It's *doing* practices that bring change into being." Thus, each week, or every two weeks, the advisor asks for a progress report on something that could be as simple as having breakfast with the family every morning. If no progress is being made, then the question becomes: what's blocking it? Once that is identified, then the client has an obligation to remove that obstacle before the next telephone discussion. The client is much, much more likely to make this behavior change if he or she knows there is going to be another telephone appointment in a week with somebody who is holding him accountable.

We'll see some concrete examples of this in a minute, but let's first address a question that is probably nagging at the back of your mind: how do you get paid for this service? Martindale follows standard coach tradition. She meets with coaching clients by telephone three times a month, and bills either by the engagement (i.e., this group of problems) or as an ongoing yearly retainer for year-round coaching. (She prefers the latter, she says, for her own practice. But advisors who want to simply begin to offer coaching may be better off working on clearly-defined projects that have a goal and an endpoint.)

Martindale notes that we all tend to offer help and advice according to our "natural way of intervening." Some of us are teachers, offering information that may help resolve the problem. Others are managers, who want to hold the client accountable for progress between sessions. Still others are inclined to try to offer help as therapists or counselors.

All of these "natural" interventions share the same fault: they promote dependence by the client on the advisor. Coaching, on the other hand, focuses on helping clients learn to change their behavior permanently, so the solution to the problem doesn't depend on the coach being there forever to teach or empathize.

No Quick Solutions

Ted Roman, who practices in San Diego, talks about a professional he has been coaching for some time. "He was working with orchestras in California, writing their music and their programs," Roman explains. "But these were all smaller accounts, and he wasn't making as much money as he felt he deserved. He's a brilliant guy, well respected in the music community."

The normal financial planning work was relatively simple, and the client might have ended the engagement with a tidied up portfolio, some insurance coverage, a retirement plan and an updated will. However, when Roman started asking open-ended questions about the client's life, it quickly became clear that what he really wanted was not a more organized financial life, but to find a way to move to the next level in his career. "I didn't have to go very far before he said, 'you know, I need to hire you as my coach, separate from our financial retainer,'" says Roman. "My vision, my goal, is I want to work with six to eight major orchestras around the country."

It was clear that this person was not a marketing demon, so Roman started the implementation phase of his life planning/coaching engagement by helping the client identify centers of influence. "We found friends and acquaintances from his work life who could get him in front of those larger orchestras and recommend his services," he says. "Then we put together a package that will help him sell them."

Inside of two years, the client had quadrupled his income and was working with several of the largest orchestras in the country.

Roman cautions that one of the first precepts of coaching, as formulated by Coach University founder Thomas Leonard, is that you should never look for quick solutions to client problems. "Somebody comes to me and says, I have a lot of credit card debt, I have trouble paying my bills" – as a financial planner, he says, "I might say, heck, take out a home equity loan, pay off those high-interest credit cards, you'll be able to deduct the interest on the home equity loan, problem solved. But," he adds, "that's just a solution for the immediate problem. The source is that they have a spending problem. And you have to solve that."

Another, related precept of coaching is that the customer is always right – even in a dysfunctional life. "Every breakdown is an opportunity to move forward," says Roman. "There's no penalty if they don't do what they say they are going to do. And they frequently don't. So the next week, I'll say, okay, what was it that kept you from doing that? You said it was important. There must be something stopping you, and we have to explore it. Every failure tells us something we need to work on."

There's a lot more to coaching than you could fit into one small book, including the contents of a 20-pound box you receive when you enroll in Coach University, the 28 principles of attraction, 40 or 50 different assessment tools, and the fact that part of the University training is a regular counseling session with 19 other students – all coaches in training – and a facilitator. You can get started on your own research on the Web (log onto www.thomasleonard.com or coachu.com.).

Roman admits that the state of the art in coaching is still being defined – in the new profession, and in his practice's interpretation of it. "I really don't know where I'm going with this," he admits. "I'm so new at it, and I am so energized by it, that it's kind of scary. I am coaching so much that it could start really supplanting my financial planning. I get turned on by it. It is more than just the numbers."

The Estate Doctor

It is also possible to apply the tools and techniques of life planning in the traditional areas of financial planning. In fact, a great deal of progress has already been made in the traditionally dry field of estate planning.

We've already talked about Scott Fithian in the context of the "virtual shopping trip." More broadly, Fithian has also found that in order to succeed in estate planning, you need to become much more personal than most technicians have traditionally been willing to do.

Why? "With estate planning, you have a volatile cocktail that includes the issue of death, which is very very difficult for many people to face logically, and family communication between generations, which is often nonexistent," he says. "The issues are highly personal. Are my children capable of managing a substantial inheritance? Have I done enough to give back to the community that has allowed me to grow my business and accumulate the wealth in the first place?"

Many advisors, says Fithian, mistake inaction for the need for more information. "If three analyses didn't clear it up, then ten are not going to do it," he says. "Any good estate plan requires clarity [the client's purpose], technical competence and management," he said. "The trouble is, most of the industry is focused only on the technical competence."

The influence of life planning on estate planning today can be seen in a radical departure from the dry numbers-oriented focus on taxes to a focus on helping people pass on their life story and their values to their heirs. This can take the form of a document that the advisor helps the client compose (or videotape), which tells the client's life story, and explains where the money came from and his/her goals for it in the future. In Fithian's experience, clients are much more interested in implementing a plan that passes on their values than one that focuses exclusively on their money, but will often do both if the two are joined in some way.

Perhaps, he suggests, they recognize that ultimately the values are more important to their heirs' well being than the assets themselves. "If you give your kids values and no money, they'll do fine," he says. "There are countless examples of that. If you give kids with well-developed values lots of money, they'll change the world. It is only [with] the children with underdeveloped or incomplete values who get money that it makes for a big problem. Because money is like fuel," he adds. "It just magnifies the outcome. It will take a bad outcome and make it worse or a good outcome and make it better."

Pyramid Power

One of Fithian's most powerful psychware tools is the pyramid, which is divided horizontally by two lines into three parts. The bottom part is labeled "how does it impact me?" The second is labeled "how does it impact my loved ones?" And the third is labeled "how does it impact everybody else?"

Fithian will draw this labeled pyramid on the back of a napkin, and then tell the client something that is powerfully reassuring. "I tell my clients that I hold myself to a fiduciary standard in representing their interests in making financial decisions," he told the group. "We first define and protect your interests, and second, we define and protect what you believe is an appropriate legacy for your family. And third, we define and protect what you believe is an appropriate social capital legacy."

Now for the powerful part: Fithian tells his clients: "I will not do anything at the third level that interferes with the first two, or anything at the second level that interferes with the first one. It is a very effective and powerful way to communicate."

Another tool is an exploratory session where the client is encouraged to communicate his or her story, but which also mixes some probing about his or her vision of the estate plan.

This puts the whole process in a much more relaxed setting. "When I do an interview, I just want to find out their unique story. Their interpretation," says Fithian. "I start out with a structure of questions about the past, the present and the future, and I let them run anywhere the emotion takes them. I don't have a plan protocol, follow this, follow that. I light the fuse, and it burns wherever it's going to go."

The session usually takes about four hours, and Fithian has it tape recorded and has an office staffer prepare a transcript. Why record the session? "You cannot ask questions and write down what they say and participate and engage in a conversation effectively, all at the same time," Fithian explains. Why make a transcript? "If you don't record it, they will never remember what they said or if they ever said it," he says. "When the clients read the transcript, they tell me all the time, 'I can't believe I said that.' Or 'I can't believe he said that. He has never told that to anybody.'"

Actually, both Fithian and the clients will read the transcript. "I circle paragraphs I think are important, they circle paragraphs they think are important," he explains, "and if we both circled it, it is important; if they did, it most likely is; if I did, it might be."

Finally, he takes out the circled paragraphs and puts them in chronological order. "It's like a whole string of pearls, of insight," he says. The important transitions in the client's life are listed, for the first time, on a document: the birth of the first child; the failure of a business; great financial success; and anxieties about the future, all of which have a direct bearing on how the estate plan should be structured.

Fithian has clearly put an uncommon amount of time into developing estate planning tools and techniques which address what we are learning to call life planning issues – the "bigger picture" issues in a person's life which, among other things, have prevented countless estate plans from ever being implemented. Listening to him, it is clear that technical expertise is not enough any more to carry people through the estate planning process. By focusing on these other issues, planners can become far more effective in helping clients take action to improve their own and their heirs' financial circumstances.

Zone of Genius

Another way in which life planning execution will differ from traditional financial planning is the range of outside professionals that the advisor will call upon in the course of an engagement.

When I first sent out questions about expanded financial planning to the *Inside Information* community, the e-mail lines exploded with stories about people wanting services that are generally outside the scope of the traditional planning engagement. Suddenly, it became necessary to find a good travel agent, or to identify somebody who could offer singing lessons. Who was in charge of the local little theater group? Which new-career-building courses, at which local schools were most beneficial? Which headhunter/employment agency could best market a career changer client to the business community? The list went on and on and on, with no apparent logic or business model.

The logic was later supplied by the Dan Sullivan/Strategic Coach program, which (during an e-mail discussion about coaching) we learned has taken an obvious insight – that all of us have special and unique talents – to its logical conclusion. To sum up a fairly complicated subject in the simplest possible terms, Sullivan has argued that each person has a certain number of tasks that they work on every day, week, month or year. Think of all these tasks as a large circle – for those who remember their algebra, this is the "set of all things you do."

Now draw a circle inside the larger circle. The area outside the inner circle, the donut shaped area at the outside of the larger circle, can be called the "set of all things you are not very good at."

Sullivan argues that you should work on delegating all of these things to somebody else who *is* good at them. (Later in this book, in the practice management chapter, we'll see exactly how this can be done in a financial planning office; for now, just follow the concept, which is probably unique to every individual.)

Now, suddenly, your "set of tasks" is much smaller. Inside this smaller circle, draw another circle, and you have another donut. This might be called the "set of all things you are pretty good at." Your next mission is to delegate all of them to people who are *very* good at them.

There is a long version to this, but the gist of it is that you repeat this process until you are functioning at the very heart of the original circle, doing only those tasks, working on only those things at which you are perfectly suited. This is what Sullivan calls your "zone of personal genius." He argues, persuasively, that if you can spend all your time doing only things which energize you, which God Himself (or Herself) created you for, then you can change the world.

And so, of course, can your clients.

I think you can see that this process of weeding out distractions and identifying what you do well, and moving your life into those areas, is exactly parallel to the life planning services that we've been describing; it may, in fact, be a better description of the career counseling service than the profession has come up with on its own.

To accomplish this journey into a client's personal genius requires the practice of delegation on a much more massive scale than has heretofore been attempted. To completely clear the decks of all "non-genius" activity will take a cast of dozens, perhaps hundreds.

Who will find these people? You will. This is actually a natural extension of what is sometimes called the quarterback role that financial planners play in their clients' lives, where they oversee the hiring of outside attorneys, tax preparation professionals, asset managers or mutual fund organizations, life insurance professionals etc., etc. – only now the role becomes more of a general contractor.

We're not building houses. We're helping people construct lives.

Marketing Your Rolodex

This is the logic behind all of these different messages I was receiving; the big picture that explains why, suddenly, they were searching for a variety of professionals in nontraditional fields.

But how do you structure this general contractor service? Is there a practice model that we can adopt?

As it happens, there is. Meet Bob Littell, who is a well-respected insurance specialist in Atlanta. Littell has pioneered a deceptively powerful concept that can serve as a model for the new general contractor role that planners will increasingly take on in this new professional cycle.

Littell has coined a term for it "NetWeaving" – which, he says, is a service that goes a full step beyond traditional networking. The concept is simple enough: you spend time identifying highly qualified professionals in your market in as many areas as possible – the very best of the best. And then, whenever you see a need for the services of these professionals, you put people in contact with them.

Littell offers the example of a computer specialist he knows who is very good, very quick, and after they work with him, people call Bob back on their knees with gratitude.

What distinguishes "NetWeaving" from "networking"? Littell introduces the slippery concept of altruism – which, he argues, defines a spectrum of behavior ranging from "disguised self-interest" to "giving with no expectation of return." Somewhere in the middle of this spectrum is a place that Littell defines as "enlightened self-interest," where "the motivation is definitely there to help others but there is at least a hopeful expectation that the NetWeaver will somehow benefit in return." Advisors who fall on the right side of the spectrum – between enlightened self-interest and giving with no expectation of return – are no longer networking. They are following the golden rule of life and building goodwill in their community.

And they are practicing an important component of expanded (Interior?) financial planning.

NetWeaving is also different from networking in the way it is applied. Littell talks about becoming a strategic matchmaker for others – to, first, spend time identifying people in your area or community who offer excellence (which is hard to define in words, but which you recognize as a combination of passion, knowledge and high standards of practice) in a wide variety of fields or endeavors. Then you train yourself to be constantly looking for the needs that these people can fulfill. Eventually, you become recognized as a conduit to excellence, and indirect but tangible benefits accrue from standing out for providing this service to others. Others in your network begin accessing the rest of it through you, as the central conduit

They also recognize you as one of them, as a master of your own trade the way they are masters of theirs.

Littell has discovered that his own practice of NetWeaving has made him, in his words, a "pied piper" in his community. "When you become a NetWeaving mentor to others, without question, it will increase your own prestige and people will relate to you differently and in a more positive fashion," he says.

More generally, Littell expects NetWeavers to reap the benefits of a diversified relationship with clients (who are the primary beneficiaries of his magic rolodex) and the community at large (which is not far behind). "If you are in the investment business and if your worth to your clients is too dependent upon the current return you are earning for them, you may be in a whole lot of trouble," he says, paraphrasing the central message of this book.

On the other hand, if you have established yourself as a strategic matchmaker as well as a resource provider and the heart of a resource network, you are perhaps the *last* person your clients would want to leave, no matter how bad things were to get.

Most advisors, alas, will have trouble moving far enough down Littell's altruistic scale to become true NetWeavers; they will become impatient that their initial efforts are not immediately rewarded. "The most basic element of NetWeaving is helping others and having the confidence to know that just like a rock thrown into the still pond, that creates ever-expanding concentric circles, so it is with NetWeaving," he says. "The consequence of that one simple good deed will have an impact far beyond the initial point of contact." (For more on NetWeaving, see *Power NetWeaving: 10 Secrets to Successful Relationship Marketing* by Robert S. Littell, CLU, ChFC, FLMI, SRM, and Donna Fisher.)

Health Care NetWeaving

In the very near future, some powerful demographic trends may start pushing planning practitioners in this direction more quickly than they expect. Several have already arisen within our own discussion forums.

Grady Cash, who practices in Nashville, Tennessee, has been thinking hard about longevity, and the possibility that the growth in medical knowledge and medical care will dramatically increase the life spans of his (and your) clients. Cash is co-authoring a book on the subject, which will talk about such alarming issues as the fact that long-term care policies have caps on the length of time they will pay for a nursing home stay – but, in fact, people of the future may need more time in managed care services than they do today.

What (Cash asked himself) are the implications for practice structure? What will the financial planner do to address the financial side of these issues?

For one thing, planners will begin to quantify these issues in dollars and cents. "Our profession will start to put numbers on good health," says Cash. "We know that by taking certain steps, that we can reduce your chances of a heart attack by 50%, and we know that if you did have a heart attack, certain amounts will be covered and others will not. So a heart attack, aside from the quality of life issues, would cost you this amount of money," he continues. "Is it worth this expenditure of time and money today to prevent these future expenses?"

With the future expenses quantified (and perhaps brought back to some kind of a present value), it becomes possible to justify the cost of bringing certain professionals into the client's life. Cash envisions planners recommending, not just the traditional attorney and accountant and life insurance specialists, but also wellness and health promoters, anti-aging doctors (which is emerging as a distinct specialty) and, of course, fitness instructors.

In conversations at a give and take meeting in Alaska, Cash discovered that other advisors are already beginning to identify professionals like registered nurses (to help coordinate the care of elderly parents), ministers, realtors and career counselors.

These ideas may seem way out of "the box," but it appears that "the box" itself is being redefined; the scope of the planning engagement is gradually enlarging. Cash is brave enough to try to define its new parameters. "I would define it as being able to assist all areas of a client's life that have financial implications," he says. "That covers a very wide range, and it gives the financial planner a justification to be involved with things that are outside the traditional planning scope. And it also, quite frankly, gives the planner a reason to back away from it," he continues. "If this is an area without significant financial implications, you can back off of it entirely."

Beyond Performance Statements

There is one other client services transition that needs to be mentioned before we move into an examination of the practice of the future. Today, financial advisors communicate the quarterly progress of their clients with what document? The quarterly portfolio statement (or performance review), which measures their investment returns down to two decimal places.

Aside from these performance numbers, what, about you, does this document convey? It says, directly and clearly, that getting superior investment returns is the primary part of what you do for them, and that the financial planning work is incidental. (If not, wouldn't *it* be on the quarterly statement too?)

This, of course, has always been a false message, but in the emerging cycle, it will be doubly so. One of the most frequent laments of life planners is that as their clients make progress, they forget where they came from. Therefore, they fail to recognize the long-term value of the planner-client relationship. No wonder so many people have been traditionally reluctant to pay full financial planning fees!

The solution is still being worked out in the laboratory of the financial services marketplace, but its outlines are becoming clearer. In the future, advisors will collect and save the document that includes their clients' initial goals, and each year they will collect new ones. And they will refer to these lists in their quarterly or annual meetings.

Thus, if the golf instructor who is barely scratching out a living sets a goal of earning $50,000 a year, and two years later is earning more than that from video sales alone, the advisor can go back to the original goal (and, perhaps, the original balance sheet) and show how two years of recommendations, suggestions and unlocking potential have made an enormous difference in the client's business.

Is there any way to systematize this into a quarterly statement? Different members of the *Inside Information* community have been working on some possibilities. Mike Daily, who practices in San Diego, would start by nailing down a client's personal, financial and life goals. Each goal would then be defined according to the five planning areas: (1) investment returns (which is what the quarterly statement already accomplishes); (2) retirement planning; (3) estate planning; (4) risk management/insurance; and (5) tax planning.

Daily can envision a software program, similar to portfolio tracking software, handling the revised reporting. Planners would use the "planning tracking" program to send out as many as five different performance statements every year. "What is most exciting," he says, "is that the comprehensive financial plan would become a working proactive document, instead of an end product banished to the fireplace mantle, oohed and awed at cocktail parties – and, sadly, never looked at again."

Nonperformance Reports?

Rozanna Patane, who practices in Maine, suggests that we create financial planning "nonperformance reports" that are proactive rather than after-the-fact. She can envision statements that look at what planning work will need to be done as a result of changes, like getting married or divorced; tax forecasting (especially in years where there are unusually high gains from securities sales or other sources); whether to convert to a Roth or not; taking those first IRA distributions; communicating new IRA minimum distributions; or updating a lifetime cash flow and capital picture now and then.

The quarterly or annual report then becomes a blueprint for what the client and advisor have on their plates for the months ahead, rather than a summary of what has been done in the recent past.

The Wealth Management Index

Interestingly enough, there is already a fairly well developed model for showing progress in the traditional financial planning (as opposed to "life" planning) areas, that was created by Ross Levin, who practices in Minneapolis.

Levin was troubled by the fact that his clients were being given quarterly reminders of his value in their investment portfolios, but no reminder at all of the progress they were making in getting their lives organized, in saving more, paying less in interest on their personal or business loans, getting better life and health insurance coverage – in other words, in the places where he was putting 90% or more of his labors.

And so Levin created a system that identifies a wide variety of issues that his planning services address, and which then tracks progress in each area. He also created a software program that tracked everything he did for clients, and gave them a print-ed "statement" showing their overall progress toward goals that they themselves had identified. This system is written up in a book called *The Wealth Management Index* (McGraw-Hill Trade, 1996). Since its publication, two software products have been developed which are able, with a little customization, to accomplish this tracking and reporting: a product called Protracker (http://www.protracker.com), and another product titled Junxure (http://www.crmsoftwareinc.com; 866-CRM-TOOL).

The basic premise of Levin's performance statement is to break down all the various kinds of work he does into broad categories, and then break those into subcategories. Then he identified the various kinds of progress that can be made in each subcategory, and showed the client this incremental progress over time.

For example, one area for each client to make progress in is the broad asset protection category, which makes up 25% of the entire index. Basically, he describes this set of goals as: *If something out of our control interferes with the financial plan, can we still complete the dreams of our clients?* A third of the category, or 8.25% of the total financial planning set of goals (33% of 25% = 8.25%) is represented by the question: "Do you have an appropriate amount of life insurance, consistent with an articulated philosophy?"

Of course, nobody just goes out and buys life insurance. There are three steps to making the purchase, which are discussed in advance with the client:

1. development of a philosophy on how much (and what kind) of coverage to buy;

2. implementation of the philosophy; and

3. estate tax analysis.

That means, at the beginning of the planning engagement, and even after the financial plan is written, clients may not yet be able to decide how much, or even if, they need life insurance protection. Why? Because they haven't really had a chance to look at the impact their death might have on their family's financial health.

So Levin spends time helping clients decide what their philosophy toward life insurance will be, and grading their current progress on a scale of 1 to 10. Notice that this doesn't presuppose that a policy will be purchased at all; the client may be able to set aside enough money that life insurance is unnecessary. There may be other sources of income–the spouse's parents, for example – who could cushion the economic shock. The point is to help the client come up with a philosophy that he or she understands and is comfortable with, and when that happens, then a score of "10" is assigned to the subcategory, and that one subcategory earns the maximum 3.71 percentage points toward the total index.

After an amount is decided on, if that amount of life insurance is purchased, then the subcategory gets another "10" and the total score goes up 3.71%.

When the client and Levin have thoroughly gone over the estate tax implications of the assets, and figured out whether additional life insurance is needed and in what form, the score goes up another 0.83%, so that (hopefully) this portion of the total index receives its full 8.25 percentage points.

Other Index Categories

Bear with me for a few more examples, because it's important to appreciate the levels of detail in which this index concept breaks down a typical planning engagement. The estate tax implications subcategory overlaps another broad category: estate planning, which accounts for a total of 20% of the index. A quarter of that (5% of the total index) involves whether or not the client's assets are titled correctly and beneficiary designations have been set up. There are three subcategories here:

1.   insuring all assets have the correct beneficiary defined;

2.   evaluating what types of retirement accounts need to be established, split or used for charity; and

3.   reviewing ownership of assets.

Another 15% of the estate planning category (3% of the total index) is earned when all the necessary planning documents have been obtained – such as powers of attorney, living wills, etc. These points are earned only after two steps have been taken:

1.   discussing the aspects of decision-making powers in case of incapacitation, life support, final wishes; and

2.   establishing written procedures for the family to execute those wishes.

In fact, this includes such details as prenegotiating the funeral and burial arrangements – because, Levin says, with all the emotions of grief and guilt, people often rack up huge death-related expenses that they realize were unnecessary when the emotions have died down.

As you can see, the financial plan evolves gradually over quarterly client meetings, when these issues are, one at a time, worked through until the planner and client have achieved perfect subcategory scores in all areas. Each quarter, the totals for all subcategories are added up, and the client gradually moves from (typically) a Wealth Management Index "grade" in the low 30s toward 100.

Taming the Logistics

Of course, management of the index has the potential to create a logistical nightmare: every meeting for every client has to be scheduled according to what subcategories will be addressed, and what the client will need to bring to the meeting. After every meeting with every client, there are action items that both the client and planner have to work through, and these have to be tracked to finality. Ideally, the database would allow a staff person to input, for every client, the steps that will be taken at each meeting, coded under the broad category in one field, the subcategory in the next, and item name in the next. The next field might show whether a document (a copy of the will, or the 401(k) statement, or the existing long-term care policy) is in-hand or needed from the client.

Is there a software program that can track all of this for you?

It so happens that ACT and Goldmine can be customized to serve as Wealth Management Index engines. But many planners prefer the profession-specific programs (Junxure and ProTracker), which both have customizable fields which can be used to enter in every single task accomplished on behalf of a client, and to print them out quarterly as a supplement to the performance statement. In addition, the score of the index can be generated on the same document, with a breakdown that shows clearly where the next year's (or quarter's) planning challenges lie.

This, of course, solves some of the limitations of the quarterly performance statement. In the near future, the Wealth Management Index will have to be adapted to the broader requirements of the life planning service. Will this take the form of a list of the original goals, and progress reports, plus a print-out of work done on those broader life goals? Will it require the

creation of personalized "life" planning indices for each individual client, based on their self-determined goals and objectives?

The laboratory is still working on the final solution, but I
have no doubt that some very good approximations can be
adapted from these beginning ideas.

Conclusion: The Convergence of Trends

This book is about predicting the future, so let's step into
the time machine and travel five years hence, and look at the
services that the typical financial planning/financial services firm
is offering to its clients.

When we land in the spring of the year 2008, we find that
the financial planning firm of the future is, first of all, doing
many of the same important things for its clients that you do
today. It creates portfolios, manages assets, and either does the
tax planning work or supervises it. Its advisors consult on how
best to incorporate risk pooling products (insurance and annuities) into the structure of the overall financial plan.

There is a new, more inclusive description of these procedural or technical services. The firm "handles the messy paperwork of life," so people can be free of it.

You see some interesting differences in the way this future
company conducts its daily routine. The financial planning firm
of the future consists of a team of professionals whose goal is for
all of them to escape the subsistence box by helping each other
determine what they want out of life and focus on the things they
do well.

Its unspoken motto is: only if you do it first, can you offer
this service to others. That has quietly emerged as the company's
biggest challenge, and the single most important focus of the
profession's efforts.

The biggest change between that future date and now is that advisors have become very serious about improving their personal lives and defining what that means to them.

In addition, in this firm of the future, traditional retirement planning is being gradually phased out in favor of career planning – where people, instead of working at a job they hate for 20 or 30 years, identify something they want to pursue and will accumulate the assets so that they can make the switch to something they never want to stop doing.

This firm of the future also makes a conscious effort to identify other professionals in the community – psychotherapists and dance instructors and travel agents and career counselors – who can help their clients in areas outside of your professional expertise.

In the background, you see that a plethora of new training programs have emerged to fill the educational vacuum on the subject of life planning, goal setting and the "new retirement." Some of these had their origins in our own time. We've already mentioned Susan Bradley's Sudden Money Institute, which offers, for a licensing fee, psychware tools, educational materials and training designed to help advisors attract and work with people who have received financial windfalls.

George Kinder, referenced earlier in connection with *The Seven Stages of Money Maturity*, also offers seminars (http://www.sevenstages.com) which, interestingly, focus not on how to work with clients, but on how to identify your own money issues and prepare yourself for your own foray into a more fulfilled life. Karen Ramsey's book entitled *Everything You Know About Money is Wrong* (Regan Books, 2001) may be the strongest book in this genre. Ramsey's seminars help people rewrite their own life script, and change their personal, self-repeated messages about money and finances.

It's not hard to see that NetWeaving, helping people live in their personal zone of genius, coaching, helping people enjoy a better life, the evolution of psychware tools, broader planning and goal-oriented performance statements and life planning (or whatever you want to call it) are all different facets of the same basic trend which will change the financial services profession more quickly, and more profoundly, than anything that has happened before.

The important thing to understand is that this convergence is still in its infancy, which means that you have time to prepare for a change in the way you structure and market your planning services.

When that change is in its mature stages (Four years from now? Five? Six?), financial planners who have been foresighted enough to adapt ahead of the curve will be in the enviable position of providing "the service that everybody, everywhere has always wanted from a professional," the service that financial planning was, from its creation, destined to offer.

Financial planning will then become what it has never been before: a mainstream service that is central to the way society functions.

As we've seen, the core of the service – basic financial planning, tax, retirement, investment and estate planning – is already in place. New practice management structures, new business models, and a full kit of psychware tools are all beginning to emerge out of these new trends.

Because of Internet technology and improved inter-professional communication, I expect these developments to be more profound and at the same time less disruptive than the (increasingly rapid) innovations that came before them. With the growth of interactive communities using the Internet, the new practice evolution will be reported on and shared among the community with enough speed to allow the profession to make a smooth transition – into its own zone of fulfillment, prosperity and genius.

Now let's see how these trends are affecting the way financial services firms are built and operated.

Interlude on *The Cutting Edge*:

"The Big Picture"

As we look at practice management issues, it helps to start with the big picture. If you are going to begin an important journey, then there ought to be some sort of a travelogue showing how others have navigated the same countryside.

It is, apparently, not an easy journey, based on the relatively small number of people who complete it. By some estimates, we have more than 100,000 people calling themselves financial planners in the U.S. market these days. Yet when I go to conferences, I see a relatively small number who seem to be way ahead of the rest. My best estimate is that this elite group of advisors has fewer than 2,000 members – just 2% of the total planning population. You read about these people in trade publications, where they are quoted and profiled. They set standards, serve on boards, and are routinely seen at the major financial services conferences. Even in difficult times, they always seem to have more business than they can handle. Yet they also seem to have time to read and think and communicate with their peers.

Interestingly enough, almost all of them are subscribers to my *Inside Information* service. (I have no idea whether they are successful because they are part of the community, or whether they are drawn to the community because it is where other successful advisors congregate.)

What's different about these people? If you could put their success in a bottle, what ingredients would it consist of?

This is a actually a rhetorical question, because people have been sending me messages on this subject for the past two years, prompted by various questions and issues that arise in our discussions. Their stories have helped me define, big picture, some of those key ingredients of success – which is surely one of the most valuable pieces of information this book can offer you in your practice.

Here's the skeletal version of all of these stories, combined to form a kind of mythic tale of success and prosperity:

"Planners Progress"

Once upon a time, there were 100 planners who started their careers in a distant jungle. As they journeyed along the road, their progress depended on how many people they could build professional relationships with, and how much those people would pay them for their services.

This was a very complicated journey. These young advisors had to make money, and they also had to provide real benefits to their clients. This was a compromise, a balancing act, and though these advisors tried to benefit both, their clients would always recognize that there was a strong element of self-interest in their recommendations and service. If they liked the planner they were working with, they'd go along and make sure he earned enough money to continue the journey. But they wouldn't ever give this person their complete trust.

In the early years of this journey through the jungle, the planners noticed a wider, shorter path, which was separated from their own path by a deep gorge. On the other side of the gorge, they could see advisors who made recommendations that were guided purely by their hearts and the desire to help their clients, and not by the revenues that their recommendations would generate. The leap itself was frightening, but even more frightening was the life on the other side of the gorge. Once they got to the other side, who was to say that their recommendations would generate the revenues they needed to continue the journey?

In the end, only 20 of the original 100 planners decided that they would test the gorge and cast their financial fate to the gods and the forces of altruism. They leaped, and crossed to the other side.

Once they landed, they realized something that nobody had told them before: that the gorge was not as wide as it had seemed. Changing from sales to service was not nearly as difficult as it looked, in part because they had been offering service (but not getting paid directly for it) for their entire careers.

On the other side, the 20 practitioners experienced a kind of freedom that they had never known existed – no more balancing act, no more compromises. As they walked forward along the new, wider path, the gods of the marketplace opened the eyes of their clients and showed them that their advisors were acting purely in their interests. And so a magical bond of trust developed between the advisors and their clients.

Suddenly, the 20 practitioners began receiving referrals from clients and local professionals, and the advisors who were able to take this leap of faith moved more quickly on their journey than the others. But though they shouted across the chasm to the advisors who were left behind, nobody else was willing to follow. After a time the two paths diverged, and the 80 advisors were again hidden from view.

As the journey continued, the 20 practitioners came to a fork in the road. At this point, they were hot and tired. For the past few miles, they had been working so hard at building their business that it had become difficult to focus their full attention on their clients' needs. Their progress, though faster than the others they had left behind, was not as fast as they would have liked.

Now, the fork in the road offered a solution, but a seemingly dangerous one. One path wound downhill and around the bend, but it was blocked by a deep chasm. The other path wound upward around a mountain, promising more hot and tired work, but there was no obstacle in the way.

Twelve advisors took the safe route and began trudging up the mountain. The other eight summoned up their courage and leaped across the chasm. On the other side, as the eight planners started down this sloping path, they began to systematically take work off of their plates by hiring an outsourcing firm to do work that they had been doing themselves, or staff people to handle specific in-office chores.

Hiring these people in a small firm was a scary leap of faith. But once they had spent the time, energy and money to free themselves up for the more important work of meeting with clients and supervising the work that was done for them, it felt as if they were walking downhill – gaining strength and energy where before they were facing burnout and fatigue.

By now, these eight practitioners were well ahead of their peers, both those who were moving up the mountain and those who were taking the longer, more difficult path on the other side of the first chasm. These advisors were following their convictions, had earned their clients' trust, were free to work with their clients without the distractions of office chores, and had the blessings of the economic winds at their backs.

But now the eight planners entered the most difficult part of the journey. The path that they traveled through now was no longer clear. It was littered with rocks, sudden dead ends, and they could hear large predators prowling about the periphery, looking for an opportunity to steal their clients and their business.

In this wilderness, where the path was replaced by a series of obstacles, six of the eight advisors trusted their instincts and luck and blundered here and there, stopping and retracing their steps when they had to.

The other two planners spent at least 10% of their time thinking about the road ahead and reading what others had to say about where to proceed and what to avoid. This, too, was a frightening risk – spending time thinking, instead of being with clients or doing office chores. But in time these two advisors learned to read the landscape. Although they never knew what they would find around the next bend, they were among the few people in the world who thought seriously about ways to make their journey – and the parallel journeys of their clients – easier and better.

If you could stand at the top of the mountain, looking down at the various pathways through the jungle, you would see 80 of the original taking an absurdly long route to get from one place to another. You would also see 12 on a more direct route that was so exhausting that even though they were well ahead of the first group, they always seemed on the verge of giving up. You would see another six who are further ahead still, on a downward slope, but who are now moving through a series of obstacles that always seem to take them by surprise, so that they are often forced to retrace their steps.

And finally you would see just two who are navigating with more efficiency, stopping to rest and think and look out at the scenery much more often than any of the others. For them, the journey is no longer a trip from here to there, but a pleasant walk with pleasant scenery that could go on as long as they are alive to enjoy it.

Sometimes these two advisors will receive e-mail messages from the other advisors, who ask how they got so far ahead of the rest of the profession. And because the story is a very long one, and hard to tell, they will simply say that they were willing to risk their survival not once but three times without any guarantee that the risk would bring them an appropriate reward. And each time (they will say) the reward was much greater than they expected.

This is what I have heard over and over again, in many different ways, from the advisors who live in that upper 2% of the profession. There are always people who predict that they will face murderous competition at some point in the future, or that their services will become commoditized. But the truth is that only a small percentage of people in this world think about the future, how to make it better, how to make themselves better, and how to make the journey more pleasant as they move forward. There will always be a shortage of those types in every profession – that is, individuals for whom every turn in the road provides not only a new opportunity, but also presents a pleasant new landscape to look at and think about. It is the Eternal Success Story, and I suspect that it exists, in the same mythic form, in every endeavor, profession and business. Chances are, on some level, this is your story, or your story in the making.

As we get into the specifics of various practice structures, I hope you'll remember that the bigger issues, the scary leaps of faith, are the raw materials of success. Everything else is details that serve them.

Now it's time to look at how, specifically, advisors on the cutting edge are structuring their practices.

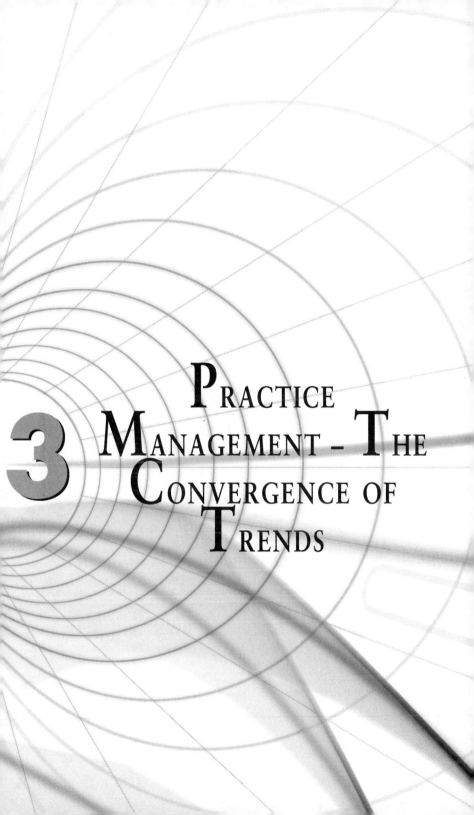

3

PRACTICE MANAGEMENT – THE CONVERGENCE OF TRENDS

L et's start by defining the term "practice management," so we can all start on the same page.

"Practice management," as defined here, is the ongoing process of creating a business that will deliver, *profitably and efficiently*, the services of financial planning.

Why profitably? Because unless the business is viable, you can't continue to do a great job for your clients, year after year. And that's what this book is primarily about: finding ways to offer terrific service.

Why efficiently? Because one important, often-overlooked key to providing terrific service is your ability to focus as much of your time as possible (with a goal of 100%) on your clients and their needs. The more time you spend filling out forms or handling downloads from the custodian, the less time you have for the important part of your job.

Efficiency also implies price – the more efficient you are, the less you'll have to charge for the same level of service, and (theoretically) the more people you can help in their financial and personal lives.

So "practice management" is the art of creating a business that will deliver you, and your knowledge and skills, to your clients, at a price they can afford. If you work in an ensemble practice (more on that later), then it is the art of bringing a variety of talents to bear on a client's life challenges.

In my experience, most investment advisors and financial planners are technicians, rather than skilled business people – which means that creating a viable business is very difficult and sometimes counterintuitive.

And, as we'll see in a moment, the practitioner today has to face not only the traditional challenges, but also some new ones. Independent practitioners will need to recognize that some of the larger brokerage firms are creating centralized, highly efficient financial planning delivery systems. This could put pressure on current pricing models. Brokers who work at these brokerage firms, meanwhile, will need to adapt their recommendations to the financial planning framework – and recreate their revenue model from sales to asset gathering, and ultimately from asset gathering to life planning services.

Advisors who primarily sell their life insurance expertise will need to recognize the demand for more holistic services, and either begin to provide those services, or create strategic partnerships with those who do. If (or when) the estate tax is repealed, these professionals will no longer be dependent on large estate cases as their sole source of livelihood.

Defining the Outcome in Advance

So how do we proceed? Let's start by recognizing the recent evolution of the planning practice, and identify the simplest (linear) trends in practice management. We will then extrapolate these simple trends to their logical conclusions. This will allow us to take a hard look at the endpoint of that evolution – what the typical planning firm will look like if current trends continue their present course.

Once we recognize the linear evolution, and where *that* is taking us, then we can begin to focus on the cyclical forces that are also influencing the planning profession. How will they change the planning practice of the future, and what needs to be done to adapt to these changes?

Then, once we have this evolutionary end-point clearly described, we can identify some practice models that were created with these end-points in mind. None of them are perfected, yet. But each offers a glimpse of how different advisors are trying to position themselves to take full advantage of the changes that are now working their way through the marketplace and society at large.

Finally, in the next chapter, we can look at concrete steps that you can take to get from here to there.

Linear Trends

The linear, straight-line part of the profession's evolution is taking us (very broadly speaking) from sales to advice. The roots of the financial services profession are in product sales: the sales of life insurance, stocks and bonds and/or mutual funds and annuities. If you look back over the last two and a half decades, you can see a clear progression from the advisor selling investment/risk management products, to the advisor offering broader guidance about investing, retirement and estate planning, to the advisor becoming a general counselor on how to achieve (financially and procedurally) a freer, better, less-cluttered life.

Each step represents a shift in compensation away from commissions toward fees – and, interestingly, also away from investments/products toward personal services.

From Producer to Advisor

The transition from commissions to fees has important practice management implications. Once upon a time, advisors earned up-front commissions for helping customers make an investment decision. But today, financial planning and investment advisory services are expected to be ongoing. That means the commission-based advisor is expected to provide ongoing service for that one-time fee. He has to bring in more clients to pay more up-front fees to sustain his business, but he still has to service the clients he has accumulated so far. Each year, he does business with 100 new clients, so his service obligation at the end of the first year is 100 people, and grows to 200 at the end of the following year. After five years, he has 500 people to watch out for, and he still has to find 100 new clients to pay the bills.

As you add more clients who have already paid you for the planning service, you add more service obligations but little or no ongoing revenues. Eventually the system breaks down.

This, more than anything else, explains why so many successful registered rep. producers eventually became fee-only advisors. They decided that they wanted to focus on 100 clients, and offer terrific service, rather than an increasingly watered down service to an exponentially growing number of people.

A few years back, I was hired as a consultant by a respected planning firm that was once highly profitable, but was now slowly going broke. We looked at the practice structure, and discovered exactly this dilemma: the company was taking on more and more clients without enough ongoing revenues to pay for the ongoing service work it was delivering to them. Yes, there were trail commissions attached to the mutual fund sales, but .25% a year was not enough to pay for the planning services the company provided to its existing clients.

They were losing money and trying to make it up in volume.

The Dangerous Producer Culture

Anybody who has been selling mutual funds these last 10 years, or making a living on commissionable stock transactions, has seen this fees to commissions trend reinforced by fund companies and brokerage firms – in the form of shrinking commissions. It is hard to remember that just 15 years ago, up-front 8.5% commissions on mutual fund purchases were not uncommon. Now I doubt many commission-compensated advisors make more than 2%, up-front, on their fund recommendations.

And, of course, life insurance professionals can look back wistfully at the age of 100% first-year-premium compensation as they struggle to make ends meet in the new age of blended and banded products, dialed-down commissions and competitive bidding for the larger estate cases. The same trend is in its recognizable early stages, and will proceed in the same direction to the same destination at some unforeseeable but preordained point in the future.

I don't think anybody argues any more that this is not a clear trend in the profession. And yet many advisors are still stubbornly resisting it. Why? And more importantly, how can this resistance be overcome in the only place where it matters: in the mind of the advisor who knows, on some level, that a transition is necessary?

Many financial services professionals have been trained in a sales culture, and through that training, they have acquired an admirable ability to push against the tide. You cannot be a successful salesperson if, when the first objection is raised to your proposal, you immediately agree with the objection and move on. A certain stubbornness is needed for success.

To help reinforce that strength of mission, the salesperson is typically surrounded by a powerful, self-reinforcing culture, whose primary business is to send encouraging messages from the home office, and sponsor mutually reinforcing messages at professional conferences. Top producers are lauded in the in-house organ, and the winners of sales contests become temporarily famous.

In effect, the salesperson exists in a kind of artificial, home-office-created reality, which makes it easier to deliver a strong message about the product and its importance to the consumer's life and well-being. At the same time, though, the home office may have other agendas. It sees a trend away from commissions, and toward more independent thinking about what the customer really needs. This trend, if left unchecked, will threaten its control over the products recommended by its "producers."

The result is predictable: the artificial reality begins to demean the trend. It does this in the form of messages orated with great confidence from the podium (to thunderous applause) and repeated in in-house organs, all saying that commissions are an important and threatened way of life, that fee-compensated advisors are nothing more than "failed producers," that *working as a fee-only advisor means leaving behind the "little guy" clients* – as if taking a $500 commission on a $12,500 fund investment is somehow more affordable than the client writing a $500 check for the same service.

The thousand voices of the "producer culture" say that *commission planning is somehow "less costly" to the client* – as if the most important practice management issue is to deliver the cheapest possible services.

In perhaps the most amusing event in this disorderly transition from commissions to fees, a large mutual fund company published a table showing that, under certain return assumptions, the up-front 4.5% commission was less costly than either a B share or a C share after a 7-year holding period. The results were published in a chart, showing the impact of the commission in each year, and the text roundly and triumphantly proclaimed that the front-end commission was the "best deal" for the consumer.

My own response was to publish a chart that showed a fourth alternative, where the advisor received zero compensation from any source. This alternative beat all the others in every single year, and was clearly the "best deal" for the consumer. The only problem with it was that it couldn't possibly work from a business standpoint. The advisor would be out of business in a year or less, and the consumer would be back to buying *Money* magazine's "12 Funds to Buy Now" advice, with unhappy consequences for everybody.

And that, of course, was the point. The best deal for the client comes when an advisor gives excellent advice and is appropriately compensated for it, so that he or she can continue to offer that advice. The argument that any particular compensation structure is the "best deal" for the client has to rest on business principles, not on which is lower than what.

Emancipation of Language

The crowning achievement of the sales culture has been to create a language that is so powerful and pervasive that it literally puts limits on the thinking of those who are under its spell. Understanding this may be the key to making the transition from salesperson to advisor.

The German philosopher Ludwig Wittgenstein has argued, persuasively, that language and thought are more or less identical; that is, the way you use language, both spoken and in your mental processes, tends to influence and perhaps even determine the way you think on a daily basis – and, by extension, your very reality. Interestingly, this same general idea can be found in the Zen sect of Buddhism, where masters teach us to be intensely suspicious of words and their restrictive influence on what we are capable of thinking and understanding.

And, of course, every self-help guru on the planet advises us to start any self-improvement program by reprogramming the words we use to describe ourselves and the world around us. You are what you think.

I started thinking along these lines after interacting with brokers and advisors in the *Inside Information* community who seemed to be having an especially hard time struggling to convert their practices from a commission basis to a fee orientation. On the outside, they seemed to have the transition licked. These were not stupid people; in fact, they were extremely successful in their current environment. They saw the future, knew that this transition had to happen eventually, and had decided to start the process earlier rather than later. They set up their offices with the right software, connected with the appropriate programs at Waterhouse, Schwab, DATAlynx or their broker-dealer, boned up on no-load funds and took their best clients out to lunch to discuss the change in practice orientation.

Then they ran into an invisible wall that prevented them from making any more progress. The transition, for some reason, never got off the ground.

Old-school salespersons and top producers have an especially difficult time getting on the other side of this particular wall for reasons that Wittgenstein or a Zen master would find obvious. As we saw earlier, the brokerage and insurance industries have developed and supported a language that emphasizes the needs and goals and income of the practitioner, rather than the client.

When I started looking into the problem, I found this harmful language in trade publications, professional newsletters, Web-based broker-support services, broker-dealer messages and the words of virtually every marketing guru in our profession. "DON'T MISS THE BIG PRODUCER WORKSHOP," one online publication advises us. There you'll hear "top producers" give you "formulas for exploding your business" this year. You can learn how to "sell" policies, "pack seminar rooms" and "close more appointments and sales."

Other messages are equally you-centered. Buy these tapes and your "personal production" will increase beyond your wildest imagination. This "selling system" will allow you to say goodbye to cold calls altogether. The folks who call you or come into your office are not "people," they are "prospects," which, in the language of the broker, is virtually synonymous with "targets." You learn "powerful prospecting techniques," or how to build a "super-profitable" asset-based business.

This language of selling is in the air that the commission compensated advisor breathes. When you think in this language (and how could you avoid it?) it is very difficult to put yourself on the same side of the table as your clients. You talk about changing your compensation structure, but the client can still sense the producer-orientation of the arrangement.

Steps to Emancipation

So if you're looking hard at the transition from sales and commissions to advice and fees (and, as we've seen, you should be), let me offer some advice that I guarantee is going to be much more effective than all that stuff you're getting bombarded with from all these gurus and motivational speakers. My advice is to change your vocabulary – and with that change, to switch from constantly looking at how *you* will benefit to looking at how you can benefit your clients.

First, eliminate the word "selling" from your vocabulary altogether. That isn't your goal. Yes, every business has to sell itself and its services. But your new goal is to find people you can help, to help them and to charge a fair (ongoing) price for doing it.

From now on, you will begin to measure your success by how much you helped them and you will talk excitedly about the successes that you and they have achieved – to other people who come to your office (leaving out the names and some particulars, of course).

If you want to call that "selling," then I won't argue with the terminology. But the term itself is poisonous.

Now let's get rid of "producer" and "production." You are not the first and you don't do the second, not any more, no matter what your home office might tell you. How does the client benefit when you measure yourself according to how many dollars have flowed through your hands from client to broker-dealer to fund? If this leaves a hole in your mental vocabulary, start thinking of yourself as an advisor, and what you do as making your clients' lives more efficient and effective. Put the focus on how your investment and life recommendations make their lives better (a better-funded retirement, for example) rather than yours (more commissions and status within your broker-dealer).

Next? Banish the terms "prospecting" and "prospect." How would you feel if I told you that you were a hot prospect for some salespeople I happen to know? You would at least feel defensive; you might very well feel alarmed or, if you're a bit more secure, you might take it as being condescending.

From "Prospect" to "Life Success Story In the Making"

Under the new terminology, bringing in business becomes a matter of spreading the gospel of a better – and better-organized – life. If that's what people want, you are there to help in any way you can. You want everybody to know that it's possible, and you want to tell him or her about your favorite success stories, in hopes that together you can create a new one.

So maybe your new terminology, to replace "prospect," is to say that everybody who walks into your office is "a potential life success story," "a happy-ending-in-transition."

Now let's get rid of all this "exploding your business" and "super profitable" stuff. It's painfully obvious who you're thinking about when you're using words like that – and it is not the client.

By now, some top producers are gloomily envisioning a life of wearing a hair shirt and putting locusts on the family supper table. In fact, the fiduciary members of the *Inside Information* community experience just the opposite. They are, in most cases, more successful after making the transition than they were before, where they dealt with the slow torture of shrinking commissions and growing client obligations. Fiduciary advisors who have made the transition typically have more business available to them than they can handle.

You could argue about some of their business practices (too many of them don't delegate enough, and most have stopped "spreading the gospel" because they have no room for new clients), but by the traditional measures of profits and business growth, they are the most successful people in the financial services community. Better yet, they generally feel great about themselves and the work they do, and enjoy the kind of client trust and confidence that most brokers would envy. They owe it to their clients to be an example of how to lead a great and prosperous life, and to be paid almost as much as the great value they've brought to their clients.

The Fiduciary Trend

These two linear trends – the shift from one-time transactional (sales) advice to ongoing service, and the shift from commissions to fees – are joined by a third: an increasingly fiduciary relationship with the client.

What does this mean? It means that advisors increasingly owe their allegiance to their clients, rather than to any outside entity. Put another way, the advisor's advice, increasingly, is intended to benefit the client without regard to any other agenda or influence.

Of course, we have not yet reached the end point of this trend, and it is possible that the profession never will. Anybody who thinks that all conflicts are eliminated with commissions should attend a give-and-take session of NAPFA, whose members are all compensated by fees exclusively. These sessions typically outline dozens of conflicts involving fee advice, and attempt to identify ways to push them aside.

As we'll see later, one of the biggest conflicts involves assets under management. When you meet with a dozen clients, and every client just happens to get a recommendation that you manage their assets, and that happens to be the primary way that you get paid, there is clearly a conflict somewhere in the decision loop. If somebody asks you whether it makes sense to pay off a $200,000 home mortgage, with assets that you are currently managing at a 1% fee, you are faced with a personal/business conflict of interest as surely as if the client were asking you whether to buy whole or term life insurance.

And, in fact, this third trend is having a further impact on the evolution of fee income. In the cutting-edge discussions that take place in the *Inside Information* community, advisors are increasingly talking about shifting from asset management compensation to retainer income. This, too, seems to be a linear trend, and there has been a lively debate about where the trend is going, and – if we can identify the terminal compensation structure at the end of it – how we can structure a planning practice today that will offer this less-conflicted compensation system.

Conclusion: Envisioning the Firm of the Future

It is not hard to envision the destination point of all these linear trends. We get into the time machine and visit the "practice of the future." Whether it is large or small (more on that in a minute), this firm is compensated exclusively by fees, which cultivates ongoing advisory relationships that last for years or decades, and which offers advice that is as unconflicted and client-centered as possible.

Now let's add the cyclical trend to this mix, and see what we come up with. The cyclical trend, as we saw earlier, will emphasize the importance of a broad financial planning service menu, and bring life planning services to the top of that menu – ahead of asset management, which has been at the top during the previous cycle.

So the firm of the future will offer the usual broad spectrum of traditional financial planning services, for a fee, and will create and monitor investment portfolios. (*Much* more on that later.)

It will, in addition, develop expertise in life planning, which is what future clients will be looking for when they walk into the office. Its practitioners will use psychware tools with as much skill as planners use planning software today.

Of course, this general outline doesn't say anything about how many employees there are in the office, or how the office is structured, how it bills for its services, how much it bills, or how the hard labor of financial planning is divided. The professional marketplace is, as you read this, filled with experiments as to how to translate the endpoint of various trends into workable business models.

That – the emerging business models – is the subject of the next chapter.

INTERLUDE ON *THE CUTTING EDGE*:

"Compensation"

Before we get to that next chapter, there are two important issues to address, which go right to the heart of whether you should believe anything you read in this book.

Issue one is compensation. As you've seen already, I believe that fees are the future compensation method for financial planners, and that it is going to be very difficult to reach or remain on the cutting edge if you are mostly compensated by commissions.

Issue two is my credibility. Am I just another biased media reporter, like all those others, who have picked up the fee mantra and spread it like gospel when, after all, thousands of advisors offer terrific advice and service while still receiving commissions?

The truth is, most advisors probably think there's no easier job than being a financial writer in the trade press. And you're right. Imagine that you've died and gone to heaven. Whenever you write columns or books like this one, your words have an instant and powerful effect on others. You have credibility simply because your name appears on printed material - which I suspect people of the future will think is some kind of religious awe in our society, unsupported by the clear evidence that *lots* of things you read in print are not just wrong but dangerously wrong.

In my own case, the subscribers to my service are well able to think for themselves, and are not foolish enough to believe everything I say. I've joked in the past that my life is full of adoring fans who send me bags full of letters that sometimes go through the metal detectors without detonating. These days, when I speak at industry functions, people hardly ever throw overripe fruit or sharp objects at the podium until after I've started speaking.

The source of animosity is always about what I have to say about fees – about (to use the words of one recent e-mail communication) my "never-ending crusade to move the profession to a fee-only compensation method."

I think this raises a fair question. Before you read further, before you trust anything I say, we should get my crusade out in the open so that you can see where my biases come from and how best you can filter them out of my book – and my columns in the future.

I'll let you ask the questions and provide answers as best I can:

First of all, where did you get on this fee-only high horse to begin with?

I guess it all started back in the mid-1980s. At that time I was editor of *Financial Planning* magazine – then the only professional magazine for financial planners – and the general population was very distrustful of the equities markets. They still remembered the awful bear market during the mid-1970s, and everybody expected a reprise at any minute. The economy was struggling with double-digit inflation, and we lived under the not-always-pleasant shadow of an incipient nuclear war.

The financial planners of the day had to work overtime trying to convince clients to put their hard-earned money into the stock and bond markets.

The ones who managed this difficult feat, and got their clients in during the early days of the bull market, really earned their commissions, with the benefit of hindsight, ten times over or more. It was a tremendously valuable service. We called it 'selling,' but back then people weren't ashamed of the term like they are today.

So you admit that there was some value to the non-fee-only approach to financial planning?

Well, yes and no. Yes, selling mutual funds was a real benefit to clients. Getting their lives organized was very important. But selling some of the other stuff, like diamonds, and, later, tax shelters and oil and gas partnerships, was not quite as beneficial.

At some point in the process, I found myself wondering whom these people worked for. The answer, sometimes, was the broker-dealer and the sponsor of the program, rather than the client. I got uncomfortable when financial planners measured success by their "production levels" rather than the financial achievements of their clients.

Not everybody was selling tax shelters.

No indeed. In fact, the people who mostly sat on the sidelines of the tax shelter craze were a small band of people who charged directly for their services, rather than through commissions. For some reason, they, as a group, took a harder look at the economics of those programs.

I used to wonder what that reason was. Now, with the benefit of hindsight, I can see that they were a little more focused on the client's well being than most of the professionals around them.

It was the first time I had seen advisors who didn't have an incentive to recommend the product du jour, even when consumers were clamoring for it.

They were holier than the average planner. Isn't that what you really mean?

I didn't say that. But *they* sure did. They formed an organization, called the National Association of Personal Financial Advisors (NAPFA), which tried to make that "holy" argument all the time in the early days. They overstated their case in a number of other ways, too. NAPFA leaders said that they had eliminated the conflicts of interest in the financial planning process. And some of them said that anybody who earned a commission was unethical.

And you believed that crap?

I don't think even *they* believed it. But remember, this was at a time when both sides were taking extreme positions. I remember a lot of comfortable chuckling at conventions and board meetings, where "big producers" who sold tons of tax shelter stuff to their unfortunate clients would dismiss the fee-only "fanatics" who wanted to do away with the gravy train. There was a semi-organized attempt to discredit the small band of fee-only advisors as a lunatic fringe, and the people being unfairly called lunatics fought back with rhetoric that was equally, but no more, far-fetched.

We remember the hot NAPFA rhetoric, but conveniently forget the other side of that argument.

There were still, obviously, conflicts of interest in the fee-only world. For example, it seemed that pretty much everybody who walked in their door needed some kind of ongoing asset management services. But as a consumer, if I had to choose between the "big producers" or the "fanatics," I think I would have leaned hard in the direction of the fanatics.

But weren't there a lot of mainstream planners who were also putting their clients' interests first, and still earning a commission on any implementation?

Yes. A lot of them are still around. Many of them are now fee-only practitioners, and virtually all of them have ratcheted up the fee side of their revenue mix. *They're* the main reason I believe this fee thing is a genuine trend.

Yeah, but only because people like you and the consumer press have told clients not to work with anybody who earns commissions.

Fair enough. We in the press have our biases. I can't speak for the consumer press, and frankly I don't approve of a lot of what I see there. But I know for a fact that I don't have the power to change peoples' minds about how they run their businesses. If you could read my mail, you'd know that the readers of my newsletter are well able to think for themselves. In fact, usually they do a better job than I do.

And they were discovering on their own that there were some clear advantages to the fee-only compensation structure.

Such as?

Well, for one thing, the profession seems to be in a constant state of adding new services. Years ago, convincing people to invest was a full-time job. Now it seems like everybody invests, and the basic planning service has gotten into all sorts of other areas – retirement planning, monitoring assets on a quarterly basis, renegotiating loans and mortgages, college planning, a host of small business issues and integrating them into the personal financial life, career counseling and the new thing my newsletter is getting into called coaching, tax work, estate work –

All right, all right. Your point being?

This is a lot of work, and it goes on more or less forever. The commission world values all these services at 25 basis points on whatever has been invested over the years, plus 2% to 3% (counting breakpoints) on whatever there is to invest this year. For clients who retire and stop putting new money away, you're basically working for less and less compensation each year.

And you're saying that's not enough?

It might be for the investment work. But for most shops, it doesn't begin to pay for all the other stuff that planners do for their clients. Hence, more money has to be paid in the form of fees. As commissions trend downward, and services become more extensive and complex, that fee percentage is constantly rising. Without any help from me or my great friends at *Money* magazine.

But what does that have to do with fee-<u>only</u> planning?

At some point, you realize that there's something illogical about this system. Why should the fund companies be pricing your services for you? Why not just set a price – typically 1% on accounts of $100,000 to, say, $400,000 – and take it all out of the portfolio each year? Or take some lesser percentage from the portfolio and have the client write a check for the rest.

The real issue here is whether you're biased toward fee-compensation in some way. In fact, you've already confessed to some biases. Care to tell us about them?

I really have two that I'm willing to confess to. One is that I am a financial consumer. When I write, I try to look at the profession from the perspective of a financial consumer, because ultimately, consumer interest and consumer needs are what drive the profession. It changes in response to those forces.

Now for bias number two. I am very strongly influenced by what the more successful, smarter, and more client-focused planners are doing in the marketplace. When I see a trend in that crowd, I report on it instantly, because chances are, I'm looking at a clear slice of the future.

Let's take these biases one at a time. How is the consumer better served by working with a fee-compensated advisor?

There's an easy answer and a hard answer. The hard answer is that if the consumer is working with a commission-compensated advisor who truly puts the client's best interests first, then there probably isn't any difference – assuming, of course, that both are equally competent. And I know there are thousands of such advisors out there.

So you admit that your bias has no relevance.

Not so fast. I haven't gotten to the easy answer yet.

The really good work that commission-compensated advisors are doing out there should be acknowledged openly, and that doesn't happen nearly as often as it should. But these people live in a regulatory structure and support environment that makes no sense for them. They are treated as salespeople by their regulatory body, the National Association of Securities Dealers (NASD), which forces every client communication to go through layers of approval by people whose agenda is to sell stuff so they can get their cut of the payout. The regulatory body assumes that everything – even, for

God's sake, *Morningstar* pages – is sales material designed to convince the client to take action for the sake of a commission.

If the commission is not their motivating factor, then the regulatory structure is totally inappropriate to who they are and what they do.

Now look at the support organization. The broker-dealers are still to some extent living in the "age of the producer." They get paid only when their reps gather assets or sell products, and the support they offer (not surprisingly) extends only to investments, not to all the advice, coaching, organizing and planning which makes up 80% of the planner's value to a client.

So financial advisors should just leave their broker-dealer and go unregulated. Is that what you're saying?

Unregulated?!? Anybody who has ever gone through an SEC audit, or dealt with the state over a consumer complaint, will challenge the idea that fee-only registered investment advisors (RIAs) are unregulated.

But (to get to the easy answer at last) I think a certain amount of NASD regulation can be safely shed when the advisor no longer earns commissions. When you manage assets for the client, or make recommendations for a fee, there's no incentive to churn the account or to make unsuitable recommendations. In fact, the incentives run in the opposite direction; you want to bend over backwards to keep the client comfortable in the investment seat.

I'll repeat one of the best lines I ever wrote: Show me a broker who has a bad habit of churning accounts, put him on salary and take away the commissions, and see if he doesn't break the habit in a heartbeat.

This may explain why each year there are upwards of 8,000 arbitration actions taken against brokers in the NASD world, but fewer than 100 similar actions against fee-compensated RIAs. The consumer is, statistically speaking, at least, safer in the hands of somebody who doesn't earn commissions than with somebody who does.

That, by the way, is why the consumer press advises its readers to look for fee-compensated professionals. They don't have the resources to find those really good, ethical, client-focused, commission-compensated advisors, and have no idea how to tell their readers how to find one with any degree of confidence. So they default to the safer (statistically) recommendation.

Incidentally, I didn't say they should leave their broker-dealer.

But I thought you said –

I envision a world, in the not-too-distant future, when the home office support mechanisms of some of the leading broker-dealers will be offered to fee-only advisors. I don't mean they'll successfully recruit at the NAPFA meetings. But they'll offer much cheaper clearing, record keeping, and turn-key asset management programs than the discount brokers do currently, plus interfaces directly with fund companies, along with attorneys and accountants on call. Advisors who hang their licenses with them today, at that point, could decide to drop their Series 7 but still remain affiliated with the broker-dealer's RIA. There will be some kind of fee-sharing arrangement that is approved by the SEC.

When that happens, you'll see a *real* trend toward fee-only planning.

Let's get back to bias number two. Are you saying that the smarter planners are fee-only, and the dumber ones still earn commissions?

I wish the world were that simple! Unfortunately, there seem to be smart ones and dumb ones in both camps. But the more successful practices are certainly gravitating toward the fee compensation structure. And the people who spend all their time thinking about planning and its future – basically, the people who have no life – have moved very strongly in that direction. Like it or not, they tend to be leading indicators for everybody else.

Of course, at the same time, they are also gravitating toward more affluent clients. That muddies the water a bit.

Aha! Are you saying that people who work with smaller clients on a commission basis should make the switch? Doesn't that leave behind all the middle-income clients who are currently being served by the planning profession?

Good question. Even fee-only advisors will admit that you can't work with non-affluent clients on a fee basis. Of course, they do it all the time, but these non-affluent people are not contributing very much to their bottom lines.

But take a second look at the economics. Somebody comes to you with $20,000 to invest. You're looking at a maximum commission of $1,000. Can a commission-compensated planner afford to do a full-blown financial plan for that? Does this person even need a full-blown financial plan?

The problem, I think, is that the planning profession can offer investment advice economically, on a commission basis, to people who are not wealthy. But all those other services are another story entirely. Most practitioners, fee or commission, are having a hard time making money in the middle-net-worth market.

Is there a solution in sight?

As you read this, there are a lot of systems evolving to help middle income people access financial planning services. We'll talk about them in the next chapter.

What about people who just don't want to work on a fee basis? They're happy in the commission world. Are you saying that they're dinosaurs?

Yes.

Come again?

In the sense that they could survive and prosper without significant change for the equivalent of hundreds of millions of years. The dinosaurs were a very successful species, and so too are fee-plus-commission financial advisors.

So let's come out and tell them what you think they should do. Instead of having a hidden agenda in your columns, get up-front and let us all know what you really think.

Somehow I've left the impression that people who are doing good work for their clients are going to have to make a significant, complicated shift in their practices, or reinvent their client relationships. They're going to have to learn to live without the support system they currently rely on. They're going to have to give up recommending the American Funds and Putnam, and work only with very wealthy clients.

None of this, in my opinion, is actually true.

Wait a minute. A minute ago you were saying–

These are trends, and they take time to play out entirely. Unfortunately, if you identify a trend, and somebody isn't already ahead of it, they feel like they've somehow fallen behind. Actually, the people who are ahead of the trends experience more trauma than those who let the pioneers take the arrows.

But you wanted my agenda, hidden or otherwise. This is a place where I commit to offering my honest views about where the financial planning profession is headed. I may be wrong; I may be short sighted or foolish. But I spend a lot of time thinking about these issues, and even more time talking with people about them. And I try to give it all back as straight as I can.

You're trying to tell us you're an objective, unbiased observer?

As much as any of us can be, which unfortunately isn't very much. True objectivity would require me not to care, and I fail that test pretty badly. I do care.

But to me, this one is a no-brainer. When I look around me, I see in the financial planning profession a transition from loyalty to product manufacturers to loyalty to clients. That, it seems to me, is the purest essence of the financial planning movement. You don't have to be a genius to imagine that this will involve a parallel transition from compensation coming from product manufacturers to compensation coming from clients.

But this is an evolutionary process, not revolutionary. And, frankly, some of the support mechanisms are not yet in place for the profession to cross "the divide." The insurance marketplace is going to go through a bloody revolution before long which will suddenly make a lot more products available to fee-compensated advisors. Other trading platforms will emerge, and the broker-dealers will continue their own service evolution, some faster, some slower.

The pioneers were well rewarded for making the transition, but they went through some pain as well – in the form of lost revenues and lost client relationships, in the form of learning curves and investing time they didn't have. Those transitional costs are going down all the time, and will continue to drop until you, whoever you are, feel comfortable making the switch.

So you're not backing off the idea that someday everybody is going to switch.

Maybe not everybody. But when I see Merrill Lynch making the switch as an organization, I know that some powerful forces are stirring in that direction, and only the most hidebound, stubborn practitioner would ignore them.

But that doesn't necessarily mean the trend will go on forever. If and when it shifts, I hope I'll be the first person to tell you about it. At that point my "never-ending crusade" will be over.

And good riddance.

By then, hopefully, I'll have found another unpopular one to replace it.

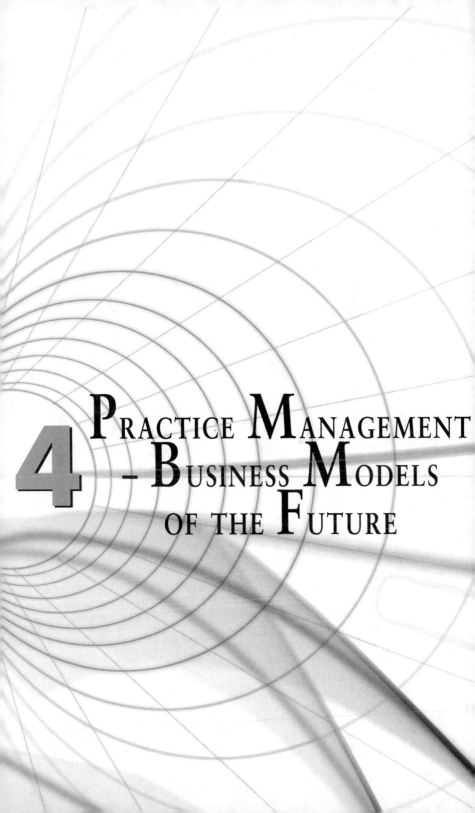

4 Practice Management – Business Models of the Future

Participants in this interesting laboratory we call the financial planning profession have been using the *Inside Information* service to compare notes, and they are discovering that the way they practice needs to fit who they are.

This makes giving specific practice management advice extraordinarily difficult. In the future, practices will not settle around a norm, but will instead be customized variations on a few basic themes created to fit the unique characteristics of the individual practitioner. Some advisors enjoy creating systems and procedures and tending the firm as a manager and overseer of the work mostly created by employees. Others want to do all the planning work themselves, and are impatient with the chores of managing others. Still others want no ongoing obligations; instead, they want to interact with clients when the clients need advice, and to be able to leave the office for a week or a month without having the phone ringing with anxious clients wanting to know how the latest stock market drop affected the value of their portfolio.

Some want to work with the super-wealthy; others with the Middle Market.

Larry Howes, who practices in Denver, has offered a very useful distinction among practice structures: he characterizes them as "thick" or "thin." The "thick" practice – the multi-planner partnership or family office – tends to have sizeable staffs and to provide a broad variety of services in-house, including tax returns, some version of financial planning, focused estate planning, bill paying, budgeting, shopping – all of which requires a large cast of employees. The principals are usually hoping to sell their "thick" practice to an outside buyer at some point down the road. Operating margins may be as low as 15% in the meantime.

The "thin" practices have as few employees as possible, out-source everything they can, give up the dream of selling to an outside buyer, and maximize their revenues. In return for the lost revenues due to an eventual sale, the "thin" practitioner can set up a defined benefit plan and put away aggressive amounts of money toward a retirement portfolio. "If you have any margins at all," he says, "then you could work for two years and make more than you would have if you had sold [your practice at the current going rates]." Margins may run at between 60% and 80% of total revenues.

You would think, with all these different tendencies, that the number of possible practice management models would be infinite. But, in fact, there seem to be four distinct models emerging at the cutting edge of practice compensation.

Let's look at them one at a time.

The Advisor as Physician (or Dentist)

One group of advisors, whose most prominent spokesperson is Sheryl Garrett, of the Garrett Planning Network, charges in much the same way as a general practitioner doctor does.

A great deal has been written about Garrett and her practice model, but the basic idea is so simple it can be captured in a couple of paragraphs. (For a more comprehensive treatment, the book to read is Garrett's own *Garrett's Guide to Financial Planning: How to Capture the Middle Market and Increase Your Profits* (The National Underwriter Co., September 2002).)

Garrett (and those in her network) has found that consumers instinctively understand the doctor's office model, and immediately (and unconsciously) recognize what is expected of them when they walk into an office with the glass window and receptionist behind it, the sign-in pad, the waiting room with magazines, the receptionist calling people to back rooms where the professional sees "patients." Perhaps most importantly, they respond instinctively to the desk on the way out where payment is expected when you leave, and where you make your next appointment.

Clients come in for a "check-up," which is not unlike the initial meeting in a more traditional planning engagement. There, they are provided a fee quote for the financial check-up, and given various questionnaires to fill out – which are proprietary to the Garrett Planning Network (www.GarrettPlanning Network.com). The results of the casework will be offered at the "presentation meeting."

Interestingly, the Middle Market client generally receives a slightly different type of financial plan than the wealthy person with a $1 million portfolio. The Garrett plan goes into budgeting and cashflow issues, credit card debt (and a plan to pay it off, using Quicken's Debt Reduction Planner), how expensive a home the client can afford (using calculators at www.FinanCenter.com), retirement projections and life insurance needs analysis (using MoneyTree Software's EasyMoney calculations) – plus an evaluation of the current investment portfolio. There may be additional visits, including "accountability meetings" for clients (patients) who are on a debt reduction schedule.

The service model follows the doctor model even further. The planner gives investment advice by way of a "prescription" that is actually written out and delivered by the client, not at a drug store, but at the local Fidelity retail office – or Waterhouse, Vanguard or Schwab, or anywhere that the local branch manager is willing to act on the advisor's recommendations without interference.

This is actually a practice management issue all in itself, since Garrett found that when she wrote these investment "prescriptions" to the local office of one discount broker in her early years, the representatives there always found it necessary to offer conflicting advice or otherwise interfere in the process. So it is necessary for the advisor who adopts this model to talk with the local discount brokerage offices, and to monitor their handling of "prescriptions" on an ongoing basis.

Cost? Garrett bills herself out at $3 per minute, and sets a goal to bill out 60% of her time. There are no asset management fees, no yearly retainers or anything else that would obligate her not to schedule appointments around a two-week vacation and simply take off into the country without cell phone or computer.

There are other ways to work under this hourly-advice compensation model. Greg Galecki and his firm in Fort Wayne, Indiana, I think, pioneered the most compelling. Galecki had agreed to host a radio program for the Fort Wayne community, and before long people were coming to his office seeking professional advice. However, the great majority of these new prospects were not wealthy enough to be appropriate for Galecki's asset management services, and Galecki was reluctant to turn them away.

Instead, he created a system whereby he would meet with Middle Market "clients" for two hours under a flat fee arrangement. As they walked in, he would have a mutual fund database and a financial planning program on his computer screen, and he would listen to their issues, work up a simple financial plan (primarily a retirement plan, showing how much would need to be saved and invested), look over their portfolio and print out reports on the current investments they were holding, and make recommendations on how to achieve better diversification or move to a more (or less) aggressive portfolio. At the end of the two hours, the "client" would leave with the best advice Galecki could offer, would pay a fee (in the neighborhood of $600), and would (as under Garrett's model) be free to come back whenever additional help was needed.

Serving the Untapped Markets

The advisors who use this business model answer the commission-compensated advisors' biggest objection to fee-compensated planning: they deliver their services to Middle Market clients. The practice structure also allows advisors to serve, profitably, the enormous number of people who aren't comfortable with delegating all of their financial affairs, but who *would* like somebody to periodically review their decisions.

Garrett refers to the Middle Market clients and "validator clients" as the "untapped market," and points out that they represent at least 80% of all consumers – a virtually unlimited market, where there is little competition. In addition, the advisors mentioned here strongly suggest that an advisor can offer much more benefit to people who are not yet financially comfortable than to a person who mainly needs his or her already-accumulated assets tended in a responsible way.

Beyond that, they believe there is evidence in their own practices that the commission-compensated model that has traditionally served the Middle Market is preventing some people from seeking financial advice. These advisors have found that their clients tend to be extremely sensitive to commissions, and are more than willing to pay for advice on a one-time basis, so long as they know there is no perceptible agenda attached to the advice.

Another advantage, unexpected at first but logical in retrospect, is that these businesses have begun to receive referrals from the local asset management-oriented planning firms. If somebody comes into one of those firms with less than $500,000 to manage, it becomes easy to simply recommend that the client work with the Middle Market-focused practice down the street.

The Advisor as Wealth Manager (or Personal CFO)

The second, best represented by the Cambridge Alliance, takes a somewhat different approach.

Advisors in this camp, who have been active in the *Inside Information* community discussions, argue that there is not much leverage in the Garrett/Galecki business model. Under the asset management system, when the portfolio value goes up (as it will, reliably, about 70% of the time), the advisor's compensation goes up automatically with it.

A second problem with the Garrett/Galecki model is that it requires clients to write a check for their planning services every time they receive advice. This hasn't been a problem for those advisors, because they don't seek out an ongoing relationship with clients other than the invitation to come in when they feel a pain in their portfolio. For an ongoing relationship, it makes less sense to write a check every time you talk with an advisor.

The solution? The Cambridge advisors, and others, are beginning to charge on the basis of a client's total net worth. This has the added advantage of allowing them to get paid for looking at the client's total investment picture – including the assets in the 401(k) plan, any rental real estate or small business assets that might be included in the overall portfolio. As the total pool of assets grows in value, the advisor earns more money automatically, and with the same (laudable) identity of interest that characterizes assets under management: I prosper when you do, and when you experience pain, so do I.

The money can be billed out of an asset management account, or paid by check each year – or credit card, which (surprisingly) many clients prefer, because they can get frequent flier miles when they pay for the service.

There are some procedural differences as well. Cambridge advisors will tell you that their practices tend to be more efficient than most because they do much of the planning work right there in front of the client. The engagement typically calls for eight to ten face to face meetings a year, each with a theme: tax planning, retirement planning, investment planning, and this aspect of the modular plan will be hammered out with the client's direct involvement.

Why is this more efficient? For one thing, it saves the usual give and take that comes when the case is written, and the client looks it over and says, "hmmm, what happens if my investments return 8.3% a year instead of 7.2%?" which necessitates a complete rerun of the numbers. That exploration takes place in the office, and is finished when the client leaves.

The process also has the effect of demonstrating the value of the service the planner provides, by engaging the client a bit in the (somewhat complicated) mechanics of planning – and also by providing more face time than the more traditional engagements.

Compensation

Billing as a percentage of the client's total net worth allows Cambridge advisors to continue to benefit from the same leverage that is built into the "percentage of assets" compensation model: as the markets go up, as clients add to their portfolios, the amount you (the advisor) charge will go up accordingly.

Second, it allows them to be paid for paying attention to the "big picture." Where the assets under management advisor might simply look at the portfolio he or she is managing, the Cambridge advisor is tracking and making recommendations on contributions to the 401(k) plan and how those assets should be deployed, and on tracking the value and economics of any rental real estate the client might own, and the growing value of a client's small business.

Of course, all of these assets are fit into an overall asset allocation model, which is built over life stages: liquid assets first; the home next; then income-oriented investments; and finally equity investments with a goal of having the majority of a client's income produced by the portfolio, rather than by his or her salary.

Middle Income Planning

Like the Garrett model, the Cambridge system has a somewhat unique focus. Detailing all of the unique features would require a book in itself, but one that tends to stand out is the inclusion of the family home in the investment portfolio, and the encouragement of a substantial home mortgage as a way to leverage this relatively safe investment. Another important distinction is Cambridge's method of identifying clients who are in different life stages: the Accumulation Stages (building the foundation, early accumulation and rapid accumulation); the Conservation Stages (financial independence and conservation) and the Distribution Stage.

How do these differ? In the Accumulation Stages, for example, the advisor's advice tends to center around saving at least 10% of annual income, having enough liquidity, having the right size (or cost) home appropriate to income level, fully funding pension plans and paying off credit card debt. From here until very late in the client's life, the traditional definition of financial planning services is bent toward the issues of less-wealthy people. Only later, in the Distribution Stage, will the focus have shifted to more traditional financial planning concerns, like advice on formulating estate planning and gifting strategies.

The Ensemble Firm (or Family Office)

The first two models can be either "thin" in Howe's vocabulary, or "fat," but the tendency is toward "thin." The "ensemble firm," in contrast, is the very definition of "fat."

The sudden arrival of the family office in the financial planning world seems to be related to the fact that a family office was an existing business model, which first originated in Europe and migrated to the United States. The original model was an advisory firm that served a single family (think Rockefellers), as a way to shelter children and grandchildren from inconsistencies in the financial advice offered by the marketplace at large, and to centralize the management of the various trust vehicles that conveyed the wealth from generation to generation. These firms were, by nature, multigenerational and provided hands-on services, including things like negotiating the purchase price of a house or a car, filing the taxes, even walking the family dog when the family went on vacation.

Today's financial planning family office offers a broad range of services to more than one family.

There are several characteristics that ensemble firms or family offices have in common.

First, there are almost always several senior planners who have a partnership arrangement as owners of the firm.

Second, clients are not clients of any particular planner, but are, instead, clients of the firm. Meaning what? When a client calls, he or she is referred to the department best suited to handle the nature of the request. In meetings, there may be three or four advisors in the room, each with differing expertise: insurance, taxes, investments etc. Clients routinely meet with people other than the senior advisor. In an extreme case, such as the Oxford Financial Group in Carmel, Indiana, each client may be assigned two teams of six specialists each, one to handle investment issues, the other to handle the family office (bill paying, tax planning and tax preparation, financial and estate planning, etc.).

Third, the firm offers more services than the traditional planning office. The firm becomes the client's private investment manager, financial planner, bill payer, banker, trust administrator and life implementer, available virtually 24 hours a day. Joe Kopczynski, of Universal Advisory Services in Albuquerque, New Mexico, has negotiated the purchase of automobiles and, for his doctor clients, helped negotiate their preferred provider organization (PPO) contracts.

Fourth, virtually all services are handled in-house. In addition to having an attorney, tax preparer and estate planner on staff, these larger firms may also have a full-time manager of household help. Haines Financial Advisors, in Birmingham, Alabama, has a psychologist on staff, who begins the life planning discussions and identifies any personal issues that might interfere or enhance the planner/client relationship. Edelman Financial Services, in Fairfax, Virginia, has an in-house mortgage broker to help clients negotiate home loans.

Finally, these firms tend to have fewer, much wealthier clients than the other firms mentioned here. It is not uncommon for an ensemble firm to have as few as 10 or 12 clients, who are (in Fort Worth planner Dave Diesslin's memorable phrase) buying a time-share in a family office. Their liquid assets typically start at $1 million; below that, the ensemble firm isn't able to charge enough to compensate itself properly.

How is the firm compensated? In most cases, there is an asset management component to the fee, often coupled with a retainer. Some firms have gone to a full retainer model, billing clients a flat quarterly fee that is negotiated up-front.

Upsides and Downsides

The ensemble firm or family office model requires that the senior planner(s) manage a substantial staff, which, of course, may take them away from the daily planning duties that may be their highest and best use. But it also frees them from the drudgery of office work, and moves them into the "big picture" realm, where they are able to take time off to strategize about their firm, and about their clients' situations without worrying whether the phone is being answered properly.

In fact, the traditional planning firm – a practitioner with a secretary and a casewriter and maybe one or two other staffers – begins to morph into the ensemble firm when the practitioner finally decides to hire an office manager and systematize procedures. Step two will be the acquisition or merger with another practitioner who aspires to have an office manager; the clients become clients of the firm at the end of the marriage, and the client base becomes large enough to make it profitable to bring the tax return preparation in-house. At some point, it becomes more cost-effective to hire an attorney to create the various documents required by the growing client base, and another planning practice may be purchased, or planners may be hired, at first to handle overflow work and smaller clients, eventually to form teams to handle different office needs.

The downside of this structure, aside from the administrative duties, is that referral systems – where local attorneys and accountants send clients to your firm and you send clients to them – are suddenly cut off, reducing what may be a significant source of new prospects.

Life Planning Issues

The life planning concept will have its most important practice management implications for these larger firms. Why?

Because part of the "mandate" of the new emergent service is to apply the goals of fulfillment and personal prosperity *to the firm* as well as to the clients. In the larger planning firms, that means, essentially, an entirely new human resources concept, where the management helps the staff identify what they want out of life, and tries to help them achieve it.

There is some (limited) evidence that this activity might help make these companies radically more efficient than planning firms have been in the past. How? Recall the Dan Sullivan/Dick Zalack concept of identifying skills and delegating away any work that you don't do competently, or that doesn't energize you. This (you'll recall) begins a long journey toward your dot of personal genius, as you specialize more and more in your core competencies.

It is interesting to note that human resource studies have, indirectly, identified this yearning by noting that staff employees typically do not rank their salary as the most important aspect of their job. The number one issue, consistently, is "meaningfulness of work."

Unfortunately, there are no comparable human resources manuals on how to achieve life planning in the office. So I asked the *Inside Information* community whether there were any procedural ways to give employees responsibilities that increasingly focused on their strengths and interests.

Surprisingly, several advisors wrote back to say that they had found workable procedures.

Boiling several responses down to their simplest terms, the advisors would recognize when the systems were becoming strained and it was time to hire a new employee. At those times, they would call a staff meeting, and have each staff member identify his or her current workday and task list, and then, on a separate sheet of paper, to draw up an ideal workday and task list. By going through this exercise, the employees would identify tasks that they felt they were not well suited to doing, that didn't fall on their ideal workday. The advisor would compile, at that meeting, a list of the tasks that different employees wanted to give up. Out of this list comes the new employee's job description.

The Outsourced (or Virtual) Office

This is the epitome of the "thin" practice.

The basic concept of the "Virtual Office" is to avoid, if possible, hiring employees, and instead hire specialist firms. This is a logical extension of the idea that all of us should try to concentrate our time on something we do very well – moving toward a zone of personal genius.

In this age of the Internet, e-mail and zip files, the traditional arguments for having employees in the office are beginning to break down, and it is becoming possible for a specialist "employee" to offer services to many firms at once. From there, it is not hard to envision a world where everybody is able to focus exclusively on an important skill that they do very, very well, and sell that service to multiple "employers."

This is not very different from the way that financial planners represent an inexpensive alternative to clients hiring a full-time personal CFO to work in their home or office.

By working with specialist employees – firms that handle office chores that are traditionally handled in-house – you find yourself dealing with people who better understand their tasks, and are more focused on them, than an employee at twice or even five times their cost. As a side benefit, you avoid the danger of losing a key employee and having to train new ones, plus all the normal hassles of employee sick days, people disgruntled with their salary or even the work of tending salary structures, payroll and FICA payments. (The book to read on this subject, written specifically for financial planners, is *Virtual Office Tools For a High Margin Practice*, by David Drucker and Joel Bruckenstein, Bloomberg Press, October 2002.)

As this simple insight ripples through the U.S. and global economy, I suspect that it will become the next driver of greatly increased business productivity.

It is perhaps harder for the reader to envision how, exactly, the "Virtual Office" would operate, since the concept is a few yards out of the traditional "small business" box. So let's look at a specific example.

Sheila Chesney, a member of the *Inside Information* discussion community, practices in Sheldon, South Carolina, about halfway along the coastline between Savannah, Georgia and Charleston, South Carolina. Among her clients are 30 doctors across three states (North Carolina, South Carolina and Gerogia), who receive comprehensive planning work that includes the usual retirement, estate, tax planning, etc., and also customized evaluations of nontraditional investments that they're considering. "One of the doctors is going to start a wellness center in Hilton Head, South Carolina, with a physical therapy center, nutrition center – and it's in a great location," she explains. "Another is investing in a dialysis machine; still others are putting money into the new construction of physician office buildings. And two clients are building fairly large homes right now, and I helped them find a contractor and handled the banking relationships."

Chesney sends her clients quarterly financial plan updates – which are a greatly expanded version of the traditional performance statement. They include updated income tax information, college planning updates and a reworked retirement model that shows the impact of the previous quarter on their retirement lifestyle. Meanwhile, on a monthly basis, she sends a fairly detailed economic review, including commentary on the performance of different asset classes and how that was reflected in the particular mutual funds her clients hold in their portfolios.

Chesney's client meetings tend not to be traditional. Since her clients are inevitably busy, and are struggling to find time to have a normal family life, she travels to their homes for face-to-face review meetings. "I have a urologist, very busy, and the last time we met was the 4th of July, out on the dock, because he got a new boat," she explains. "We talked about the new boat and things. I really work around what they need, more than my own practice location."

Now here's the punchline: Chesney provides this level of service with an office staff of zero.

Portfolio Downloading at a Bargain Price

How does she do this?

Let's start with the portfolio downloading work, which in most offices is handled by an office staffer who is also doing a lot of other routine office chores. "I have a friend in the business who, every six months she's training a new employee to handle her Centerpiece files," says Chesney. "It's hard to find somebody who is good at doing Centerpiece, and you really don't need that person for very many days out of the month – unless you're going to give them lots of other things to do."

The alternative? Krisan Marotta, proprietor of Krisan's Back Office in Charlottesville, Virginia, handles all Chesney's Schwab reconciliations and quarterly reporting. (krisan@krisan.com; www.krisan.com). "They set up a little web site for you, a secure web site where they download a zip file every Friday night with all my reconciliations," Chesney explains. "I pick it up on that web site and download it, and it unzips into Centerpiece, and Centerpiece updates all the accounts."

Total cost: $12 a client (up to 6 accounts per client), or, for Chesney, about $600 a month – which, as she points out, is less than the cost of an employee.

There are other benefits as well. "Krisan knows things about Centerpiece and the downloading process that I wouldn't be able to train somebody to do," says Chesney. Better yet, she doesn't have to constantly worry about losing an employee and training another one, or paying somebody during those times when the workload is slow.

Remote Planning

What about the financial planning work? For that, Chesney works with Naomi Scrivener (nscrivener@cox-internet.com) of BackOffice Solutions, whose only job is to input data into financial planning software (she uses MoneyPlan and Integrate). "A new client calls, I send him out a number of things including a questionnaire and a data checklist," Chesney explains. "When they send it all back, I scan it into my system and e-mail it to Naomi. She sticks all that information into a file called Dr. Jones – or whatever."

This, understand, is a scanned handwritten file. "I don't do any typing at all," says Chesney. "I also scan their wills, their account statements, their insurance policies, everything Naomi needs to build her file."

Of course, nobody ever gives all of their information in the first round of these processes, and so Chesney and Scrivener have a process for handling that as well. "She will enter everything in and find whatever is missing," says Chesney. "She will send me an Integrate file with as much information that she has been able to garner, plus a little memo that says, here are the things we are missing with this client." The next time Chesney meets with the client, she brings the Integrate file as it exists, "so I can show them how important it is for us to get good, complete data," she says. "Here are the things we need right now. And on a quarterly basis, you will continue to need to send me stuff, but I will always have a list for you."

Remember those quarterly financial plan updates? Those, too, are mostly created in Scrivener's office. "I send the Centerpiece information from Krisan over and Naomi uses them to update the plan," says Chesney. "At the beginning of the month, she sends me a checklist for each client with the required updated information, and I follow up with the client to get it to her."

Isn't Chesney uncomfortable giving up the creative planning work? "What Naomi does for me is not necessarily the creative part," says Chesney. "She could, but I want to retain that because I handle planning a little bit differently than most. What Naomi does is excellent, accurate data entry – and, more important, she verifies the integrity of the data. No garbage in/garbage out. Then she and I together discuss how the data looks in the plan, discuss any "what ifs" that we should run, and then I do all of the planning from there."

Total cost for up-front planning data entry and quarterly plan updates that are more comprehensive than the normal performance statements? Roughly $600 a month.

Investment Planning Outsourced

What about the investment planning? What about those monthly reports on the markets, the economy, and the funds that clients hold in their portfolios? Chesney believes that this is one area where her firm adds value for her clients. "Very few people come to me with any kind of a well designed portfolio," she says. "I take them through my philosophy, talk about tactical asset allocation models, we talk through their tolerance for risk, and then we choose a portfolio model."

As it happens, the materials on risk tolerance come from *Advisor Intelligence*, the service offered by Littman/Gregory for $1,500 a year, and the model portfolios are largely adapted from AI's recommended list – which, of course, also have specific mutual funds included. "We build an investment policy statement where I've kind of reworked AI's," says Chesney, "and then on an annual basis we talk through what has changed, do we need to make any adjustments, etc." The monthly reports are adapted from the AI monthly reports, credited but also customized. "AI provides more due diligence and mutual fund information than any client of mine would ever want or need," says Chesney, "and I often supplement it with articles that I find in other publications."

Add it up, and Chesney's various staff services are costing her in the neighborhood of $1,350 a month. Her Centerpiece staffer is an expert, her casewriter is an expert, and the portfolio/research work is handled by experts.

Next Frontier

And she's not quite finished with the outsourcing. Remember, Chesney still has to get clients to supply their quarterly information, which is more a hassle contact than a financial planning call.

The plan is to outsource that service to Sherry Carnahan, of Total Office Solutions (totaloffice@neo.rr.com; www.totaloffice.cc). Carnahan is more of a generalist; her firm handles a variety of secretarial, clerical, and general office chores for financial advisors.

In this case, the task is relatively straightforward "Sherry is going to take over the responsibility of taking Naomi's 'here's what I need' list and going back to the client and get it," says Chesney. "I'm not good at that; it is time-consuming and clients forget." In fact, if all goes well, Chesney will install a server some-time early next year that both Scrivener and Carnahan can access directly, to pull information back and forth, and eliminate Chesney as the middleperson. Carnahan can also send out the market commentary that is adapted from Advisor Intelligence's reports. "I can rewrite it and send it over in a PDF file." she says. "Sherry has my stationary there, so she can print it out and put it in the envelope and mail it."

Estimated cost for Carnahan's involvement? About $500 a month.

The Real Value

But (some of you may be asking) where's the value-added here? What is left for the planner to do?

"I continually try to upgrade the level of service that I provide by educating myself and trying new things," says Chesney. "I believe that the level of expertise that most clients run into is mediocre. I want to be the best."

Best at what? "What clients are paying me for is the really creative wealth building and the support that tells them that they really can do this or that, because we're doing it together," says Chesney. "And for the contacts that I make that bring new opportunities to them. They pay me for strategizing with them and being a sounding board, not putting together two-inch thick financial plans. Maybe one of the important things that I do for them is to encourage them to step out on a limb a little bit."

Chesney also feels that it's important to set an example, and keep her own life flexible and uncluttered. Having worked as a systems analyst with IBM in Connecticut before career-changing to financial planning, she and her husband are enjoying uncommon freedom. "I didn't want to be physically tied to an office with staff sitting there waiting for my next direction," she explains. "I often work from my home, work long hours and variable hours – very often in the evening. I have dogs and I love being around them when I work and I have a horse and like to go out and ride sometimes in the late afternoon. Sometimes I want to work from my office in town. I travel to see my clients regularly and wanted to be able to work from wherever I am. So the 'Virtual Office' structure has been my goal," she says, "and so far it seems to be working."

Growth of Outsource Firms

Because of the expansion of online communications, and the (very early stages) trend toward personal specialization, I think it is possible to argue that the "virtual firm" will become one of the most popular business models of the future. In the near term, however, it may be the slowest to get out of the gate, simply because it will take time for advisors to shed their habit of handling all office chores in-house, and become more comfortable with the electronic connections with outside service providers.

I think the virtual firm may also be the model that offers the most freedom for the practitioner – both personal freedom, and also freedom to pursue the expanded engagement that is now tentatively labeled life planning.

One determining factor in the growth of virtual firms is how quickly a variety of specialized outsourcing firms can develop in the marketplace. When I asked the *Inside Information* community to nominate their favorite outside service provider, I discovered that there is a small, but very healthy community of outsource firms and advisors who are beginning to use them.

Other planners who happen to have a particular expertise will provide some of this. We've already talked about Pamela Christensen and the fact that advisors can refer clients to her budgeting service, and how Sherry Hazan-Cohen outsources the chore of inputting client checkbook information into Quicken. But Hazan-Cohen is also serving as a life planner for clients of another local planning firm, on a referral basis. The benefit? "The biggest frustration most planners encounter is when they give great advice and make great plans, and nobody does anything," she says. "After working with me, clients are more likely to do what they tell them to. They send me people who seem to have an inability to follow-through with the plan, often because they haven't defined what they want out of their life and the planning relationship."

For Hazan-Cohen, the benefit is the ability to focus on the kind of client work she prefers, with clients she didn't have to spend time marketing to bring in the door.

To make the chain more complicated, Hazan-Cohen outsources some of the evaluation work to Dr. James Gottfurcht, the Los Angeles-based money psychologist who administers a 44 - question "Psychology of Money" profile which, Hazan-Cohen says, makes it much easier for the coach and planner to understand what might be blocking clients from achieving their goals or fully participating in the planning process.

"Part of the exercise is to identify the six psychological money traps," Hazan-Cohen says, listing them from the acronym RAPIDS: Rationalization, Avoidance, Projection of Blame, Idealization, Denial and Splitting."

With one client, the profile revealed an inability to break down the achievement of goals into individual steps. "He came to me with $65,000 in credit card debt, and he shut down, because he didn't see how he could ever pay it off," she says. "Once I realized what the problem was, I could say, here, do this, one month at a time, and you'll be out in nine months."

Outsourcing Performance Statements

Most of the initial activity seems to be centering on out-sourcing the portfolio downloads – the service offered (as we saw earlier) by Krisan Marotta. Nancy Gire, of Strategic Advisory Services in Orinda, California, reports that in the early years of her (and her husband Paul's) planning firm, she felt "like a prisoner of any employee we could find with the smarts to manage the system."

To make matters worse, the company experienced a computer crash and had to recreate its client records from scratch – a process that Gire describes as "a nightmare."

This led the Gires to look around, and identify a Vista, California firm called Asset Management Solutions, owned and operated by Mike Kelly (mkelly@assetsolutions.com). Gire says her company currently has 75 clients and 142 client accounts, trading primarily in mutual funds. "The most exotic things we'll ever see are stocks and some short positions," she adds. But there's that one client whose Great West VA contract was purchased through Schwab, which Schwab, inexplicably, does not provide downloads for. It has to be entered manually from printed statements – a task that AMS handles as well. AMS also helped create the performance reports that Gire designed for maximum readability.

In all, AMS charges SAS $815 a month – calculated as a base fee of $425, plus $2.75 per account.

Scott Leonard, of Leonard Capital Management in Hermosa Beach, California, pays a slightly higher monthly fee to have AMS handle the downloads on 150 client accounts (through Schwab and DST FanMail), but in his case, AMS also does manual entry on client 401(k) statements every quarter, so those assets can be included in the quarterly reports. "It helps them get a clear picture of what they own and how everything is allocated," says Leonard.

Other Platforms

Right now, AMS supports just two of the "big four" client management software programs: Centerpiece and Portfolio 2002 (now an Advent product). However, the company downloads data from any custodian that those two programs have an interface with, including Schwab, Waterhouse, Fidelity, First Trust DATAlynx, DST, LPL, Bear Stearns, Raymond James and Pershing.

Advisors who use dbCAMS can work with another outsource service provider: Derato, Fontalbert & Associates. Company principals Sandy Derato (sandy@plannersconsulting.com) and Candy Fontalbert (candy@planners consulting.com) both worked as senior executives with Financial Computer Support, Inc., the parent company that produces dbCAMS.

Derato's firm currently works with 70 different planning offices, offering services that range from routine client downloads to quarterly clean-ups of client data to manual entry on those accounts that require it. What do the clean-ups involve? "The Hartford just announced that they're changing all their CUSIPS and client account numbers," says Derato. "That is going to hit every user of every software package. Meanwhile, Scudder has absorbed the Kemper funds and changed the better part of their CUSIPS – and anybody who is not prepared for stuff like that is going to have a big mess. Things like that happen all the time. It drives people crazy."

Although Derato's firm works primarily with dbCAMS, it also handles downloads for Portfolio 2002. Like AMS, they will download from any company that those software products support. The list of downloads they're working with now includes Schwab, Waterhouse, Fidelity, First Trust DATAlynx, DST, SEI, FNIC and Nathan & Lewis.

Derato, Fontalbert charges differently from AMS; the cost is a flat hourly rate of $25 an hour, with a clear estimate up-front. "Somebody who has 3,000 clients is going to pay $1,500 a month or more," says Derato. Somebody who has 200 clients and wants routine downloads, the cost is going to be more like $600 a month."

Advent/Axys customers, meanwhile, can outsource their portfolio download work to Pacific Financial Services in San Diego. "They are quick, responsive, will do manual work, charge reasonably and offer the options of printing reports yourself off the web and/or posting PDF files for clients on your website," says Katherine Campbell, who practices in San Francisco.

The technical, hands-on contact person at PFS is Jeff Abadie (jabadie@pfsreporting.com), who estimates that the company is currently working on 10,000 client accounts from 20 different planning/asset management offices. Like the other companies mentioned here, PFS will do downloads from anybody supported by Advent; at present, the company downloads daily from Schwab, Waterhouse, Smith Barney, DST, National Financial Services (Fidelity), Pershing and Bear Stearns.

The least expensive option is to allow PFS to keep all the data on its computers, and send out PDF files by disk or over the web, so the advisory office can print out client statements. For an additional fee, advisors will be able to tie into Advent's online BREU system and have daily access to any of the reports that Advent offers. Abadie would need to know how much manual input is required before quoting an exact fee, but the base charge for downloading and housing the data is $60 a month per account. The full gamut of Advent reports will cost several hundred dollars a month – some of which goes into Advent's pocket. "We pay for them to log on through Advent," says Abadie. "For that, our pricing really reflects their pricing."

Planning in Paradise?

Within these four very different business models, we are likely to see an incredible diversity of individual styles and adaptations, as advisors begin addressing their own personal life planning issues. Earlier, we saw how Alice Bullwinkle had cut back on her personal hours and reserved more-than-the-usual-amount of vacation time as a way of living the new retirement. Other "thick" firms may decide to outsource their portfolio downloading tasks, while "thin" firms may form virtual partnerships or revenue-sharing arrangements.

The broader, more complex trend will be for advisors to take the traditional planning role, and then shift it around to suit their personal goals and personal definition of a pleasurable life. Thus, Sheryl Garrett has created a doctor's office-like planning practice, in part because it allows her to offer planning services to the Middle Market, in part because it allows her to close the office for two weeks at a time so she can put on her hiking boots and disappear into the mountains.

In order to understand the planning firm of the future, it is helpful to also look at some of these adaptations. What does life planning look like when the financial advisor is applying it to herself?

Not long ago, I moderated a panel discussion on this subject – in, of all places, Maui, Hawaii. I could see that this was a group of terminal workaholics by the nearly perfect attendance over the three-day conference – while, less than 200 feet outside the conference facility, the sun beat down on warm tropical beaches shaded by palm trees. There was also evidence of this workaholism in the fact that the same objection kept coming up over and over again: *"I can understand why I'd want to create 'paradise' for my clients, but why should I want to do that for me?"*

In the panel discussion, Kathleen Cotton, who lives and works in the Seattle area, talked about how she routinely operates her planning practice for six weeks from a condo on the beach in Puerto Vallarta – something she now does twice a year. This is not, she stressed to the group, a vacation (she takes those too), but a regular part of her working life.

What's the difference? "On a vacation, I don't call the office every day or answer my e-mails, and clients can only reach me for emergencies," she says. "When I work at a remote location, it's business as usual."

Well, almost. Cotton has a small staff in her office who take phone calls and answer most of the simple questions for clients. If clients call with any significant issues (which is not a daily occurrence), then the staff person will take a message, contact Cotton at her cell phone, and she will return the call. Cotton also takes her laptop computer and connects with the Internet, so she can respond to client e-mails for two hours each morning. "I received portfolio allocations on one client from the people in my office, and I reviewed them and sent them right on to the clients," she says. "They were not even aware of the fact that I wasn't in the office. It didn't matter to them."

A second panelist, Nancy Nelson, spends three months a year in the mountains of Costa Rica or Chile. She basically echoed Cotton's remarks, and showed the attendees a "traveling office" which consists of two carry-on bags containing a laptop computer, cell phone, a variety of electrical outlet connections and phone jacks (different countries have different standards), and office supplies like paper clips and scissors. "People always ask me how I can work outside of my office, and they're expecting me to have a lot of technology solutions," she says. "But the phone, the computer and an Internet connection are really all you need. That and somebody in the office to take the local calls."

Interestingly, Nelson and Cotton both found that the biggest barriers to working offsite were in their own minds: they imagined that clients wouldn't want them to be working out-of-town, and they imagined that there would be things they couldn't do because they weren't in proximity to the computer that downloads client performance and transaction data.

The truth, as Cotton put it, is that working remotely is so out-of-the-box that most planners reject the idea before they realize that it can be done. Nelson added that "we're a little like the employee who is afraid to take a vacation, for fear that people will find out that he isn't actually needed around the office. But the truth is, we're just being insecure."

Long-Term Project Work

After they were doing this a while, both planners had actually found some powerful practice benefits to spending weeks offsite. Cotton offers the simplest and perhaps the best reason. "One thing I know about this industry is that it will burn you out if you let it," she says. "It is very intense work that we do." Spending time away from the office, in a tranquil or beautiful setting, is a way to recharge your batteries without stopping work.

Nelson offered a second benefit to off-site work: it gives you a way to "stress-test" the staff. "I recommend that even if you work in your basement for two weeks, that you spend a little bit of time away from the office and see what breaks down," she says. "It's the best kind of disability insurance you can have, because you find out what the staff is totally relying on you to do, that maybe they could learn to do if they had to."

As a simple example, she had gotten into the habit of always opening up the office in the morning, and turning the computers on and checking the phone messages – and somehow came to believe that nobody else in the office (or, indeed, the world) could do this simple task. As long as nobody else was ever asked to, she may have been right.

"Someday," she said, "something could happen that will make it impossible for you to go to the office for a week or two. This gives you a chance to prepare for that, so it doesn't cripple your practice."

That's two potential benefits. Here's an even bigger one. Both Nelson and Cotton use their off-site time to work on long-term projects. These are the things that you never seem to have the time to get around to when you're working in the office – like long-term planning for where you want to take your business, and how to implement new ideas.

Cotton and Nelson both made the point, in the conference setting, by pointing to all the practice-building ideas the planners in the audience were getting from the speakers. "Then you go home and you don't have time to put any of them into action," Nelson says. "If you have a time on your calendar set aside for these things, and a place to work that is relatively free from distractions, then you know you'll get around to them."

Of course, this is also true of all the great ideas that you run across in the course of the year. Many planners will save them and then, years later, will go through the pile and catalogue their missed opportunities. Cotton and Nelson know that they will be able to take that file away at least once a year, go through it and make plans for how to incorporate these ideas into their lives and practices. As a result, they become more efficient collectors of new practice/life building ideas.

Other long-term projects are fit into this time as well. Cotton spent time in Puerto Vallarta working on her next book. In 1990, Nelson reviewed her asset allocation strategies, looking at what would have happened to her client portfolios if this had been 1970, or 1971, or 1972, and examining how she could reallocate assets so the portfolios would hold up better under times of stress, without giving up too much of the upside. "I ended up creating laddered bond components of all my clients' portfolios as soon as I got back," she says. "And as it turned out," she adds with a nod to the catastrophic bear market that had just begun then, "it couldn't have happened at a better time."

Finally, Nelson is able to use this time to catch up on her reading. In fact, she will often put aside all the various magazines she receives – again, knowing that she will get to them when she takes her off-site trip. Just having the time to read through the professional literature is valuable, but she quickly discovered that there was a huge value to having all of the material pass across her eyes at once – what she calls "the smell test of time." "I had a chance to read what the portfolio managers were saying six months ago, and comparing it with what actually happened," she told the audience in Maui. "Most people don't remember what was said three or four or six months ago, because they have the latest message or article in front of them. But it's a great way to figure out who is credible and who is consistently right with the benefit of hindsight."

Accelerated Office Work

But how do you hold client meetings when you're in Puerto Vallarta or Costa Rica? You don't. What you do (and this is a downside to working remotely) is accelerate your client meeting schedule before you leave and after you return. So instead of seeing one client a day, you might see two or three before you leave. Similarly, if a new client comes in (both Nelson and Cotton are taking new clients, but not actively seeking them), then you want to get the initial meetings in before you leave, and maybe accelerate the planning work so you can do a presentation before you get on the plane.

One member of the audience asked whether it would be possible to work remotely during the practice-building phase, when you are taking on new clients regularly, and meeting with prospects. The answer was a qualified "yes." Most planners aren't going to be able to incorporate remote work into their practice while their children are still attending school and/or while their wives and husbands are working a day job. So the opportunity will generally come to advisors who have a mature practice. But the panelists seemed to think that a six-week hole in your meeting schedule could be overcome by creative scheduling of appointments before and after, and by putting clients on a waiting list while you're out of town.

What about the staff? Don't they get jealous that you're in Costa Rica while they're holed up in the office? Cotton and Nelson both addressed the question squarely, and both said that this is not their experience. If anything, the people in the office feel trusted and empowered when the advisor has enough confidence to leave them in charge for six weeks. But Nelson told the audience that she, personally, would use this as a criterion for whether a staff person is working out. "If you don't trust them to handle things when you're not there," she said, "do you really want them working for you?" The obvious answer: maybe not.

Conclusion: The Space Outside the Box

When the session was over, I found myself wondering why more advisors aren't taking advantage of this opportunity. It became clear from the audience questions that most of the barriers to working remotely are psychological and self-imposed; they are not coming from the clients, the staff or the demands of the office environment itself.

This, I think, also reflects on the practice management trends of the future. Advisors of the future will be primarily fee-compensated, and will offer advice on subjects that increasingly are detaching from investments and products and expanding into the broader sphere of their clients' lives. At first, they will step fearfully into these changes, but the loudest objections they are likely to hear are those coming from their own minds. Hopefully, with time, the inner voices will grow quieter, and the practice management revolution will accelerate in a thousand directions at once.

In the coming cycle, increasing freedom of advice is going to be matched by a growing freedom of practice. As we take our time machine forward a half-decade or so, we see a lot of convergence around these four basic practice models. But we also see the principals exploring the space outside the box in their personal and professional lives – just, of course, as they are encouraging their clients to do.

INTERLUDE ON *THE CUTTING EDGE*:

A Worst Case Scenario

Before we continue with what I believe is the most important practice management information in today's advisory profession, let me offer another big picture assessment of the profession. This time, I invite you to look at what would happen if my client services and practice management predictions turn out to be wrong. What could possibly arrest these trends (I asked myself), and what would be the logical consequences?

The answer appears in front of us as a kind of "nuclear winter" for the planning profession.

"A Keynote from the Future"

"Greetings fellow investment advisors. As the opening keynote speaker to the 2023 Success Forum, I want to welcome you all to the Moon, where I'm sure you enjoyed your pre-conference golf outing. I am as excited as you about yesterday's announcement that the citizens of the planet Jupiter have decided to adopt the CFP designation as their primary financial planning credential. In fact, I've just been informed that, now that the Jupiterian planners have been granted three rotating members of the CFP Board of Governors, their ruling council has decided not to declare war on humankind after all.

My talk today is not about the future of the financial planning profession, but of its past – specifically, 20 years ago, in those long-forgotten days before the yearly company audit was replaced by online financials delivered through Bloomberg terminals. It is hard to remember now, but this was before the fifth reinstatement of the estate tax, three years before the Life Insurance Reform Act mandated the same contract disclosure requirements as home loans.

The year 2003 was, in many ways, an interesting period in the long history of our profession, a unique transitional point where planners missed a golden opportunity to become more relevant and central to the global community. We can only wonder where we would be today if they had chosen more carefully, and resisted the obvious and ultimately destructive temptations of the time.

Some of you may remember those days when the Internet carried primitive typewritten messages rather than streaming holographic images. Financial advisors then were primarily asset managers – who generally recommended mutual funds for their client portfolios. Twenty years ago, the limitations of these vehicles – largely unchanged since the 1930s – were beginning to become apparent. Global price data was beginning to arrive in real-time, yet most investors still owned funds that disclosed the contents of their portfolios twice a year. Despite rapid customization in most service industries, the mutual fund investment still forced millions of very different individual shareholders to hold exactly the same portfolio and realize exactly the same tax consequences.

Some of you who worked in the marketing side of the fund industry back then may remember that there were too many mutual funds vying for our business. It was impossible to get the attention of advisors with anything other than great long-term performance or extremely low costs – and we all know that these have always been rare commodities in the investment business. Nobody said it publicly at the time, but what the marketing people really wanted, deep down in their hearts, was a way to pay advisors to recommend their funds, using either hard or soft dollars.

Most of you saw Federal Reserve Chairman Abby Joseph Cohen's statement yesterday, where she warned of possible global deflation if the 40-year recession in Japan should once again carry the country's gross domestic product (GDP) levels into negative territory. It is interesting to remember that the U.S. experienced a comparable level of investment gloom from the summer of 2001 to the spring of 2003, first with the bursting of the Internet bubble, later with a gradual tightening of accounting standards that led most of the S&P 500 companies to restate (cut) their earnings by half or more. To take just one example, AOL Time Warner – the precursor to today's AOL-Microsoft-Disney-Fidelity – reported $1.493 billion in earnings in 2001. Two simple accounting reforms would have taken that figure down to just $384 million.

During this period of gloom, a few advisors began to de-emphasize the investment side of their services, which (they argued) could be commoditized, and which were never as important as the personal services that they were beginning to provide. But most of the profession persisted in its investment orientation, and began searching for ever-more-exotic investment concepts that would give their clients the false hope of double-digit real returns. Of course, investors were increasingly hungry for the very opposite of those qualities that make a great investment: sizzle and flash. All of a sudden, hedge fund managers who were willing to promise great returns suddenly became more marketable – and easier to recommend by advisors. A few hedge fund promoters who figured out how to share their revenues with advisors suddenly held an enormous marketing advantage over their competitors.

As the mutual fund died, new, less regulated investment alternatives took their place as the investment vehicles of choice for financial planners everywhere. For the next five years, these hedge fund promoters made significant under-the-table payments to those advisors who chose the easy path of selling their flash and sizzle into the greed of the moment. Because there was so much money to be made in dealing out these false promises, the life planning service went dormant, and the trend away from commissions (or product-related compensation) was stopped in its tracks and ultimately reversed.

There were some warnings of the terrible professional scandals that followed. Several news articles told us that the hedge fund industry was taking in more money than its managers could handle. Others pointed out that hedge funds didn't have to report their holdings even to their own investors, and undisclosed soft dollar compensation was an accepted way of life in the hedge fund world.

When several of the largest hedge funds were finally exposed as naked Ponzi schemes, the financial planning profession went on a long, dark trip through lawsuits and self-recrimination. Client losses weighed heavily on our prestige. Decades of positive press suddenly turned viciously negative, as story after story told of how advisors had taken ever-higher under-the-table revenues for selling Ponzi shares to their clients.

It has taken us 20 years to climb back out of that credibility pit and once again convince investors that we are their most trusted advisors.

It is hard to imagine what heights the planning profession might have scaled if we could have somehow avoided that investment trap, and made the transition from investment planners to a broader service menu that helps clients achieve a better life. That is why I urge all of you who are here today to recognize that investment performance is out of our control, and that helping people set goals and achieve their definition of success is the most valuable service our profession has ever offered.

Over the next three days, we will spend much of our time studying the nuances of the Tax Simplification Act of 2022, which adds 2,900 pages to the Tax Code. Our keynote economist will assess whether President Jenna Bush's new campaign to unseat Saddam Hussein could trigger a global oil shortage, and a respected climatologist will challenge us to consider whether the blistering December heat wave in Alaska is or is not conclusive evidence of global warming.

But I ask you to consider the lessons of history as you evaluate these new trends in our ever-changing profession. Twenty years ago, the planning profession somehow forgot that our reputation is our most important business asset. We cannot afford to ever make that mistake again.

Thank you all."

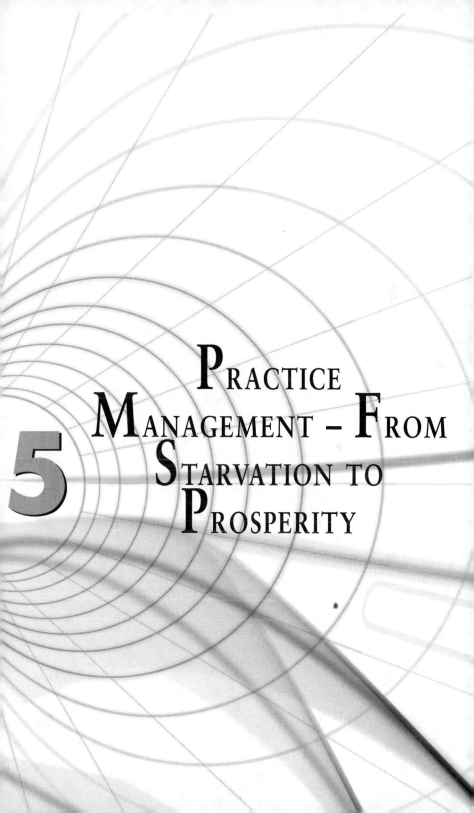

5

Practice Management – From Starvation to Prosperity

The practice management guidance is only half-complete when it points out the destination. It also has to create a map for how to get there.

The reality is that many advisors will not immediately adopt any of these practice models, but, once the goal is clear, begin to evolve their existing practices toward the termination point of trends of the profession.

In fact, many have started down that path, only to discover that something, somehow, isn't working for them.

In my *Inside Information* community discussions, it has become clear that many advisors have run into an invisible wall, where they embrace the ideals of the future, but seem not to be able to make a living in that practice space. I call these people the "starving idealists." We should pause a moment and recognize that this nearly invisible segment of the profession actually makes up the great majority of the profession at any point in time.

The "starving idealists" are defined as *people who have offered good service at a reasonable price for years and sometimes decades, who have somehow never been financially rewarded for the work they've done.* For them, the extended bear market has been a crusher – and it has made them wonder whether there isn't something missing in their business equation.

"I always thought that if you offered great service at a reasonable price, that was the perfect business model," one advisor wrote to me. "You go to conferences or read profiles in the trade magazines, and it sounds like everybody else spends zero money on marketing and the phone is always ringing with new people who want to do business with them. Is there any other business in the world that works that way?" he asked. "If so, what am I doing wrong? Why can't that be me?"

Thousands – maybe tens of thousands – of consumers have received help and service from countless starving idealists around the profession. Many of these consumers have gone on to become prosperous and financially free, while those who gave them advice have failed to achieve the same goals.

Recognizing the Struggle

Something is clearly wrong with this equation. But what?

In one of my weekly e-columns, I asked the *Inside Information* community what they would say to these people: what advice they would offer out of their own experience. That message attracted almost 900 responses, which still represents our all-time record (more even than when I took a poll to see how many members of the community were reading the messages on a regular basis).

Many of the responses were simply confirmation that this person was not alone in feeling depressed about his business achievements. Hundreds and perhaps thousands of advisors looked at my brief profile of the starving idealist, and it was like looking at themselves in the mirror.

Taking a line from the article, some of the respondents referred to themselves as the "other 90%"– and said, in one way or another, that until I wrote this brief e-column, they thought they were somehow unusual. One longtime advisor said, "in an odd sort of way, I find it comforting that I'm not the only planner struggling."

Another advisor captured perfectly the dilemma that many are facing. "For the past 22 years I have made an effort to help all who came to me regardless of their position in our economy," he wrote. "By giving so much of my time for free, my name spread among those that no other planner or planning agency was willing to shepherd. I have worked with over 150 couples to resolve and prevent bankruptcy. All the while, what little commission income I was generating from the middle income clients was eroded by reduced commissions on products and increased overhead and insurance."

Their situation is made much, much more uncomfortable by the articles we read in the trade press, which always, without exception, profile successful advisors. It is not the profiles themselves that do the damage, but the fact that every advisor who is profiled seems to be dealing with more business than he or she can handle, has a large staff and mysterious systems in place which take care of much of the procedural workload, and works primarily with clients whose portfolios are no smaller than $1,000,000 in size.

After reading these profiles over the course of years, it is hard not to come to the unconscious conclusion that practically everybody else in the business has found the right formula. Even though we know, on a conscious level, that these profile subjects are not a statistically valid sample, and we know that the magazines deliberately look for people who have achieved some form of success, the fact that we never, ever hear about the "other 90%" makes advisors who are struggling for business success feel lonely and isolated.

Only the Successful are Visible

So if you are one of the starving idealists, the other 90%, then perhaps the most important message of this book is an acknowledgement that you are not alone. In fact, you are in the majority. Most advisors, like you, are still trying to figure it out.

I'll mention a second, less important conclusion in passing. One of the e-mail messages told me that there was a good reason why only the most successful planning shops were ever profiled. Who [he asked rhetorically] wants to read about failure? What can you learn from them?

On the surface, the statement makes sense. But when you look under the surface, you realize something that I consider to be very important. The profiles that we read of successful advisors have not, in fact, taught us very much. Very seldom do they tell us about the advisor in the "struggling idealist" stage of her practice, and what she did to overcome the same challenges that the rest of us face. You never, ever see a nitty-gritty, step-by-step analysis of how the successful advisor got from point A to points B, C, D and E, where the phone rings without any marketing effort and they are routinely quoted in the *Wall Street Journal.*

Surely there must have been some terrific business decisions made along the way, but we are never told what they were. Instead, we are told about this person's practice *now*, after success has been achieved. It's like showing what the trapeze artist does in the air, without explaining how she trained to acquire these skills. The result is entertaining, but ultimately not very helpful.

The Definition of "Success"

Some of the advisors who responded to my e-newsletter made a point that ought to come before any practice management advice is offered.

Before we start helping the "other 90%" of advisors build larger firms and big client bases, we need to ask them whether this is what they really want out of their practice. And we need to recognize that certain definitions of "success" are tossed around the profession and accepted without question – even though they shouldn't be.

I myself fell into this trap with my careless reference to the "top 10%" of planners. Measured how? Some advisors told me that they probably belong in the starving idealist camp based on the revenues they generate, but they don't consider themselves unsuccessful.

This message was, of course, powerfully reinforced by the terrorist events that had taken place two days before my e-newsletter column went out. "Will any of us remember the status or compensation, the kind of car or home that any of these people had that lost their lives because of this most recent act of domestic terrorism?" American Express planner Alan Ayers asked me in one of the first return messages I received. "I can only speak for me," he said, "but the friendships, the kindness, the caring and the time spent together sharing that which is most precious of life is what 'at the end of the day' matters most. Can it be more comfortable? Can it have burled mahogany or walnut finishes? Can it provide private school and education? Yes, but I am thankful for clients and peers that have taught me the true values of life."

"I don't drive a fancy car or live in a fancy house," Kelly Buck wrote me. "But I have been blessed with many people (clients) who have donated their time and expertise for my various personal projects for no charge. My family is proud of me. I am very rich, just not in a monetary sense. I thank God daily for what I have and I don't worry about what others are doing."

Others made equally valid points. "I love my business and my life," Jerri Hewett wrote. "Material wealth became a lot less important to me several years ago."

Wrote Harold Templeton: "Those whose only desire is a large house in an exclusive neighborhood will never be satisfied. As professionals, we teach our clients to set priorities. Have we forgotten to follow our own instruction?"

Some e-mail responses told me that, in order to define success on their own terms (less revenues but better quality-of-life; working only with clients they enjoy working with, etc., etc.), they had to deprogram themselves from the definitions of "success" that are beamed out from the broker-dealer world. Their broker-dealers (and trade publications who cater to their interests) tend to laud the "top producers" whose skills (these advisors told me) often lie more in marketing than in service.

Measuring "Success" by Revenues

The dark side of this emphasis on revenues and sales is that advisors are drawn by these messages to aspire to become like a person whose scruples are open to question. "It's sad that our industry sometimes rewards the most morally bankrupt among us," Rick Kagawa wrote to me. "The planners that have the largest sales seem to get the lion's share of the ink in publications. Sometimes I personally know that these people have made their money with a concept or idea that I would never think of buying myself, let alone telling a client about."

Scott Young had moved over from the medical field, and was appalled at what he found. "In my previous career, you made it to the 'top 10%' by contributions to the field, publications, new treatment designs, things you have come up with to better facilitate the treatment and healing of patients" he says. This clearly is not like the "top producer" standards offered by some members of the broker-dealer community.

In fact, the comparison with other professions makes it clear how strange the planning profession's emphasis on revenues as a measure of "success" really is. "Imagine if the medical, CPA or legal communities only honored those who made the most money, not those who provided the best new ideas or the best service," Paul Wolf wrote in an especially eloquent message. "Surgeons would be given awards, not based on a new surgical procedure they invented or the skill of their technique, but instead on how much income they made in a year. Imagine going to your doctor's office and seeing awards she had won for earning the most revenues – as many 'financial planners' proudly display in their offices."

In a follow-up e-mail, he suggested that I explore for myself what I mean when I talk about the "top 10%" of planners. "Would you say the 'top 10%' of doctors or lawyers?" he asks. "How about engineers or accountants? What would it mean to say the 'top 10%' of family practitioner physicians in the country? Examine how you define this for our profession. Is it by income? Size of practice? It is doubtful you mean by this the best financial planners by services provided, skills or ingenuity." Or, I would add, quality of life.

The clear message from these advisors to the starving idealists is this: first define what you mean by "success" and "personal fulfillment." If you want to create a large planning firm, go for it. But I suspect that many people who have been working hard to get into their broker-dealer's elite list may read this and take a deep breath of relief. Increasing your production may be their goal, but you may feel like there are more important things to do with your life. If you do, recognize that this is an equally valid (many would say *more* valid) way to approach your business life.

This is so important that it bears repeating. Take the time to define what you want out of your career as a financial planner, and make sure that your goals are not being determined or manipulated by the messages you receive from the outside.

Then, with your own personal definition of success in hand, move forward toward it.

The Fee Solution

One of the clearest messages I received in the various e-mails is that down markets like the one we have recently been experiencing tend to be much harder for people paid via commissions than those who charge fees.

I heard this message from advisors on both sides of the fence. "This year and last have been tough on the pocketbook because of a lack of new money," confessed David Sakata, a commission-compensated advisor who practices in Moorpark, California.

What makes it harder for planners who work on commissions is the fact that their scruples are actually costing them money compared with other professionals down the street. "It doesn't help when I hear of some dirtball who churns his client, all for the sake of an easy commission," Sakata adds. "Even if I leave this business (and I may soon)," he says, "I will walk away with a great sense of accomplishment because I can honestly say (before God and others) that I did what was best for my clients, first and always."

Some commission-compensated advisors have recognized this tension between the interests of the client and the need to get paid, and tried to work out a system of rough justice by trading enough each year to pay themselves what they think their services were worth. "I do a lot of ongoing planning work for my clients," one advisor wrote. "Each year, I look at the accounts, and will shift assets from one fund to another, equivalent funds to pay me for the services."

This message led to an e-mail discussion, where I suggested that this logic can lead to wholesale churning, depending on how you value your services. Who is to say that this year his financial planning work isn't worth double what he was charging last year? The response was defensive but honest. "My overall compensation comes to about $50 an hour," he said on a subsequent e-mail. "There are a lot of planning shops around here charging a lot more in fees than that."

However, this "solution" to the revenue dilemma flies in the face of the idealistic financial planning culture, where even commission-compensated advisors are moving to the same side of the table as their clients. If this minor churning isn't in the clients' best interests, then the starving idealist won't do it. That's what makes this person an idealist to begin with. We don't need to cite chapter and verse of the rules of the National Association of Securities Dealers (NASD), or the fiduciary concepts enforced by the Securities and Exchange Commission (SEC), to reject this approach to getting paid on an ongoing basis. The starving idealist has already rejected it out of hand.

Pitfall of Success

As it happens, you don't need a bear market to find yourself having these kinds of problems, where you are working essentially for free. You can also get there by becoming very successful at bringing in new money.

Come again? Take the case of Jack Best, who practices in Rochester, New York. Best was, by most conventional measures, extremely successful; he wound up with 900 clients who had bought life insurance contracts or college education accounts or executed rollovers of various sizes. His goal was to meet with everybody twice a year personally, but as the client list grew, he realized that he'd have to have five client meetings a day just to meet that goal. Never mind getting anything else done.

Best was living the nightmare of the successful producer: he was collecting up-front revenues and then providing service, forever, for a growing list of people – and, to pay the bills, he also had to expand the number of clients, get new prospects who would commit new money, and who would add to the number of people he would have to provide ongoing services for. The circle had no obvious end to it; it went around and around, until, theoretically, he would be meeting with seven, eight, or 10 clients a day in order to meet his twice-a-year-meeting commitment. And, of course, the spiral wouldn't stop there.

What to do? Get off the merry-go-round. Best talked with his clients about the dilemma, and discovered that they were more than willing to pay him a fee for his services. "I recognized the evolution of the financial planning profession," says Best. "The bull market increased account values to levels many clients could never have imagined. Clients now wanted more attention and some occasional handholding. They wanted my time and were willing to pay for it. They had changed," he says, "and I had not."

If the goal is to get paid on an ongoing basis, and bring in revenues even when new money is scarce, then the simplest solution is to charge an ongoing fee for planning and related services – which is why, as we saw earlier, it is the trend in the profession.

Success in a Year or Less

There were many success stories offered in the *Inside Information* e-mailbox, and some that were heartbreaking; Jim Stark offered one that had both elements. "For the first 20 years of my career, I gave free financial profiles hoping to get commissions on products the client might need," he wrote. Then the clients would take his document and shop around for the lowest price to implement it. "Needless to say," he says, "I rarely got the sale."

Then, last November, he left the major insurer he had been working for and started with a firm that helped him structure his business on a fee and commission basis.

"I should have done this years ago," he wrote. "The same clients that I sold some investments and life insurance to (worth around $2,000,000 to $3,000,000) were now willing to hire me for $5,500 to fix their estate, financial, retirement and business succession plan. When I deliver the plan, I am now looked at as their professional financial advisor – not a salesman. When it comes time to implement the strategies they select, they don't shop around."

This change, you will note, took place in less than a single year. "I have since given away over one hundred of my small clients," he reports. "I now work smarter – not harder."

Robert Errico spent months creating a system of tracking his time spent per client, and then evaluated the fees received from each client versus the time expensed per client. The result opened his eyes – and his conclusions should be noted by anybody who thinks financial planning is a functional loss leader for product sales and commission revenue.

"It's astonishing how much time we spend per client answering questions, doing service interviews, providing tax information and other issues," he wrote me. "If your goal is to provide a high level of service to clients, then you must be compensated for this, or you will be bankrupt. An advisor must operate his or her planning practice as a business, which means not being afraid to charge high fees for service and, if necessary, turn prospects away. We all enjoy helping our clients, but we must also help ourselves."

Experienced advisors said that they experienced two primary benefits after switching to fee compensation:

Benefit 1: They don't starve when new money dries up.

Benefit 2: Their services to their existing clients improved dramatically. This, in turn, leads to increased business with less marketing effort, because clients who get more attention are more willing to recommend you to their friends and neighbors. "I can spend much more time preparing for client reviews," says Best, "and the referrals continue to come, because the more regular nature of my own income stream enables me to focus on the needs of the client across the desk rather than on the prospect in the waiting room."

The referral argument is sometimes challenged, but usually by people who don't get a lot of referrals, and who haven't experienced firsthand the positive referral dynamic. John Schram noted that many advisors are under the mistaken impression that people are motivated by price when they make recommendations to their friends and relatives, but in fact price may be the last criteria that people use when deciding to recommend an advisor. "I have to assume that your caller has been under the assumption that if he doesn't charge much for his services, the referrals just walk in," Schram writes with a perceptible shake of his head. But those who receive referrals will tell you that the high-touch, high-service issue overwhelms all other factors – and especially price.

Trapped?

Others told me more or less the same basic story that Best did about his conversion to fees. John Ritter worked for a firm that gave away planning as a loss leader for its commission revenue. "First year commissions were not amortized over the life expectancy of the client," he says. "Rather, they were consumed immediately to feed the hungry beast that had been created. Any thought of transitioning to fee-based compensation was immediately dismissed because of the 'certain company death' that would result."

In fact, in my conversation with one of the starving idealists who triggered my initial e-newsletter, I made the same suggestion – that he convert to fees. But he had done some analysis that shows that if he gives up his 6% commissions in favor of 1% ongoing revenues, he'll be out of business before he gets enough ongoing revenues to survive. He's trapped!

Transitional Strategies

Or is he? I received responses from a number of advisors who switched their compensation from A and B shares to C shares – which they regard, rightly or wrongly, as the equivalent of the asset management fee that fee-only planners assess on their client portfolios. (There is a rebuttal to this assertion, which leads to a very long and interesting argument which, I have decided, is beside the immediate point at hand.) The key to the conversion (which is *directly* on point) is that they didn't move every bit of their business from up-front to ongoing revenues all at once. "Most of my systematic monthly investment plans purchase A or B share products," says Richard Barca. "As of a couple of years ago, most of our large 401(k) rollovers are positioned into C shares. This helps me build my residual income, so I can stay in business in the future."

John Schram took the time to identify the opportunity cost of not having made this transition 20 years ago, when the starving idealist started in the business. "I did some quick HP12c calculations assuming gathering of $1,000,000 per year on average for twenty years and growing that asset base by 8% on average every year. Based on that, our starving advisor would have $50 million under his wing. He would have over $100,000 per year just in 25 basis point trails alone if he'd recommended a diversified mutual fund portfolio."

This, in effect, was Mark Leibman's approach as well. Leibman reports that he made the transition easier by starting to recommend Putnam's M-class shares, to earn a lower 3% up-front commission and a higher 65 basis point trail. Then he began recommending 2% up-front commission C shares, and mixed in 1% C shares as well. As the recurring revenue became larger, he gave up front-end commissions altogether.

"My business plan was simplicity itself," Leibman reports. "If you book $100 a day in recurring income every day for 1,000 days, you end up with $100,000 in recurring annual income. This is only $10,000 a day in C share business! 1,000 working days – less than 4 years! At first you may have to work in a little front money, or do some insurance business, but the rewards are perpetual."

Old Way vs. New Way

Of course, the transition is made more quickly if you can convert some or all of your existing commission clients to a fee basis. Charlie Kares wrote with some advice on how to explain the change in compensation structure to these existing clients. "I explained the 'old way' versus the 'new way.' "The old way," he says, "was that the client was limited to only commission-paying products, and their portfolio would not be actively managed. I told them it was 'cross your fingers and hope nothing goes bad with your mutual funds, because I could not make changes in their portfolio without them paying a sales commission again.' I also told the client that there are many very good no-load mutual funds that I could not recommend because I wouldn't get paid for the sale of those funds."

How did he describe the "new way?" Under the new way, he says, the client would be able to buy almost any mutual fund as a no-load. "Now that the churning issue does not exist," he says, "I can be free to actively manage their account and make changes for them so that they stay in the funds best suited to achieve their goals. Additionally, I told the client that the quarterly management fee would be automatically deducted from their account."

Simple, but effective: Kares reports that he was able to convert every commission account over $50,000 to a fee arrangement.

The Payoff Down the Road

Mike Schafer, who practices in Independence, Ohio, offered a rare glimpse of a planning office at exactly that transitional point: his firm, which had been spun-off from a prominent estate planning company and was less than two years old when he wrote to me, and is being built on the fee-only model. Painful? Hell yes, says Schafer. "On a $1,500,000 account brought in during July," he writes, we will not see a dime until we take a prorated quarterly fee in October. Compare that to any big upfront commission and you realize that we aren't getting any immediate benefit to cover our costs, let alone pay ourselves."

But he can see the payoff down the road – and it's more than just money. It is also security. "We will be able to tell what we are going to earn on an ongoing basis as long as we have this client," he wrote. "The fact that we are 'feeing' the account requires regular contact, which makes people know that you are still working for them. When people know you are working for them and doing the right thing (i.e., recommending changes that do not generate a commission) they are more apt to bring referrals. We think we have a sound long term model," he says. "The more reoccurring revenue our business holds, the more valuable our business (should we decide to sell). While we are trying to grow now, we know down the road that we won't have to worry from year to year where our next client is going to come from. I think that is the danger," he concludes. "When the market/trading dries up, those that depend on it suffer. We suffer now but are creating a revenue stream that at some point, we may be able to stop taking clients."

Ritter found the transition to be much easier when he started charging up-front planning or case writing fees. "I went from preparing comprehensive plans for free (sounds like the internet - lose a dollar on every sale and make it up on volume) to charging $500," he says. "That was two years, and three price increases, ago. We now charge $1,250 for a comprehensive financial plan, and use this as a qualifier to determine if a person is willing to pay for solid advice."

Trainable Clients

This is interesting, because you typically read in the trade press about how the most successful firms have given up planning fees. Many of the largest planning shops are (as reported) doing comprehensive financial plans for their clients, and letting the asset management fees pay for that up-front work. And yes, these established advisors tend to be the most visible and most-often-profiled advisors in the business. But from my experience in talking with advisors in the trenches, and from many of the e-mails I've received, this is actually a minority practice. Most advisors charge an up-front fee for the planning work they do – which, they will argue, takes away any sales pressure for the client to "implement" the plan with them.

Bill Ramsay, who practices in Charlotte on a fee-only basis, is one of the few fee-compensated planners who agrees that the assets under management compensation structure is pretty much identical to the roughly 1% that C-shares pay, and that doing a financial plan mainly to get investment business (whether commission or asset management) represents "planning with an agenda" – a conflict of interest that he's uncomfortable with. *All* of his compensation is for planning work.

Will clients pay fees for planning work after you've trained them to expect it for free? According to the messages I received, some clearly will not, but you will be surprised at how small this percentage is. Ramsay reports that when the client is paying for the initial planning casework, then the dreaded "obligation to do business with this person at the end of the planning casework" was eliminated. "I think the (fee) relationships are actually more mature," he says. "I'm sure some salespeople would be insistent that the up-front planning work is done to show the 'need' to buy, but that sounds like the outcome is predetermined – certainly not an objective relationship."

Mike Lafferty echoes Ramsay's comment that advisors themselves are harder to convert than their clients. "Clients are very trainable," he says. "If you can't afford to do it all at once, start with new clients. Realize that at some point you will have to drop those clients who will not convert. I actually turn away more prospective clients than I take," Lafferty continues. "I refuse to work with anyone who does not value my time or wants to haggle over my fees. I would rather work with 100 clients who value my time than 1,000 who don't."

Charge a Fee, Get Respect

Eliminating that conflict, said one advisor, was the best thing she ever did for her own business, and for her self-image as a planner. And, she said, it really helped her sort out the clients who were willing to work with her from the ones that simply wanted some free advice – a sorting process that she found impossible to do when she was paid by commissions, and which caused her to spend as much as 60% of her time unproductively in the early years of her practice. As Mike Noland, in Marietta, Georgia says: "It eliminates the tire-kickers." And if they won't implement after completing the plan, the planner doesn't starve.

If the financial plan is a loss leader designed to lead to other sources of income, then not charging for it may, paradoxically, be reducing your income potential. Barry Doll, who works in Port Orchard, Washington, reports that his firm used to do financial plans and advise these people for free (some of them pastors, some elderly on fixed income, some just starting out). "What we found out," he says, "is that if we do not charge anything, they have made no investment and typically do not value and implement the plan."

So, over the last year or so, Doll and his firm have started charging these people a reduced charge for their plans (although they aren't told that it's reduced). "Since they have paid for professional advice, they typically follow through with the recommendations," says Doll.

Other advisors echoed this same theme, which might be stated as: "You only value what you pay for." Ronald Smith, who practices in La Jolla, California, wishes every advisor would muster the courage to charge a fair price for his or her services. "In recent years many planners fell into the trap of trying to offer boutique services to all at bargain basement prices," he says. "We (planners) have to educate our clients that great service comes at a reasonable (not cheap) price. Any compromise to this premise promotes the 'starving idealist' syndrome." In other words, starving idealists are perpetuating and reinforcing their own situation when they cut their fees.

Finally, a few advisors noted that the conversion to fee-compensation is inevitable as the planning profession becomes a profession. You can decide for yourself whether they make a good case, but I find it persuasive. Mike Lafferty made a career change from the legal profession, and worked with Morgan Stanley Dean Witter and, later, American Express. His impressions were that most advisors are trained to sell, and are culturally uncomfortable with offering advice without an agenda.

This, he says, will have to change before advisors can earn the trust of their clients and the status of professionals. "I don't care how you slice it," he says, "professionals do *not* sell. If I, as a lawyer, recommended a course of action to a client because it benefited me, I would be disbarred." Later in the letter he advised the starving idealist to move his compensation from being tied to the sale of a product. "Your advice," he says, "is the product."

The Confidence Spiral

Smith also noted that his best clients never fight him on the fees he charges. This has given him the strength to reject clients who do. "Prospects who do fight the proposed fees are encouraged to keep looking for an advisor who does cheap work," he says. "It's perfectly reasonable to reject business that will drive your business into the ground!"

Bruce Miller takes a similarly tough approach with the fees he charges. "I set the rules for billing and collections as my first topic item," he says, "and insure that we agree to it before we get started."

This, however, will strike some starving idealists as too easy. They recognize that there's a chicken-and-egg situation here: the more business success you achieve, the more revenues you bring in, the more confident you are about the value of your services, and the more able you are to reject prospects who are looking for as close to free service as they can get. On the other end, if you're not making a living in the business, you tend to grasp at any planning work that comes your way, and take on people who are ultimately unprofitable.

The question becomes: how do you stop the negative spiral, and gain the confidence to turn the spiral around?

It starts by recognizing the problem.

Bruce Keefe, who practices in La Jolla, California, thought he detected a symptom of low self-esteem in the original subject of the original e-mail, particularly in the advisor's decision to "Give every client who walks in the door, no matter how little or how much they have to invest, a full financial plan and a portfolio with the best funds I can recommend."

"We live in a society where price determines value," says Keefe. "To 'give' (or severely discount) his work will accomplish nothing more than to demean him and his products. I'm sure everyone will think he's a nice person, but they will not respect him. Why? Because he establishes his 'value' by his price, and why would his customers value him any higher than he does himself?"

"The same defeatist attitude is found in the phrase 'My clients are typically middle income and very resistant to paying fees.' I believe our friend, for whatever reason, doesn't think he is deserving of those fees and he transmits that feeling to his clients. Since the starving idealist thinks of the fees as a problem," says Keefe, "his customers will also."

Undervaluing Your Service

Marilyn Capelli Dimitroff, who has been the subject of a number of articles in the trade press, can relate to the starving idealist syndrome – because she lived under it in the early years of her career. She thinks that a lack of confidence is endemic in the planning profession. "One factor common to starving idealists is chronically undervaluing their own benefit to clients," she says. "If the planner doesn't think he or she is worth it, the client won't either."

Mark Leibman points out that many advisors find themselves backed into a corner on revenues, where they have such an investment in loss-leader time that it has to be paid for by a product recommendation. When products are recommended purely for the revenue they will provide to the advisor, it is hard to feel confident about the ultimate value-added. "I've seen the victims of the idealists – massive free work for periods of time, followed by an inappropriate sale of a second-rate variable annuity to catch up," says Leibman.

Scott Dolitsky comes to the problem from a unique perspective: he has been a trainer for planners, and has noticed that a lot of advisors lack the self confidence to sell their services or any investment products – a process he calls "creating a reality that is void of rejection." "I am sure my success rate is due, like all my interactions with clients, to the fact that if I believed in it, they tend to believe it," he says. "If [the starving idealist] truly believes he is providing a top level service, then he deserves to be paid a fair wage."

The Power of Small Course Corrections

This raises what I consider to be one of the most interesting points about the planning profession – a point that I wish every advisor, and particularly the starving idealists among us – could understand.

Whenever I talk with planners who have more than 30 years in the business, who typically have worked with some people for 20, 25 or 30 years, they are utterly confident about the value of financial planning advice. They have seen how their advice, leveraged over a time period measured in decades, accomplishes enormous differences in the lives of their clients.

As one veteran advisor put it to me: "I have people I've worked with for 20 years, and over that time, with my help, they have tended to save a little more, invest a little more wisely, pay a little less for more and better coverage, plan a little better for their future and spend a little more time deciding what they really want out of life." All these "little mores" added up to something remarkable, he says. "I've seen my clients retire with millions of dollars, earlier than other people in their companies who earned more than they did, who couldn't afford to retire."

The lesson: just a 1% course correction, each year, over a 10-year period means a huge difference in the end of the journey.

That is the ultimate value of financial planning advice; the little adjustments, changes and bits of timely wisdom make the difference between a life that achieves financial success, and one that does not. The advice along the way is worth much more to the client than anybody today is charging for it.

A few advisors noted that as they spent time finding better ways to communicate the value of their services, they became more confident about charging an appropriate price for them.

"I have educated my clients, and continue to purposefully educate them in every work session we have together about the importance, process, and deliverables of personal financial planning," wrote David Carter, who was once a starving idealist but now makes a successful living working with a Middle Market clientele. "My clients are told that part of everything that they pay me is 'tuition,' and that the more they learn, the farther we will go together." He adds that his stated thesis is to get his clients retired and keep them retired since, as he says, "that is the primary purpose of most middle income level clients' financial/investment objectives."

Most articles on the subject of client communication will stress the importance of creating an "elevator sentence" – that is, a one-sentence communication of what you offer to clients, short enough that if somebody asks you what you do on the elevator, you can communicate your value before they reach their floor. (An example of an elevator sentence is: "I work with successful people who have stress in their lives, to help them make work optional rather than necessary.")

As Carter makes clear, the elevator sentence is only a beginning. As clients work with you for months and years, the planning profession is going to have to get much, much better about communicating its value to its clients. Some advisors sent me messages complaining, "People don't really recognize the value of financial planning services." The only possible answer to this complaint is: whose fault is that? Is it the fault of the client that he (or she) doesn't see how your work is benefiting him (or her)?

Strategic Alliances

A few of the e-mail respondents noted that, as they converted totally to fees, there were suddenly a lot of opportunities to work with outside firms and deliver financial planning services to their (these other firms') clients.

If you're a starving idealist who hates to market, this may be the best avenue to explore.

For example? One of the most interesting phenomena to emerge in the profession is something I call the "remora firm," named after the small fish that routinely hitches a ride with larger fish and eats food that the larger fish finds unattractive. Earlier in this book, we saw this with members of the Garrett Planning Network and the Cambridge Alliance. But it also works for advisors who are not part of a cooperative system.

Two advisors, in different parts of the country, sent me messages saying that when they converted to fees, they prepared themselves for a huge struggle – and then suddenly struck gold. In both cases, a local, much larger planning firm identified their little company as a place to refer out prospects who came to them without a lot of assets – people who aren't worth millions, and who don't qualify for the larger firm's asset under management service.

"I'm working with middle income people who are primarily referrals from a big fee-only firm down the street," one told me. "The relationship now brings me more business than I can handle."

Why would the large firm bother to find a home for these prospects that it finds unattractive? The prospects may be friends or relatives of existing clients, who need or want planning service, and the larger firm doesn't want to turn them away altogether. Or (as is often the case) the principals at the larger firm may be uncomfortable simply turning away people who have sought out their services.

Stages of Transformation

Of course, the more common strategic alliance opportunities lie with companies that want to offer financial planning to their customers, but who have, for a variety of reasons, found it difficult to start up a planning division internally.

An excellent example of this comes from Michael Fischer, who wrote what amounts to a mini-case study of how to transform yourself from the starving idealist situation into success in several easy steps. They offer a rare snapshot of how each stage of the transformation took place.

"I have been a CFP for nearly 20 years now and for many of those years I felt just like your starving idealist friend," Fischer wrote. "I did what I considered to be great work and I always went home after what was usually a very long day with a feeling of great pride about what I did and how I did it. I sometimes felt frustrated over the fact that I did okay financially, but I never got over that hump that I saw so many of my colleagues achieve in terms of creating personal wealth. I felt embarrassed at times that I was a financial planner and I wasn't getting ahead financially in my personal circumstances."

Does this sound familiar? Fischer went on to say that he has an excellent reputation in the industry and has held almost all of the board positions in both the former IAFP and ICFP. In fact, he was currently serving on the FPA local chapter board.

Fischer made the transition to fees, and exchanged short-term pain for a stabilization of his income. Then he made the decision to create a larger critical mass, and found someone who had a similar firm to merge with. "Amidst the perils and occasional disadvantages of having a partner," he wrote, "there are some real benefits. One, major benefit is expense sharing. I now have more support resources with about the same level of expenses for support staff, computers, software, etc."

With staff came other opportunities. Fischer learned to begin delegating many tasks that he had earlier thought to be an important part of his personal relationship with his clients. For example? "I used to take a great deal of time calling every client to schedule their quarterly reviews," he says, "thinking that they would be offended or find it too impersonal if my staff called them." What he discovered, instead, was that his clients enjoyed getting to know other members of his firm, and that they respected him (and his time) more when he started treating his business more like a business.

This benefit might have been expected, but another was not. "I found my staff started taking their roles more seriously as they became more intimate with the clients," Fischer wrote. "In spite of all my delusions to the contrary, delegating a small task like that improved my business and gave me more time to do the important things. I have since learned many similar lessons in delegation. My staff now prepares many things that I formerly thought only I could do adequately. In fact, they have shown me ways to do them better and more efficiently. This has also freed up more of my time to think more creatively and put my energies into the more important areas of my business – which is where I belong."

Over time, Fischer began to raise his fees and stopped being apologetic about the fact that he needed to get paid for his work. "Mind you," he says, "I was still probably one of the lower cost providers in the area, but I was making more money that I did before."

Raising his fees had several visible impacts. "One, I began to take myself more seriously and I started doing even better work," he says. "Two, my clients and prospects started taking me more seriously and our relationship strengthened and became more professional. The quality of the work became as important as the personal relationship with the client, and the personal relationship was not sacrificed in the process. As one of my original clients put it when we talked about the higher fees: 'I am not going to be better off if you go out of business.'"

Even so, the major breakthrough was still to come. "I finally had to admit that we were terrible at marketing," Fischer wrote to me. "I had begun to build a really great system, but I didn't have enough volume of clients to put into the pipeline."

Here's where the strategic partnership enters the picture. Fischer and his partner met with a local third party administrator of retirement plans – a company that wanted to offer investment advisory services to clients. "Their experience was that many of their retirement plans and individual clients were receiving crummy service from their advisors, and they felt that the only way of assuring quality of service was to offer it themselves," he says. "They hired a number of people and it failed miserably, for many reasons. Finally, their attorney suggested that they link up with a firm that was already providing such services and find a way to share revenues." After some negotiations, a partnership was born.

The Missing Ingredient

This proved to be the missing ingredient to Fischer's business success. "Now," he says, "we get a steady stream of pre-sold referrals and we don't have to spend our time and money on marketing efforts that were rather unsuccessful. This relationship has helped us focus our efforts on several types of clients and build a system for servicing them. Many of them report that they have never experienced such service, and it is resulting in a significant amount of new referrals. "We are also," Fischer adds, "developing solid relationships with the new clients' existing advisors, and are beginning to see additional referrals from them as well."

"This new business," Fischer wrote, "has allowed us to expand our staff, and thus has meant no disruption to our existing clients. In fact I would say that our old clients are receiving better services through many of the advances that have grown out of the relationship with the third party administrator. I know that I spend much more of my time doing research, analysis, and developing presentations that I was hard-pressed to do before. I am allowed to do more of what I really enjoy and value, so I am even happier about my work. I now leave the office at a reasonable hour on most days and I seldom work weekends any more. Even my golf game is better! In addition," he adds, "over the past four years, my personal income has increased each year to a level that I feel good about and I am building the net worth I always believed I should have."

Fisher adds one more note that I think is worth passing on. "I know just how your 'starving idealist' feels, and I encourage him to not give up," he says. "If you're not good at generating the volume of business that gets you where you want to be, admit that. Once I faced that reality and stopped making excuses for myself, the rest became rather easy. I was then more willing to give up part of my revenue stream to someone who was, and achieve the best of both worlds."

Some of the themes of this story – converting to fees, developing the confidence to charge a fair price, and, of course, the strategic partnership, have been reinforced by earlier messages. Others – reducing overhead and gaining economies of scale by sharing office space or merging with another advisor; overcoming a resistance to delegate; and facing your own limitations and allowing others to take over a part of your business functions – will be echoed and reinforced in the next two sections of this chapter.

Business Issues and The Clientele

Bruce Rawlins, who now works with one of the larger insurance companies, offers a simple, soul-searching question to advisors who are relentlessly determined to work with a Middle Market client: Why?

"When I went into the insurance/financial services business in 1991," he reports, "I had no desire to try to go after the 'high dollar' client. I wanted to serve middle America. What I found out was that although I believe my clients appreciated my advice and service, it is not feasible to serve this market unless you are willing to work night and day, which I was not. Unless something changes," Rawlins warns, "the successful planners are going to have a limited number of medium to high net worth individuals, with middle America continuing to be under served."

Matthew Dow Teems puts this even more clearly. "Financial advice is a luxury that some can afford and some can't," he wrote. "I wish they would find a way to make Ferraris cost $10,000, but don't count on it. I don't mean to sound insensitive, but this is similar to the problems in the health care industry. Everyone complains about rising health insurance costs, yet everyone wants Ferrari-level health care. No one wants to publicly state the obvious, 'Citizen 1 can afford top notch _____ (fill in the blank: health care, financial advice, housing, etc.) and Citizen 2 has to make do without.'"

Nor does Teems believe that the middle income person is totally left without resources. "As much as I fight the financial press over who provides the best advice (us or them), they do a good job of broadcasting the basics," he says. "I firmly believe that a lower-to-middle income person, with a sincere desire to get ahead, can find enough direction in the media, books, and newspapers to build a sound foundation. If members of our business want to provide top level, time-consuming advice to people who can't afford to pay for it, I applaud their philanthropy," he concludes. "I just can't afford to feed my family operating as a non-profit organization."

Middle Market Profits

Even so, some of the best responses I received were from advisors who have made a good living working with a Middle Market clientele. One of the best came from David Williams, whose e-mail handle is "planman." Williams decided to start his planning practice in rural northeast Oregon on the theory that if he was starting from scratch anyway, why not build his business in a place where he wouldn't mind retiring?

The total market (from one end of the valley to the other) contains 25,000 people; the wealthy are individuals with $100,000 portfolios. "I believe I can make a bigger difference in the life of the retiring school teacher with an $80,000 tax sheltered annuity or the young couple who needs a plan to protect against death or disability, than I can with somebody who has more than they can ever spend. I explain 529 plans, Roth IRAs, and medical savings accounts more than I do multigenerational estate planning," he says, "yet when we go to educational conferences, we are taught to trample rabbits while hunting for these elephants."

"I have colleagues in Seattle and San Francisco who have $500,000 minimums," he adds. "I think you hit it right on the head that our industry focuses on those other 10%; the other 90% of us work for people whom the elite of the industry won't call clients."

Surely this market represents a challenge as great as any starving idealist could hope for, and the fact that Williams earns commissions would seem to make him doubly handicapped. Yet he reports that he's been financially successful even through the downturn. One part of his success (here's that theme again) is ongoing revenues; he converted many of his recommendations to C shares and went through a difficult 15 months before emerging with an ongoing revenue stream. (He still recommends B share funds for clients investing less than $10,000.)

A more important key to success appears to be Williams' candor about how he gets paid, and his outspoken desire to sit on the same side of the table as his clients in all their financial and personal challenges. "I have a staff of three, and I am sincere in telling clients that I'm financially responsible to my staff," he says. The last year has been hard, he admits, and his clients have lost money. "I've lost two or three clients this year, and in each case we parted on good terms," he says. "On the positive side, we picked up more than a dozen clients from wire house 'salesmen.' These clients came because of our reputation of financial planning and, more important, our relationship with clients. It's fulfilling for my staff and I to maintain a love affair with our clients."

"WE" Focused

Several e-mail responses I received to the "starving idealist" syndrome said that the problem lay not with any of the things I mentioned above, but simply with the fact that many advisors just don't know how to run a business.

"There's a big difference between knowing how to provide financial planning services, and knowing how to run a successful business," one advisor told me. "As a profession, we tend to focus all of our attention on the former, and none at all on the latter."

"Many of these people are missionaries, not business people, more involved in preaching the good news of planning and investing than having any fundamental concept of business and analysis," adds Mark Leibman. "I give away more advice than anyone I know – but I figured out how to turn my avocation into a business. If I do great work but can't stay in business, I failed the clients who depend on me, so job one is to take care of my business."

I suspect that many starving idealists often hear their peers telling them that they need to develop business skills, but we are never told exactly what that means. The e-mails I received were full of highly specific business advice, which makes it clear that we are not talking about rocket science.

For example, several advisors suggested that our starving idealists look for immediate ways to cut expenses. Rob Isbitts, from Weston, Florida, says that when the top line is not controllable, then you have to move the other lever. "Find advisors in similar situations," he suggests. "By sharing office space, technology, even staff, they can all reduce expenses, and increase the bottom line."

Sherry Hazan-Cohen, who referred to herself as "queen of the idealists," offered similar advice: move to a home office and eliminate 95% of your overhead. She also suggested that the starving idealist practice what he or she preaches: get out of debt, get a written financial plan and stick to it.

Another example: Jeff Bright suggested that the starving idealists keep track of the time they spend with each client. "If he looks at his commissions and divides the hours worked with a client," he says, "Chances are he'll find that he makes $10 an hour for some and $200 an hour for others. How fair is that to the people who are paying $200 an hour?"

More importantly, he says, how smart is it? Earlier in this chapter, we heard a lot about advisors who are clearly too "*me*-focused," as Bright puts it. But, he says, advisors at the other end of the spectrum are too "*you*-focused" for their business health. They are giving too much and getting too little.

"The great advisors," he argues, persuasively, "are *we*-focused;" they improve their clients' lives and are paid well to do it."

Time Limits

Is there a procedural way to determine whether you are too "*you*-focused?" Maybe. Michael Klonsky confesses up-front that he has tendencies in that direction. "I'm a firm believer in spending time with clients," he says. "However, there is a limit as to how much time one can spend."

It may be possible to calculate that limit precisely. Bill Verhagen would sit down with a client and determine how he could help them, and then, if the relationship was intended to be a commissioned one (he also has fee clients) he would calculate the commission revenues and divide that by the $75 an hour that his time was worth. "This gave me the total amount of time that I could spend in hours working for that client," he says. He would take these hours and allocate them according to the following activities:

1. Time needed to find that client (e.g., how much prospecting time did it take on average to obtain a client?).

2. Initial meeting time (fact finding and relationship building).

3. Time needed to deliver and review recommendations, product sales, etc.

4. Estimated time to service the client during that year.

5. The time that was left that he could spend working on the plan.

"If I did not force myself to an allotment of time, I could work all week on a plan," he says, noting how quickly that would bring him to the starving idealist's financial position. "By limiting my time," Verhagen continues, "I forced myself to deliver an appropriate plan to each person based on what they were paying for. Those who paid for a "spec" plan received a complete, but simplified plan. Those who paid for a "custom built" plan with all the spreadsheets and ancillary computations got what they paid for."

"In time," Verhagen concludes, "I found each client was pleased with what they paid for. Many clients who started out small have since grown with me and updated plans have developed additional detail that was really not important to them when we first started our relationship. If the person asking you for advice has really been in the business for 20 years, I suspect he could do a bang up job for a client with a yellow pad and a one-hour meeting. He needs to define what his client needs and how he can best provide it."

Mike Lafferty points out that too many advisors are doing menial work that they could hire out at minimal cost. "Realize that your time is all you have to offer," he says. "If you value your time at $150 per hour you should never be doing $10/hour tasks like typing letters to clients." Another advisor offered what I think is a brilliant suggestion: he said that every time you do something around the office, ask yourself how much somebody else would pay you to do that kind of work. If the answer is less than $50 an hour, then the task is a good candidate for you to delegate.

David Bernard, who practices in Aurora, Colorado, wrote to say that he practices this on a daily basis. "Every time I observe a function in my practice, I first ask, 'Who can I get to do this function for me, hopefully without charge?' Next, I say, 'OK, if I have to do it myself, can I get the computer to do it?'" Between the asset managers he works with, his broker-dealer and

Morningstar, a lot of his investment analysis work is now automated.

The Gift of Business Talent

Some of the messages I received suggested that the starving idealists lacked something that might be called a "business talent," which some people have and some people do not.

This is another one of those things that is almost never defined in a satisfactory way. What do you mean by being a talented businessperson? What would a person with business talent do that the rest of us would not?

You won't get a precise definition here, but you might get something more useful: a concrete example or two of what separates those who are naturally gifted from those who are (for whatever reason) not. Several advisors told me that for the naturally talented businessperson, failure is the key to success. I frankly didn't understand this concept at first (I'm not one of these gifted individuals either), but after some follow-up e-mails, I realize that this is perhaps the most profound insight you will read in this book.

The advisors who have business talent experience roughly the same degree of failure as the rest of us, and just like the rest of us, it tends to come randomly and with little preparation or warning. The difference is that these business/talented people do two things that most of the rest of us don't:

1. They set aside time on their schedule, on a regular basis, to think about the problems they have, and their goals, and how to achieve them. They also reserve time from their daily tasks exclusively for fixing long-term or recurrent problems.

2.   Successful people regard any setback as an opportunity to move forward.

The best example of this came from a planner named James Cannon, who sent me an e-mail saying that he had been compensated primarily by load fund commissions – until they dried up in the last 18 months. You would think this was the end of the world, but, he says, "The downturn in the market over the last 18 months or so has been a blessing to me, because it forced me to learn new things in order to stay ahead of the competition."

For example? "Over the last year I have trashed most of the models and have had much greater success since doing so. I study economics, finance, business trends and consumer trends in an attempt to gauge market trends. By the end of May this year, I had the majority of client funds in cash, bonds, and a few small value funds. Over the last month all my clients have seen great value in this approach and are advertising for me."

Now that we've laid out some basic tips and techniques for refining the starving idealist's business model, some readers are shaking their heads and saying: "This isn't for me. Whatever made me think that I wanted to run a business in the first place?"

In fact, for advisors who have limited business skills and limited desire to develop them, the best solution might be to operate in an environment where others tend the profitability issues. "If it turns out that he can't operate financially as a planner on his own, he can to look at becoming an employee of a good firm," says Marilyn Capelli Dimitroff. "There is a growing demand for good planners (CFPs) by growing firms. If he doesn't have the mark," she adds, "he should get it."

Resistance to Coaching

Many advisors said that the very best single piece of advice they could give to others was to hire a business coach or personal life trainer to help them overcome their own personal limitations.

Interestingly, many of the members of my *Inside Information* community rejected this idea out-of-hand the first time it was presented. They responded that they didn't have time, didn't have the money to spend, or didn't have problems that need "fixing."

This resistance to hiring an outside advisor in things they are not skilled at is almost certainly one of the strangest things about the planning profession. Isn't the profession founded on the principle that people should delegate difficult areas of their life (like personal finances) to outside experts (us)?

Then why are we reluctant to take our own advice, and why are we resistant to hiring outside professionals to help us overcome our own areas of incompetency?

We believe everybody should come to us for this service. But we wouldn't be willing to buy it ourselves.

There was a second interesting irony in the messages that came back. When financial advisors become consumers of their own services, they get a very different perspective on the services they are currently offering.

Meaning what? A disturbingly large number of advisors took my advice to heart, looked around their communities, and then came back and told me that they couldn't find anybody they, themselves, would want to hire. And, they said, it caused them to take another look at their own services, to see whether they (if they were an outsider) would want to hire themselves to provide the services they were seeking.

Several of these advisors eventually found a coach outside their communities, and one of the first items on the agenda was to learn how to provide this service to their own clients. Of course, other professions already have this kind of system built into the training structure. Psychologists must go through psychological evaluation themselves before they can offer services to the general public.

David Carter, whose message was mentioned earlier in the section on communicating the benefits of planning to clients, has worked out what I think is a tremendously creative way to handle – and pay for – consulting services. He routinely buys consulting time from more successful firms than his. "This is a good way to identify the strengths and weaknesses of a particular practitioner's efforts," he says.

Then he turns around and, with the perspectives of other successful firms in hand, offers his own consulting services to smaller financial planning and accounting firms all over the country. The one helps pay for the other, and everybody benefits.

The Value of Coaching

Tracy Beckes, a business coach who works with financial advisors, offers the same essential point.

"If you want to be a coach, hire a coach," she says. "It's one of the first tenets of any profession: be a recipient of the service you want to offer. Become coachable. I'll say with a lot of my planners when I start working with them, 'do you have a financial planner?'"

Beyond that, there seems to be a fundamental misunderstanding among many people about what, exactly, coaching or life planning is. Beckes believes that she, personally, was lucky to have been an athlete in high school and college because it allowed her to experience the process of having other successful people share their secrets of success in an environment where this was considered socially acceptable. "I always had a team of coaches around me coaching me," she says. "Later, I looked back and thought, wow, why didn't I have coaches in other parts of my life when I was younger? It wasn't until I actually started doing it that I started thinking about and understanding the value of coaching services."

In her own practice, Beckes encourages her clients to work on creating what she calls an "effortless, outrageous practice."

Where do you start? In the earliest stages, the goal is to get clear about what an effortless, outrageous practice means to you. For everybody, the definition is going to be at least slightly different – and, in most cases, it will also be very difficult to define at first. Beckes has found that most planners are trapped by their own assumptions about what a financial planning practice "should" look like, and how it "should" function, which makes it hard for them to freely identify what they actually want to happen in their business. "We unconsciously adopt these ideas and beliefs and sometimes we operate from them long past their actual useful life and service to us," she says. To make matters worse, she has found that her planner clients tend to have a very hard time determining the things they, personally, happen to be really good at. "They're hidden in plain sight," she says. "Because they are so easy and natural for us, we absolutely don't see them. Or if we do, we think of them as unimpressive."

So you should begin your own life planning journey – the business part of it, anyway – by taking a fresh look at your business life, and try to see beyond the assumptions and blind spots that might be hemming you in.

Does It Energize Me?

But how? Beckes suggests a relatively simple test for each advisor to give him/herself. You pay attention to everything you do in the office, and as you are doing it, you ask yourself: "do I feel energized or drained as I do this?" If you feel energized (perhaps during a client meeting, or when you're speaking in front of a group of people at a marketing seminar), then this is something you want to do more of. "Typically, when you're working in areas you're really good at, time flies by," she says. "Probably the most important thing you're doing for your firm is using your creativity – packaging your ideas and concepts and products and services, and delivering them to clients on a moment by moment basis. It's a very creative act. So when you get clear and focus on the few activities you most enjoy doing, and the ones you're most interested in, you're actually starting to access your creativity."

"Planning," says Beckes, "is the daily practice of creativity."

Of course, when you run across activities that are draining your energy, then your first goal is to list them, and then find ways to delegate them to somebody else. This is often much easier to say than it is to do. "The main reason why people don't focus on their natural abilities is because they try to do everything themselves," Beckes argues. "They start clogging up their schedule with activities that literally hundreds of other people could do."

You might imagine that you're the only person in the entire planning profession who is so bogged down with busywork that creativity is nearly unthinkable. But Beckes has statistics that suggest that the average professional has 200 to 300 hours of backlogged work on his or her desk. "Think about all the journal articles to read, all the projects you're working on, all the client issues that you're resolving," she says. "It's vitally important that you free up your energy by getting all of that off your desk."

How? "Almost all of the planners I work with are extremely competent and capable and can do a lot of things, which is their biggest trap," says Beckes. "Just because you can do something doesn't mean that you should. Learning how to say 'no' is one of the more important skills for creating an effortless, outrageous practice."

This point is so important that Beckes repeats it with greater emphasis. "The inability to say 'no'," she says, "is the main reason why people don't live the lives they want and create the practice that they most want."

You can, of course, delegate these hundreds of hours of backlogged work – and the ongoing tasks that put them on your desk to begin with. But before you do that, you might consider an easier solution. "You could," Beckes suggests, "simply delete that item. Is it one of the few core activities that produce the best results in your practice? Remember that the quality of your life depends on making good, clear decisions."

Preconceived Income Limitations

The effortless, outrageous practice is not just about time and delegation; it is also about money, and your relationship with money. Beckes has found that many of her planning clients walk in with preconceived ideas about how much they "ought" to be earning, and are limited by these internal definitions of what they think about their value and worth. "I ask people to suspend all their thoughts and ideas about fees for a moment," she says. Then she suggests that you think about what it truly costs to deliver your service. The list includes your ideas, your life experiences, and the wisdom you have accumulated. It includes the educational sessions you attend, the actual cost of your office and overhead, and also the health cost of stress whenever you take on new business.

"I contend that almost everyone is undercharging for his or her services," she says. "The key thing for you to consider is: do you feel fully compensated for the value and benefit that you're providing your clients?"

Some readers may be wondering how this relates to the satisfaction you get from your work. But Beckes has an answer.

"When you feel fully compensated for what you do, it has a whole different feeling inside," she says. "You show up. You do a better job. With some clients who are reluctant to pay you, you feel defeated; with others, who are paying full value for your services, you feel energized."

In her coaching activities, Beckes has found that there are two key areas that advisors need to address before they're willing or able to make more money per unit time of work. The first is basic self-esteem. "A lot of time, what stops us from being fully compensated is that we aren't certain about the true value of what we're providing," she says. This is an area you can work on yourself and/or with coaching, but Beckes also thinks there's a feedback loop with clients that you could be tending more closely. If you ask for more money, often the clients have no problem with paying it, and you realize the value of what you're providing. "I just challenge people to try bringing on a few new clients at a higher fee, and just living with that for a while," she says. "It's surprising the psychological and emotional impact of being well-compensated for what you do."

Communicating Value

And the second area to address is communication. "How well are you communicating the value and benefit of what you're doing?" Beckes asks. "Sometimes that one adjustment, just getting clearer about it and communicating more clearly with your clients what you're doing for them, can make it easier for you to start making more money."

Finally, Beckes talks about self-care. How important is this? "Phenomenal self-care is the foundation for an effortless, outrageous practice," she says. "When you take good care of yourself, then and only then are you able to provide great service for your clients."

This is an enormous subject, but Beckes offers a few practical tips for addressing it. One of her clients made up a list of the seven to ten things that he was most stressed about, and made a commitment to eliminate them. Not reducing or modifying or changing them, you understand, but completely eliminating them from his life.

Another is to find a location that energizes you. Some people, Beckes says, receive vitality and energy from a lake environment, or living on or near water. Others prefer to live in a city. The list of possibilities is endless, but Beckes has found that most of her clients haven't bothered to identify their ideal environment, much less make an effort to move their office there.

As you make progress from your current position toward a greater realization of life planning in your own practice, you recognize that the goal is to create a practice that authentically reflects who you are when you're at your very best. You are focused on the things that you most enjoy doing, and your work energizes you, rather than draining energy and leaving you tired and dissatisfied at the end of the day. And your clients are able to truly access the best that you're offering.

One insight that comes as you move deeper into life planning is that there is no logical end point to the process; that you will keep evolving and improving and keep seeing new goals the further you get. Beckes has a terrific way of expressing the fact that life is a journey with no fixed destination. "Even if you get a great foundation for an effortless, outrageous practice, it's constantly evolving, and there's constant opportunity to learn deeply about yourself and to move through more issues," she says. "I think this is the gist of the human experience."

Beckes offers some advice for how to select and work with a planner/coach. "The key thing is to take responsibility and make sure that you get what you want out of the coaching relationship," she says. "Make frequent communications about that with your coach. And if they don't respond, then you know they're not the right person for you. What I look for is somebody who will truly take responsibility for collaboratively partnering with me to create what they want in their lives."

We started with the premise that this was the first step toward offering life planning services, and Beckes reinforces that. "If you want to be a coach, then hire a coach. Be a recipient of coaching," she says. "When I start coaching with my planning clients, I say to them, 'do you have a financial planner?' You have to be a recipient of the services before you really understand how to deliver them to others."

It sounds simple, but your life planning activities start in your own office. "The more you move through issues and blocks that might be stopping you," says Beckes, "the better you're going to be able to take your clients through these things."

The Tragedy that Changed a Life

What happens when an advisor works with a coach, and actually implements the advice? Are there any existing practices that show the results of that slippery (seldom defined) concept of "delegation?"

Some years back, I was privileged to moderate a panel that consisted of one person: Floyd Green, a planning practitioner in Raleigh, North Carolina. Green told a deceptively simple tale. He operated a thriving financial planning practice in Raleigh and – like most of us, I think – ran it with a typically workaholic lifestyle right up until the day he and his bicycle were hit by an automobile operated by a drunk driver. Paramedics who put him on a respirator and flew him to the nearest hospital in a helicopter brought Green back to life. Green told of a darkly humorous moment that too many readers will recognize in themselves: he woke up in the intensive care unit 24 hours after the accident, emerging from a coma that might have become a permanently vegetative state, stared at his wife blankly for a second, and then immediately asked for his Daytimer.

Among his physical injuries was brain trauma that required a "no compromises" period of recuperation. His doctor told him that if he tried to work more than 20 hours a week, the healing process would reverse itself and the brain damage could become permanent.

So Green faced an unusual dilemma. He wanted to keep his planning practice alive, but he had to find a way to cut 30 hours of his own work time out of his weekly office routine.

He was absolutely forced to find a way to get his practice radically more efficient in a hurry.

Skipping to the ending a bit, Green managed to accomplish all this and more, and discovered along the way that he had been (before the accident) psychologically resistant to giving up busy-work, and to delegating what he considered to be key tasks to his staff.

He had been, in other words, working 50 or more hours a week for no good reason.

In the years that followed, Green actually increased the level of service to his clients while cutting his hours in half. In the process, he got his life back, rediscovered the joys of family relationships, vacations and leisure time. "My goal here is to convince you," he said to the audience, "that you don't have to go through brain surgery to get the same results." He was there to share the lessons he had learned.

Creeping Dysfunction

So how did he do it? At the time of the accident, Green was following the standard boutique model of a planning practice: he had four staffers who were basically leveraging his own expertise. His goal, after the accident, was to see if the leverage could be stretched out – and how far. "First thing I did was ask myself the basic question: what are the results that make us money?" he told the group. "How do we earn income? Well," he answered himself, "when I meet with clients. When I meet with *new* clients. Bringing clients in. I'm the only one in the office, fundamentally, that can do that, at least at a level that will keep us going. I'm the one who needs to meet with clients and introduce our services, make recommendations, do new investments. It didn't take rocket science – or, as I now say, brain surgery – to figure out that that's what I had to focus my attention on."

Green then made a list of all the things that he thought somebody else could do. This forced him to confront a basic dysfunction in his business life, which had gradually sucked him deeper and deeper into the minutia of his company.

Listen carefully here: I suspect it is a dysfunction that creeps into the lives of most financial advisors as their practices grow. "In retrospect, the process made me realize that I tell myself lots of lies," Green confessed to the audience. "I think for many of us there is a peculiar kind of psychic payoff in all the frenetic business of our lives. There's a payoff that says, you know, because I'm so busy, I must be really important. Nobody could be as busy as I am and not be a really important person. Well, I've had to kill some of those lies and say, you know, it's just not true."

Delegation Made Real

One thing that Green cut away was the case writing activities, which he had long since convinced himself that only he could do properly. "Between the first and second meeting, we would create what we called the proposals," Green said. "I was the one who was drafting proposals. I'm on my computer spending probably five hours, on average, drafting a proposal. Well, I quickly decided I couldn't do that anymore. That's not what my clients are paying me to do. They're not paying me to sit on a computer and draft investment proposals. They're paying me to have a process that makes sure that the recommendations are the appropriate ones for them, but they're not paying me to pound away on a computer."

At this point in his presentation, Green introduced Scott Bush to the audience, and Scott stood up kind of deferentially. "Scott and I sat down and I said, Scott, I can't do these anymore," said Green. "If we could find a way where you would take over all the proposals, that would cut out five hours for every new client." Suddenly, Scott was empowered, not only to take over a crucial piece of work, but also to use his own creativity to figure out better ways to get it done.

"This might not surprise you, but to me it was amazing," Green told the group. "It wasn't long before the proposals were being generated faster. I asked Scott the other day, how long does it take you now, once I give you the information you need, to prepare a proposal? He said 20 minutes. Maybe on a rare occasion, an hour."

The audience laughed, and then Green added the punch line: "And they look a lot better now. Today, I'm proud to put our proposals in front of our clients."

New Ideas from New Sources

There were other examples that basically illustrated the same theme. When Green finally liberated his staff people to think about how to improve some aspect of the office tasks, and gave them responsibility for getting them done, they responded with something that worked better and more efficiently than Green expected. For example, Green had been rebalancing portfolios using a hand calculator. Scott created a computerized system that basically generated reports on all clients in (compared to the old way) no time at all.

The insight here is that employees may be the best – and least-consulted – authorities on how to make your practice more efficient.

In most financial planning practices, any new time-saving innovations, or improvements in efficiency and quality, have to come out of the mind of the company's founder. Of course, this is the same person who is working 50 hours a week on all sorts of chores, who is often too distracted to think about anything more complicated than getting out this next performance statement in time for a client meeting at 2:00, and who has always done it this way. It's a miracle that any practice innovations ever come out of this person's hectic life – and if they do, it's usually because they found time to get away from the office and talk to people at conferences.

In other words, you may unknowingly have become a bottleneck to progress toward goals that you never find the time to fully share with your staff people.

But Green found something miraculous: that his staff people are as smart and creative – and interested in the business – as he is. All he had to do to unlock their creativity was give them full responsibility for getting something done – with him as the judge of whether their results measured up. This, I think, is a concrete example of that slippery idea of "empowerment" that we're always reading in management books. If you can manage to give up tasks that don't absolutely require your involvement, and convince yourself that maybe, just maybe, somebody else in the office can do them as well as you could, and give up the invisible self esteem crutch of busyness, then suddenly you're on the road to getting your life back.

Green used the term "shift" to describe this empowerment process. "A shift is a permanent transfer of authority and responsibility for results in a certain area. It's not delegation. Delegation, to me, is you [arrive] in the morning and give people their responsibilities for the day," he said. "You have to figure out what everybody is supposed to for the day. I never do that. We completely shifted areas of responsibility, not for jobs, but for results in each particular area."

And, believe it or not, Green found that job satisfaction actually rose as more responsibility was shoved off of his desk. "The process took all four of our staff people to a significantly higher level of ownership of what we're doing," Green said. "They were actually happier and more satisfied with their work than they had been before."

The Rule

Eventually, the process was codified into an office "way of life" that was designed to protect Green from expending any of his precious 20 hours on unnecessary activities. "There is a rule in the office now that any client issue only reaches me after it has been evaluated and nobody else in the office can do it," he said. This, he noted, is the opposite of the default position in most practices, where any client issue is immediately referred to you – the principal of the firm.

"We're just kind of the default person to do it," Green said. "Now, anything that ends up in my bin, or on my voice mail, whatever, has to be something that just no one else, either from a licensing or a compliance perspective or whatever, can deal with. And on those rare occasions when something comes to me and I realize that somebody else could do it, I kick it right back." Eventually, they refined the system so that when a task came up, the staff would have to answer why it had to be done. This revealed a number of things that people were spending time on, but which really weren't necessary – filing certain pieces of paperwork when the computer already had the same information, or filing things monthly when quarterly summaries would work just as well.

Conclusion: What's Next (For You and Your Clients)?

At the most recent FPA Retreat, which is a meeting of many of the most successful planning practitioners in the U.S. market, the hallway "buzz" was exactly on this subject.

What's next?

Over the three-day conference, this question echoed back and forth with increasing volume across the hallways, around the bar, in the after hours suites, over lunch and threaded around the "under the trees" discussions.

"What's next?" It proved to be a remarkably flexible question, meaning very different things to different people. For example:

"I've suddenly reached the point in my life where the survival of my firm is no longer in question. I'm not concerned at all about the Mark Hurley reports that say I'm going to be hounded to extinction by giant financial services firms, because I have more clients than I need or want already, and my biggest problem is finding ways *not* to take on more new business than I can handle. I never expected to get to this place in my life, yet I am working harder than I want to, at the same ironic moment when, financially, I no longer need to work at all."

"What's next? Where do I go from here? And how do I get there?"

Or: "I'm working 55 hours a week and most of it is administrative work; I hardly have time for my clients any more. The business can't seem to function unless I'm in the middle of the office directing traffic and making decisions that seem obvious to me and confusing to everybody else.

"What's next? What can I do to get back to real financial planning, which is what attracted me to the business in the first place?"

Or: "I'm reaching that stage of my life when I only want to work half-time, so I'll be able to travel, devote time to my hobbies, write a little and spend more time with my spouse.

"What's next? Do I sell my firm, or do I bring in a partner and turn the company over to her for day-to-day management."

It seemed as if the entire financial planning profession was experiencing a simultaneous mid-life crisis. For the first time, significant numbers of planning practitioners are facing the same success issues in their own lives that their clients have been bringing to them for two decades – and, irony of ironies, they don't know what to do.

A long time ago, in my *Inside Information* newsletter, I wrote a column that attempted to define something basic in our profession. It talked about how, when I was editor of *Financial Planning* magazine, way back in the 1980s, my staff and I consciously looked for the magic elixir that would make practices successful.

What was it that separated the successful people from the unsuccessful people? If we could find that, then we would have done a real service to our readers.

But we never found it. What we discovered was that everybody was doing everything differently. There were a hundred different marketing approaches, dozens of different practice structures, as many different areas of expertise and client focus as there were readers of the magazine. There was no common denominator between this successful practice and that successful practice – and so we wrote about all the successful practices we could find in columns entitled "practice management," "practice marketing," and "practice profiles," hoping that some good ideas would find their way to our readers by osmosis.

After working with the *Inside Information* community, I now realize that we hadn't stepped back far enough. If we'd stepped back one more step and looked at all those successful practices, what we would have discovered is that they had all had a goal. And they all set aside a certain amount of time to make their lives better.

That was the elixir. It was the very simple touchstone that transmutes our lives and practices from lead to gold.

The many suggestions that have been offered by ex-starving idealists, and by coaches and practitioners, who have gotten their lives back, really invite you to join their journey toward the place where your future intersects the future of the profession.

You will be guided by the same simple questions that your clients want to answer in their own lives. How do we, day to day, become more efficient? How do we make our lives simpler? How do we get our lives back so we have time for fun, relationships, friends, travel, and that precious thing which is inadequately described as the joy of life?

How to we recover these things when our time is sucked away into the black hole that a boutique practice threatens to become?

The practice management challenge of the future is to join hands with your clients and start on a journey that only you can define.

INTERLUDE ON *THE CUTTING EDGE*:

Fighting the Power of the Press

Most of the best professional investors I talk to believe that the financial TV shows do an incalculable amount of damage to lay investors, by touting hot stocks, and by making it seem as if short-term data and information has significance or value. Some have gone so far as to call this daily diet of titillating white noise "investment pornography."

This interview represents what I wish somebody, somewhere would say on one of the financial TV shows, in between the touts, predictors of the future and talking heads. It will never happen, of course. But when I first published it, I got an incredible reaction from the *Inside Information* community, who rushed to share it with their clients. It made a point that nobody had managed to make quite so directly: that investment pornography is inevitably bad for your financial health.

(Concerning the advice on Treasury Bonds, Please note that this mock interview was originally published in mid-2001.)

"The Fantasy Interview"

CNBC: I'm here with Bob Veres, who I think might be the only financial commentator in America who wears his hair in a ponytail. Mr. Veres is publisher of a newsletter service for financial planners called *Inside Information*. Welcome Bob.

VERES: It's a pleasure to be here, Dan.

CNBC: Bob, with the Fed about to meet on Thursday, where do you think interest rates are going to go in the next couple of weeks?

VERES: That's not a relevant question, Dan.

CNBC: I beg your pardon?

VERES: Even if I KNEW which way interest rates were going, with absolute certainty, any investment move I'd make based on that information is bound to be fool-hardy and reckless.

And I thought you knew that I don't have the ability to foresee the future. I put it right there in my bio. If you want my honest opinion, I think what you just asked me to do is beyond human capabilities altogether. And most professional financial planners would strongly agree with me.

CNBC: Yes... (Recovering quickly) Well, I'm sure our panel of economists will be happy to answer that question for us at 2:00 eastern time. So, Bob, what do you think of Lucent Technology's latest round of layoffs?

VERES: Doesn't make any difference to me. I think overall I'm around 13% technology right now, and I'd guess Lucent is one of about 150 stocks in that part of my portfolio. Two different fund managers are probably looking at that issue for me right now.

CNBC: Can you comment on the market activity so far today?

VERES: That's completely irrelevant to serious investing. Why don't you ask me about Treasury bonds, instead?

CNBC: (instantly wary) Treasuries?

VERES: I like them right now. I think a lot of financial planners do.

CNBC: (with no noticeable enthusiasm) Really.

VERES: Really! Because they're starting to get a little scarce. Because, even though we had this huge tax cut, the actual Treasury revenues are going to increase pretty dramatically over the next ten years – even before the estate tax kicks back in and clobbers everybody with the mother of all bracket creep. That's because the economy, despite all the obvious recessionary signs, is actually still growing, and more likely than not there will be more business activity on which to collect revenues next year than there was this year.

CNBC: And that means...?

VERES: They're going to continue to pay down the deficit over at least the next five years, even if we take the very lowest end of the projections.

CNBC: (becoming impatient) And...?

VERES: Fewer Treasuries will be issued each year than the one before it. And you know, Dan, that in times of economic uncertainty, the whole investment center of gravity swings toward the safer stuff, and you don't get much safer than Treasury bonds. So you have a gradual, tectonic, unstoppable shift toward an asset class that is becoming increasingly scarce. Supply and demand might shift just enough to give a slight edge to the Treasury bond investor.

CNBC: (Staring in amazement for a second.) You call THAT a hot tip?!?

VERES: That's about as hot as it gets in the financial planning world, Dan.

CNBC: (quickly) Well, I suspect that many of our viewers are not quite as excited about Treasuries as they are about the latest dot-com disaster, which will be the subject of a special report–

VERES: Which is exactly the point.

CNBC: I beg your pardon?

VERES: Where did you ever get the idea that investing is supposed to be exciting? It's all right to enjoy it if you want, but every exciting thing you do with your portfolio is probably going to be harmful to your future financial health. That's why I like 10-year Treasuries at 5%, because I suspect that this will come to 3% over the inflation rate until the bond's maturity, which, at the ice cold bottom of my portfolio, is a pretty good return and will cover a lot of the mistakes that my mutual fund managers are inevitably going to make.

CNBC: (becoming slightly more interested): So our viewers should rush out right now and buy Treasuries?

VERES: I'd say they could build their position from 2% of the overall portfolio to maybe 5% sometime in the next year or so. There's really no hurry.

CNBC: Oh. Well, ah, Bob, I'd have to say that you've been the most unexciting guest we've had on this program – at least since I've been affiliated with it.

VERES: That's quite an achievement. Thank you, Dan.

CNBC: We still have about 20 minutes to fill here before I bring on the next guest, who is a respected mutual fund analyst with great insight into the undervalued stocks that could go up by as much as 120% over the next 12 months–

VERES: Oh, my gosh!

CNBC: What.

VERES: Dan, if this person has somehow managed to come across valuable inside information that is material to the price of these stocks, then he's obligated to notify the SEC. And of course he's absolutely prohibited from trading on it. This man may be a criminal!

CNBC: As a matter of fact, some of the industry's most respected money managers share their insights with us on a regular basis.

VERES: Wow! But maybe they're just pretending to have material inside information. Have you ever followed up on their track records, to see if investing in the companies they recommend would have beaten or even equaled the market's overall performance?

CNBC: I really think we need to get back on the subject here. Is there any other advice you'd care to share with our audience?

VERES: Sure. (Looking into the camera) You should all turn off the TV and get a life. Or at least watch something that isn't actively harmful to your investment health.

CNBC: Excuse me!?!

VERES: I've only got a few more seconds, so you viewers listen carefully, and maybe you should get out a pencil and paper and write down what I'm going to say. All day long this program that you've been watching has been teaching you every single investment bad habit known to the business, and the longer you watch, the longer it's going to take you to recover the wealth it's going to cost you.

CNBC: Ohmigod! Ohmigod! I think it's time we took a–

VERES: (quickly, sensing time is short) The very best long-term investment advice I can ever offer you viewers is to stop watching this rubbish. And while you're at it, stop reading the white noise in your local newspaper and cancel your subscription to all but maybe one investment magazine, so you always have a general idea what's going on.

CNBC: Yes, well, I believe we've run out of time for this segment. After this commercial break, we'll bring you a quick rundown on the day's news, where a leading economist tell us which way interest rates are going to move, and an analyst will tell us all the great things about a hot young company that his firm has just taken public.

Thank you, Bob. Those security people over there will be only too happy to throw you out the window, while I have a word or two with the producer who arranged to have you on the show...

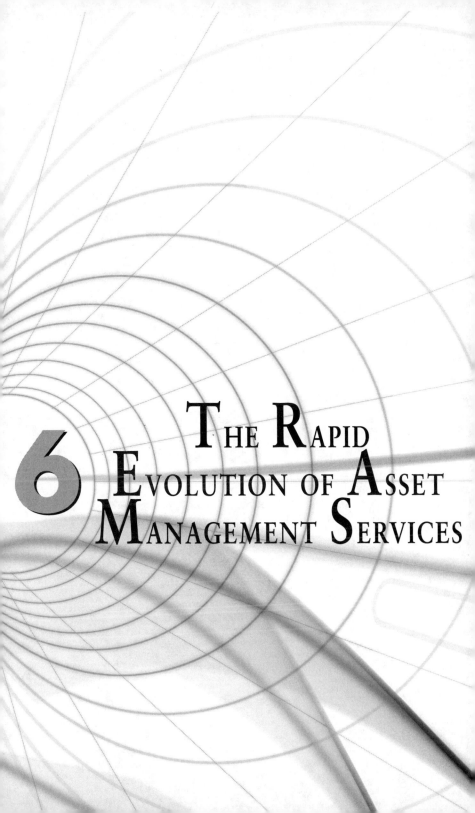

6 THE RAPID EVOLUTION OF ASSET MANAGEMENT SERVICES

I n today's profession, no single client service is changing faster than asset management. At the same time that this service is being demoted from the top of the menu, it is also beset by new challenges and a host of potentially important new services.

Once upon a time – only about 15 years ago now – most financial advisors believed that the most important service they offered their clients was identifying mutual funds that would, going forward, significantly outperform the market as a whole. That was the goal of investment management across the length and breadth of the profession, and today we hardly remember the outcome of that grand experiment.

The remarkable outcome was that tens of thousands of professionals – with above-average intelligence, a growing array of databases and analytical tools, and decades of personal and professional experience in the markets – all failed to beat the indices.

Following the Trendlines

This ongoing failure had a profound effect on the profession, which really hasn't been written about – at least not directly – in the trade and consumer press. Indeed, it led to a quiet, very gradual evolution in how advisors picked mutual funds.

Just as we did with practice management, we can also trace the linear part of this evolution and identify the end point where it reaches its logical limit.

Early in the days of the electronic mutual fund databases, the profession began what we now refer to (somewhat contemptuously) as "chasing hot performance." However, this contempt is misplaced. At the time, it seemed entirely logical that the managers with the best short- and long-term track records were the best in their profession; recommending their funds was much like placing bets on the top tennis player or golf professional.

Before that time, it was very difficult to identify which track records were superior; now, suddenly, the information was laid out clearly for the professional advisor.

And so advisors put their clients' money into the funds with top quintile performance, and experienced the disappointment we referred to earlier.

As it became clear that past performance alone wasn't a clear indicator of future returns, advisors began moving their attention to other issues – creating screens that identify, with increasing precision, things like consistency of returns, manager tenure, operating expenses and the ability to keep the fund's holdings in a consistent style box.

As time went on, advisors' returns grew ever closer to the frictionless, costless returns of the indices they were benchmarking against. As the trend became visible, a small but significant minority of advisors recognized where the trend was heading, and simply moved to its logical conclusion. They stopped evaluating and recommending active mutual funds completely, and offered their clients a blend of low-cost index funds.

Spinning our Wheels?

In an effort to find out how many advisors were ahead of this trend, I wrote a series of interactive e-columns for the *Inside Information* community, asking planners to identify, as precisely as they could, where they were spending their time and what their investment value-added is today. I found that the profession is now (as you read this) very nearly at the end of one evolutionary path, and about to start down another, very different one.

In response to the first e-column, more than two hundred advisors shared their current fund screening techniques with me. Many confessed that they spend less and less time on the screening/fund selection process as time goes on. In fact, a majority of the messages I received said that the advisor can usually add much more value, per hour worked, by counseling with clients and helping them with the things they have more control over: budgeting, taxes, making more informed life decisions. I think Bill Christy, who practices in the greater Philadelphia area, did the best job of articulating this position when he said: "We should spend less time spinning our wheels on screening techniques and more time and energy on our clients and their unique problems."

Jack White, who practices in St. Charles, Missouri, added clarity to the argument. "The more time we spend educating our clients that our goal is achieving their well-thought-out goals, and not beating this or that index," he said, "the more progress that we are going to make helping people understand this financial planning process."

Communists and Active Managers

Until very recently, the only people who were articulating the endpoint of this trend were a small but very active "cult" of indexers, many of whom recommend the funds offered by Dimensional Fund Advisors (http://www.dfafunds.com) founded by Rex Sinquefield, who coauthored the landmark study of equity returns with Roger Ibbotson. In fact, Sinquefield coined the phrase that sums up the view of the indexers as bluntly as possible: "The only people who don't believe in the efficiency of the markets," Sinquefield told a financial services audience, "are the North Koreans, the Cubans and the active mutual fund managers."

Investment management, to the indexers, meant creating a diversified portfolio of index funds for their clients, using modern portfolio theory software (called "optimizers" in the trade) like RAMCAP or Allocation Master, and rebalancing these portfolios on a regular basis to keep them at the specified allocations. It was taken for granted that the lower turnover and lower expense ratios of the index funds would, over long enough periods of time, deliver returns above those earned by all but a handful of (lucky) portfolio managers – managers who, they would argue, cannot be identified with any certainty in advance.

The debates within this group tended to center around how often to rebalance the portfolios (Annually? Whenever the portfolio had strayed by more than 5% from the targets?) and whether to input forward-looking returns into the optimizer (and, thereby, guess about the future), or use historical averages (driving by looking in the rear-view mirror).

Since then, there has been a groundbreaking article that, I think, takes the argument a step further. It points out, systematically, the advantages of indexing over active management using the very databases that advisors once relied on. And it goes even further and points out that both arguments against the use of optimizers may be correct.

The article, "Changing Equity Premium Implications for Wealth Management Portfolio Design and Implementation," was written by Harold Evensky, and was published in the June 2002 edition of the *Journal of Financial Planning.* Harold's credentials include, in addition to two decades in practice, the authorship of what had been regarded as the definitive argument for asset allocation, *Wealth Management: The Financial Advisor's Guide to Investing and Managing Your Client's Assets* (Irwin Publishing Co., August 1996).

Diversified – and Expensive

Evensky started with a simple premise that we've already discussed elsewhere in this book: if returns are, in fact, going to be lower in the future than they have been in the recent past, then what does that mean for investment planning going forward?

His first conclusion (very simple, and obvious in retrospect) was that the impact of taxes and trading costs would be greater on a lower-return portfolio than they have been on assets that are earning double-digit returns. The lower those future returns are going to be, the more obvious the costs will be.

This led Evensky to conclude that the traditional diversified portfolio of mutual funds, each devoted to its asset class, is too inefficient for taxable investors. "Our clients, unlike institutions, pension plans and sheltered institutional accounts, are affected by taxes – lots of kinds of taxes," he says. Some of these taxes arise from the normal friction of life. "If they want to take a big chunk out, I may have a position that has a big loss, but I can't take it all out of there because now my portfolio is completely out of whack," Evensky points out. "I've got to take a little piece out of every part of it. I am very likely to be generating taxes in order to get them the money that they need because they live in a real world."

Other frictional effects come from the way that traditional multi-manager portfolios are operated. "A manager may focus on the portfolio. They may be very tax efficient within their portfolio," Evensky argues. "They're using lot basis accounting. They're trying to sell these losses, but they're not paying attention to what any of the other managers I've selected are doing."

Meaning what? "I've got a large cap growth manager and he's got a portfolio of stocks," Evensky explains. "One of their stocks doesn't do terribly well, so it's no longer a growth company. It sort of drops into that mid-cap range. That manager sells it; my core manager buys it. It's not doing real well at all. The core manager sells it; the value manager buys it. And now it starts picking back up, they sell it, core buys it and it does great. Core sells it, growth buys it. If you think about what's happening in my one client's portfolio," Evensky concludes, "I've got the same stock moving all around the place, up and down and back and forth because no manager is paying attention to what the other one is doing."

Of course, the same travels are taking place with index funds. The same stock may bounce back and forth at the interface of the large-cap/mid-cap division, or at the mid-cap/small-cap line, being bought and sold and bought again as the price rises and falls. Or a small stock may rise to become a mid-cap stock, then become a large cap stock, and then drop back again.

Evensky concluded that until you find managers who have 10% turnover or less, the benefits of tax efficiency are really not significant enough to affect the portfolio. If you add in the need to rebalance the portfolio every so often, the result that you get with the diversified mix of active managers – and also with diversified mixes of index funds – is a very tax-inefficient, high turnover portfolio.

The Cost of Friction

To test this hypothesis, Evensky took a hard look at the costs and the potential for excess return of various possible portfolios. From a search of the literature, he was able to create a remarkable table (see Figure 6.1), which estimates trading costs – including the typical cost of the spread between bid and ask prices – for a variety of different asset classes. He found that different asset classes tended to have different bid-ask ranges, from 30 to 90 basis points (.5% to .9%).

Then he created a hypothetical diversified portfolio, estimating the turnover that is normal to each asset class (127% a year for a large-cap growth fund; 61% for a large-cap value portfolio and so forth). This average turnover was multiplied by a low estimate of the typical bid-ask spread plus trading costs (70 basis points in small-cap growth portfolios; 30 in large-cap value funds), and then Evensky multiplied the two numbers by the percentage that the portfolio is invested in each asset class.

The result is a very conservatively figured total trading cost of roughly 46 basis points a year on the overall portfolio. (You get this number by adding up the figures in the last column of Figure 6.1.)

Then Evensky calculated the cost of active management – basically an average of the expense ratios of funds that financial planners might use minus the cost of an index alternative. He did this for each asset class, and then, again, weighted those numbers by their percentage of the total portfolio (see Figure 6.2).

His conclusion: the cost of active management is roughly 72 basis points.

Finally, Evensky calculated the tax drag on his hypothetical portfolio. Here, he looked at the tax costs of a diversified portfolio of index funds (which, he argued, is going to be lower than what the active managers are generating), and came up with a figure of 25% of the returns, on average, per year. (See Figure 6.3).

Add up the three numbers, and you get 1.37% a year as the "cost" of investing in the traditional way.

And so the question becomes: can the advisor find a way to add enough value to the investment process to offset this 1.37% annual drag? The indexers clearly cannot, because they aren't attempting to add returns. They only capture the returns offered by the market. So the question really is: can the advisor select active managers astutely enough to overcome this annual expense figure?

If the answer is "no," then Evensky suggests that we look for some other way to organize client portfolios.

Figure 6.1

Estimated Trading Costs of a Generic Portfolio

	Portfolio Weighting	Trading Turnover	Costs	Weighted Portfolio Cost
Large Capitalization				
Growth	20%	127%	60 bp	.13%
Blended	20%	77%	40	.08
Value	20%	61%	30	.06
Small Capitalization				
Growth	15%	137%	70 bp	.10
Blended	10%	51%	30	.03
Value	15%	77%	40	.06

Reprinted with permission by the Financial Planning Association, *Journal of Financial Planning*, June 2002, Harold Evensky, "Changing Equity Premium Implications for Wealth Management Portfolio Design and Implementation."

Figure 6.2

Estimated Cost of Active Management (generic portfolio)

	Portfolio Weighting	Passive Expense	Active Expense	Weighted Portfolio Cost
Large Capitalization				
Growth	20%	0.2%	1.1%	.22%
Blended	20%	0.2%	0.6%	.11
Value	20%	0.2%	0.4%	.08
Small Capitalization				
Growth	15%	0.2%	1.2%	.18
Blended	10%	0.2%	0.3%	.03
Value	15%	0.2%	0.6%	.09

Reprinted with permission by the Financial Planning Association, *Journal of Financial Planning*, June 2002, Harold Evensky, "Changing Equity Premium Implications for Wealth Management Portfolio Design and Implementation."

Figure 6.3

Tax Drag of Representative Index Funds

	Turnover	Expenses	Trading Costs	Tax Efficiency
Large Capitalization				
Growth	127%	0.8%	0.5%	.87%
Blended	77%	0.2%	0.1%	.93
Value	61%	0.7%	0.5%	.65
Small Capitalization				
Growth	137%	1.3%	1.3%	.47
Blended	51%	0.5%	0.5%	.79
Value	77%	1.0%	0.9%	.73

Reprinted with permission by the Financial Planning Association, *Journal of Financial Planning*, June 2002, Harold Evensky, "Changing Equity Premium Implications for Wealth Management Portfolio Design and Implementation."

Perfection Still Falls Short

Is the answer "no?" And how would you determine that?

Evensky imagined that the advisor could fill each asset class with all of the managers who fell in the first quartile of returns, for that asset class, over every three- or five-year period. Basically that means he assumed that an astute advisor could get, consistently, quarter in, quarter out, the average return of all the managers who were in the top 25% of all returns for each asset class.

This astute fund picking would have gotten, interestingly enough, a 0% excess return in the large-cap growth asset class, but for some of the other asset classes, the benefits would have been considerable:

Annualized Excess Return
Relative to S&P 500

Large-Cap Growth:	0.0%
Large-Cap Blend:	0.3%
Large-Cap Value:	1.3%
Small-Cap Growth:	0.6%
Small-Cap Blend:	2.2%
Small-Cap Value:	4.6%

Tally it all up, and you discover that if the planner who is somehow able to choose brilliantly and get top quartile performance for each three-to-five-year period, he would have gotten an excess return, above the indices, of 1.3% a year. This (the reader has already noted) is *less than* the very conservatively calculated expenses of the traditional multi-class actively managed fund portfolio.

Evensky ran a complicated Monte Carlo analysis on the distributions of returns, and discovered that, even if he were to achieve the top quartile-average performance going forward, there was less than a 10% chance that he would be able to add more value than the portfolio was costing his clients.

"The efficient frontier," Evensky says, "doesn't work in a taxable environment. The current model is clearly tax inefficient or tax oblivious, and if returns are lower, that is going to make a monumental problem. In the future, the old way won't work."

Core and Satellite

So how will advisors construct portfolios in the future?

Evensky suggests that instead of many managers, each with his/her own piece of the portfolio, advisors put the bulk of the portfolio in "the total market," which might be the Russell 3000, plus an equally broad international index fund. This is the core of the portfolio, where stocks are free to migrate from large-cap to small-cap, growth to value without having to be bought and sold by different managers. There would be little or no rebalancing in the core. It is automatically rebalancing itself.

Then Evensky suggests that the planner add "satellite holdings" to the portfolio. Here, you're free from style consistency; you're simply looking for managers who you believe can add after-tax, risk-adjusted alpha – that is, returns that are high enough to beat the 1.37% (conservatively estimated) drag they are imposing on the money allocated to them.

Interestingly enough, this also frees you from patience. "In the past when we hired a manager, if they were style-consistent, we were extremely patient," Evensky says. Now it's: "we hired you for a reason, and we'll give you some time," he continued. "If you don't do it, at least we're going to have Uncle Sam absorb part of that loss and move somewhere else. For us, it's a totally different kind of mindset."

After that, Evensky suggests that clients are going to have to take more risk to get similar returns to the long-term averages, that this tax-efficient strategy may affect whether stocks or bonds go into the IRA and compound tax-free, the use of immediate annuities in retirement portfolios, and the idea that with lower returns, advisors are likely to have trouble charging as much as they have in the past.

Let it Go

What is interesting here is that Evensky is still hanging onto the satellite portions of the portfolio, going through elaborate investment screening processes and chasing incremental returns even though the tide of history seems to be moving away from that expenditure of time and energy. When I posted this information for discussion in the *Inside Information* community,

Mike Haubrich, who practices in Milwaukee, Wisconsin, advised Evensky to eliminate the satellites altogether. "Let it go..." he said.

Creative Indices

If we enter the time machine, set the clock forward 10 years, and study the financial planning practice of the future, we are likely to see a radically transforming effect brought about by these more efficient portfolios. Advisors of the future will spend a great deal less time creating their client portfolios. The optimizers will be gone, and so too will be the elaborate mutual fund databases and screening techniques.

There will still be debates about indexing vs. active management, but the active managers themselves will be different from what you see today. Boutique management firms will create quasi-index portfolios. Instead of cap-weighted portfolios (where more money has to go into the stocks that are going up, leading the fund into discredited momentum investment strategies), they will offer synthetic indices that hold very large baskets of stocks without weighting them by capitalization. They will trade very seldom, and the management fees will be down around the current cost of index funds.

In fact, the trend is already with us today. The various exchange-traded funds offered by Barclay's and Merrill Lynch will be joined by other, quasi-actively managed offerings at the same prices (20 basis points or less in management fees), which can be bought and sold through any discount brokerage firm.

A relatively new concept, Folio, may take transaction costs down to zero. A firm called FOLIOfn (http://www.foliofn.com) creates baskets of stocks that advisors can customize and put client assets into. The Folios can even hold fractional shares of stocks, making it possible for relatively unwealthy investors to own highly diversified baskets of stocks. When an advisor wants to trade a stock out of all client portfolios (to harvest tax losses, perhaps), he sends a sell order to FOLIOfn's trading desk, and this sell order is matched with any buy orders from other Folios. To the extent that the orders are matched in-house, there is no transaction cost.

If the orders cannot be matched, then FOLIOfn aggregates all of the buys and sells from all the Folios and takes them to market twice a day in very inexpensive block trades – which are covered by an ongoing custodial fee.

Indeed, as we step out of the time machine into the future, we are met by a bewildering array of interesting portfolio mixes, shared and discussed online between different advisors, who have developed their own proprietary indices that may invest in a broad range of stocks from (to take one example) all over the Far East, but which will only include small-cap issues from the Japanese. Other advisor portfolios are diversified, not across traditional asset classes, but across industry sectors; still others are broadly diversified, but systematically underweight or overweight different industry sectors or asset classes based on whether, by historical standards and valuation models, they are more or less expensive than the norm.

We will discover that much of the creativity that once went into selecting fund managers has gradually, over time, bubbled up into creative indexing, with much of the friction eliminated from the client portfolios.

The Rock in the Middle of the Herd

In addition, investment managers are beginning to add a variety of new services for their clients, which will become a mainstream part of the investment management "offer" in the future.

Such as?

One fairly traditional service has received a renewed importance (and emphasis) during the market bubble and subsequent bear market. The basic concept is this: if the professional advisor is doing her job right, she always finds herself speaking contrary to the prevailing moods of the market.

When the tech sector is roaring, you are preaching a bit of gloom and the value of diversification. When the bear growls, you are the rare optimist about long-term investing, advising clients to maintain their course and buy stocks that have gone on sale.

You advocate caution and optimism precisely at the time when each is most out of favor, and you are always vindicated, even though proof of this wisdom can be delayed for years.

In one of our memorable e-column discussions, Robert Horowitz, who practices in Stamford, Connecticut argued that the real value-added of an investment advisor is what he calls "fighting the conspiracy" – that is, ignoring the chorus of voices in the press, on radio and television, at cocktail parties etc. that try to lead you away from the initial asset allocation and get you to buy or sell at the wrong times. "The really difficult job is sticking to a rationally-developed portfolio despite everything that goes on," he says. "There are incredible pressures out there not to do that. Fighting the conspiracy is at least half of what you're getting paid for, on behalf of the client and also in your own mind."

Interestingly, the sheer difficulty of maintaining your investment equilibrium is nowhere discussed in the financial services professional literature, even though it may be the hardest thing that financial planners do in their professional careers. What is equally interesting is how easy it is to simply turn your head up from this page, stare blankly at the wall for a second, and realize that you know exactly what "the conspiracy" has been telling us in a thousand different ways recently. Its voice has been eerily clear and insistent. "Emerging markets don't make sense," says Horowitz. "The world has changed [as a result of whatever recent events have taken place]. The United States is fundamentally superior to all other countries and always will be. In the new global economy, only large companies are able to thrive. The markets are down: sell. The markets are up: buy."

"As people hear that over and over," he says, "they start to believe it. And then they start adjusting."

The pressure, which you can't really measure in terms of time, to break the asset allocation, becomes enormous.

Over time, "the conspiracy" wears down the resistance of the client, and then the client wears down the advisor. "The true value of a good advisor," Horowitz continues, "is this conviction. It is one thing to say it, and another to really, truly have it inside you so you can stick with it when everyone else is bailing out or following their clients' worst instincts."

The "S" word

Horowitz has a word for people who are not able to stand up to "the conspiracy" on behalf of their clients – or who never try to in the first place. It's not a word to use in a family publication.

He calls them *salespeople.*

"To me, this is really what distinguishes the professionals from the salespeople, at least on the asset management side," he says. "You get a client who says, 'hey, I want to be fully invested, and I don't want any of this international crap.' And you say, well, I don't think that is a good idea. But the client insists. So if you are a salesperson, and you are getting a commission and a trail or an asset management fee paid quarterly, and your goal is to protect your income, not necessarily to protect the client, what do you care? You switch them out. You protect yourself, but you're giving in to the worst instincts of your clients."

Notice that this distinction between the salesperson and the real advisor – that is, somebody who follows the line of least resistance versus the person who follows the line of his/her own expertise and convictions – doesn't have anything to do with compensation structure. Horowitz is a member of the National Association of Personal Financial Advisors, and knows a number of NAPFA fee-only advisors who fit this "salesperson" definition. "I think many advisors convince themselves that they are doing the right thing," he says. "I speak to people who tell me that international diversification no longer makes sense. These are not people who have been practicing for six months. These are pretty established people."

The Day Trading Benchmark

This ability to hold our ground against the flow of the herd is, by definition, rather rare and precious (if everybody had it, then there would no longer *be* a herd). It also makes the members of our profession a little bit lonely, a little bit apart from the mainstream.

The price of wisdom is a high one: Throughout your life and your career, you will be saying, over and over again, the very things that people don't believe and often don't want to hear. With all the satisfaction that comes from helping people achieve their goals, there comes this burden that our profession must willingly bear, because you cannot have one without the other.

But this service may prove to be the most valuable of all, in terms of raw returns.

How so? Few advisors I know will be so bold as to claim that they can offer as much as a 1% excess return per year from all their fund screening and manager selection activities. But most experienced advisors can boast that their clients generally earn something close to the returns the markets are generating. Compare this with my favorite benchmark. According to the best statistics compiled by the press, more than 70% of everybody who actively day-traded during the bull market of the late 1990s went broke – while the market was going up faster and longer than it ever has before, and maybe than it ever will again.

Broke! Here we have a real-world illustration of what people who get really interested in investing will tend to do on their own, without the help of an outside professional. If you can guide your clients well enough that they don't go broke when the market is going up, then you've beaten an important real-world benchmark. If they don't go broke when the market is going *down*, then you have made an immense contribution to their financial well being.

The Portfolio Chef

Is anyone developing procedural methods to help clients endure their time on the investment roller coaster?

Stephen Barnes, of Barnes Investment Advisory in Phoenix, offers an intriguing analogy.

Suppose, he says, you walk into a restaurant for a good, nutritious meal, are promptly seated at a table, and after the usual discussion with the waiter about your meal preferences, the waiter comes back with a plate of what appears to be green slop, with ground up bits of what appear to be vitamin tablets floating stickily on the top. You look up from the plate in distress, timidly ask whether this is what you ordered, and the waiter assures you that this meal has been formulated according to the latest nutritional principles, with an optimal mix of every relevant vitamin and mineral using 70 years of dietary data.

"It's very good for you," the waiter says. "Dig in."

At that moment, do you:

(A) Throw the entire disgusting mess at the waiter and escape from the restaurant?

(B) Pretend to eat until the waiter is out of sight and then make a fervent promise never to visit this restaurant again?

(C) Decide you could do lots better in your own kitchen, with a popular book on nutrition and maybe a few Internet buddies to give you pointers?

(D) Chow down, because, after all, this is the optimal mix according to 70 years of nutritional history?

The correct answer, in case you were wondering, is (D), at least according to the reasoning that most financial planning professionals use when designing investment portfolios for their clients. "If you were to dump a nutritious meal into a food processor, blend it and serve it to the client, then they would get all the necessary nutrients," Barnes argues with perfect (if facetious) reasonableness. "The chef may suggest that the manner of preparation makes no difference because the nutrition is, well, optimized. Isn't that all that matters?"

Not in Barnes' view. "The typical process leaves plenty of room for improvement as far as the client enjoying the meal," he says. "As the maitre d' my partner is responsible for the relationship with the client and she ensures that we understand each client's nutritional requirements. I see myself as the chef, with primary responsibility for optimizing nutritional content, but also for making those meals pleasing to the eye and the palate. That's the value-added beyond the sterile optimization/indexing."

Barnes' partner happens to be his wife Kathie, who holds a master's degree in counseling. Barnes himself has the CFP and CFA designations; both husband partner and wife partner worked at John Hancock's headquarters before starting the firm in Phoenix, with the idea that a small boutique financial "restaurant" could offer much better service and a more pleasing menu than the big chains. Other staff includes an office manager who runs the office so Barnes can focus on the "cooking" and Kathie can focus on clients. A researcher does the more intellectually-complicated equivalent of chopping up the vegetables for Barnes, and the account services person cleans up and makes sure the dishes are washed – literally chasing down stray dividends and transfers, and seeing that the forms are filled out completely.

Gourmet Portfolios

So what do these gourmet portfolios consist of? Instead of mutual funds, Barnes prefers to buy individual stocks on behalf of his clients – or, at least, those clients who have more than $500,000 in their investment portfolio. The idea here is that clients are more likely to identify with an investment that is earning its way in the economy, rather than a faceless money manager or an index fund.

The account may earn index-like performance; indeed, the construction of the portfolio deliberately attempts to capture the broad movements in the market. The overall return may well mimic the broadest Wilshire indices.

That's the nutritional side of the meal – which, obviously, could be reproduced with a portfolio of index funds or the use of Folios, for advisors who have less wealthy clients.

The "flavorings" are how Barnes is able to get his clients interested in the "meal." As investment manager and chief financial chef, Barnes is able to engage his clients' attention in the actual business operations of the companies they own, and the markets they exist within, through two primary communication pieces.

"Every week we send out a one-page note on what is going on in the marketplace," Barnes explains. "We look for one or two interesting things to write about, so clients know what's happening to their portfolios in a general way. The original idea was to preempt calls about what's happening in the markets, and it has done its job in that regard," he adds. "But what we didn't realize was that there is some entertainment value in these mailings – the equivalent of 'taste' in the portfolio 'meal.' These weekly e-mails or faxes are enhancing the experience for the client," he says.

The second piece is sent out regularly, but not on a specific schedule. Here, the focus is on one of the individual stocks that most clients have positions in. "For example, if we own Microsoft," says Barnes, "we can send out a note that says, this is what is happening, and we thought it was important enough to tell you about it. This was really intended to inform and educate and preempt questions, but it has become another enhancement of the client's experience."

If this sounds like a lot of work, well, the reader may have already noticed that a tremendous amount of market-specific, sector-specific and even company-specific information is passing across your desk every day, sent by active fund managers and available through a growing number of clearing firms that are vying for your business.

Even so, selecting the information sources and compiling the information is an extra chore – one way to spend that time and energy that is no longer being used to screen the universe of active fund managers. Barnes argues that a gourmet restaurant's staff works harder than the people selling nutritional supplements at the local health food store. "Health food is a commodity," he says. "What a chef produces has a value-added that goes beyond nutrition." This value-added could be the key to survival and prosperity in a business landscape where financial services chains are setting up "financial eateries" on every street corner.

And (perhaps more importantly) this value-added tends to help clients bond with their portfolios, recognize the reason why they are investing in the first place, and makes them more likely to continue the course they've identified without the emotional swings that come when you are reacting to numbers rather than company stories. We know we are not going to be poisoning people, and maybe this won't prove to be the most nutritional meal as the future unfolds," Barnes admits. "But if it keeps their financial lives healthy, and they keep coming back, we'll keep tweaking it as we learn more."

The Information Tsunami

It's not a great leap from this trend to a broader one, which has implications for the advisor's role in society as well as in clients' lives.

What trend? Take a look at the sudden proliferation of information in our little corner of the world. Twenty years ago, when I got into this business as editor of its primary trade magazine, consumers had their choice of *Money, Kiplinger's, Barron's,* the *Wall Street Journal* and (sometimes) investing columns in *Fortune* and *Forbes.* Today, a consumer who wants to stay on top of all the investment information put out by the media would have to read all of those publications plus *Investor's Business*

Daily, plus the investment columns in *Business Week, Smart Money* and three different mutual fund magazines, plus watch 24-hour coverage on CNBC and CNNfn, plus monitor in real time the consumer investment-related chat rooms hosted by Morningstar, Motley Fool, Yahoo, TheStreet.com, MSN Money, InvestorsUniverse, MetaMarkets, Excite...

And, of course, the next question for these sleepless consumers becomes: how far down this information well do you want to drill? How often should you check out the "Invest in Tunisia" site, or the regularly updated web information offered by the General Investment Authority of Yemen?

As this incredible proliferation of information continues to rise exponentially, consumers everywhere will begin to tune out the white noise and search hopefully for ways to focus on what's important. There will emerge new services (not unlike my own Media Reviews service for the *Inside Information* community) that filter through the information and report on what is truly relevant.

Increasingly, journalists will be writing, not for audiences of consumers, but for professional filters of information, who decide what to pass on to their overwhelmed readers.

By popular consumer demand, these filtering organizations will, increasingly, fit two important criteria:

1.   they will know the consumer investor personally, and know this person's personal financial situation; and

2.   they will have a detailed, professional knowledge of the field that they do the filtering in.

Who will these filters be? Most financial journalists don't meet the first criteria, and many don't meet Criteria 2. In fact, as you look around you, you begin to realize that you, yourself, are going to become the source of information for financial consumers of the future. Who fits our criteria better than financial planners?

As we step out of the time machine into the future, we suddenly realize that financial planners themselves are subscribing to news sources and filtering mechanisms, and are themselves offering weekly or monthly updates to their clients, telling them what's going on in the investment world, what's relevant, what to watch out for.

Delegating Information Management

Are there any models for this type of information filtering service? In fact, there are several.

Bob Frey, who practices in Seattle, offers not a weekly, but a *daily* market report to his clients, with information pulled from various online sources. His own comments are found at the back of the report, and they generally advise clients not to take the daily movements too seriously.

Others, including Sheila Chesney and Rich Chambers, who practices in Palo Alto, adapt the monthly *Advisor Intelligence* reports for their clients.

And there is currently at least one turnkey service that offers a steady stream of articles that planners can send to their clients. The service is from a Long Island based company called Advisor Products (http://www.advisorproducts.com), which also sets up web sites for financial planners.

The Advisor Products organization has assembled a board made up of financial planners, who suggest article ideas and sources of information. The articles – typically five or six a month – cover subjects you will never see in the consumer press: buy and hold investing, the importance of asset allocation, the downside of 529 plans – basically the financial world from the viewpoint of senior advisors. Subscribers to the service can go to the AdvisorSites web site and download them or order them to be incorporated into a newsletter that can be mailed to clients, or have them automatically posted on their own web sites. Recently, the company has begun handling e-mail lists for advisors, allowing the advisor to simply select what he/she wants to send, and provide a weekly news service to clients – with your company's own banner across the top.

Distribution Strategies

While Barnes and a handful of other advisors are perfecting their portfolio cooking techniques, and pioneering their own information synthesis and filtering activities, other advisors are exploring the implications of those demographic trends we talked about earlier.

Of all the investment worries raised by the advisors who have been sending messages to me from the *Inside Information* community, the scariest, in my opinion, came from Bobbie Munroe. Munroe pointed out that, with advances in medical technology, future retirees could be looking at more than 35 years of living off of their retirement portfolios.

Indeed, it's possible that a 55-year-old will take early retirement and then live to 120. We hope that this person's financial planner has a strategy for making her money last for 65 years under a variety of potential investment scenarios. Yes, it's possible that in the "new retirement" era clients will be working at least some of that time. But they may still be drawing down their retirement portfolios to supplement their income, and they may decide to leave work altogether or become disabled at some point in the retirement years.

This, I think, represents an entirely new and important frontier in the financial planning profession, a new investment planning service that has gotten very little attention in the profession. Up to now, planners have been mostly focused on accumulation scenarios using modern portfolio theory, dollar-cost averaging and dynamic asset allocation. But what do we know about distribution strategies in retirement? How much can we take out of a portfolio, each year, with relative certainty that the money will still be around if the client happens to celebrate his 65th year of retirement?

So far, the state of the art looks a bit primitive. Bill Bengen, who practices in El Cajon, California, has written a great series of articles that essentially make three points:

1. Liquidating at roughly the rate of return you expect the portfolio to deliver would be a disaster. Bengen ran spreadsheet after spreadsheet showing that even if the markets deliver 12% a year over time, a couple of bad years in a row will cripple the portfolio to the point where the client taking 10-12% a year will sooner or later have to find part-time work at McDonald's to supplement his cat food diet.

2. If you want some certainty that the money will last for at least 30 years under all circumstances, then you can take out no more than 4% of the original portfolio in the first year, and then convert that to a dollar figure, and then index this living expense figure to inflation. So if you have a $1 million retirement portfolio, you can be relatively certain that if you spend $40,000 a year, adjusted for inflation, you almost certainly won't outlive your assets over a normally volatile 30-year

period. Bengen's analyses don't go out any further than that, but another study (I'll get to that in a minute) suggests that this distribution level may be pretty safe as far out as 40 years.

3.   Bengen's articles also suggest that you want to be between 65% and 80% (roughly) in equities, in order to combat the twin enemies of inflation and volatility over a long retirement. Get too far off of that balance, and the safe distribution amount starts to drop. (The four articles in this series can be found at: http://www.journalfp.net/fpajournal.)

Reverse Ammunition

Most of you probably glazed over that last couple of sentences, and were instead imagining what your clients are going to say when you gently break this interesting news to them. "Let me get this straight: I've accumulated a $1 million portfolio," they will tell you, "and we expect stocks to deliver roughly 10% a year returns," they will continue, "and yet you're telling me that I can only spend the equivalent of 4% of my money each year."

The word "bonehead" has a high chance of showing up somewhere in this conversation.

Unfortunately, the last 30 years don't give you much ammunition for making your point. If somebody retired in 1970 with $1,000,000 invested in the S&P 500 (to keep the numbers simple) she would have $40,000 to spend in the first year, $41,600 in the second (assuming a 4% inflation rate) and she would be living on roughly $135,000 during calendar 2001 – safely avoiding McDonald's and cat food.

Even with the bear market returns of the last few years, the client's portfolio would have grown to something north of

$11,000,000 – which suggests that, at some point, your client could have started taking out a little more income without busting the bank.

And it could be "worse." For the sake of curiosity, I reversed the sequence of returns from 1970 to 2001 and ran the same analysis. Under those circumstances, the portfolio would have grown to more than $28,000,000.

Systematic Distributions

Clearly, the 4%-indexed distribution is interesting to study, but not flexible enough for clients who have to live in the real world. A more sophisticated distribution system comes from Bart Boyer, who practices in Asheville, North Carolina. Boyer suggests that the client take a more aggressive 6% of the original portfolio in the first year, and then apply some rules to future distributions.

> <u>Rule 1:</u> If the market returns are high enough to replace the money the client took out of the portfolio (if the portfolio has grown despite the distribution), then the next year's distribution will be 6% again – which should be a higher dollar figure (6% of more equals more).

> <u>Rule 2:</u> If the market returns were too low to increase the principal (or, of course, if they were negative), then the retiree would simply live on last year's income – essentially freezing his or her lifestyle until the principal recovers to the point where a 6% distribution is higher than the previous year's income distribution. As we'll see in a minute, that means that after a bear market, the income might be frozen for several more years, until the positive years bring the portfolio back up to where it was before.

> Rule 3: If there's an extended bear market, then the frozen
> distribution should never exceed 12% of the portfolio.
> That means that under extreme cases, the client might
> have to reduce her lifestyle expenditures in order to
> protect the income-generating power of the portfolio.

Boyer sent me several spreadsheets, and I constructed my
own based on his analyses. We start with $1,000,000, invested
aggressively in an all-stock portfolio. (We both used the S&P 500
as a proxy.) In 1970, the retiree is living on $60,000 – 6% of the
original portfolio. Since the returns that year were somewhat
anemic (4.01%), that's also the amount this person is living on
the following year.

The next year (1972), the portfolio distributes $63,621; the
following year, the distribution is $71,879. That takes us up to
1973, when stocks go through a devastating two-year bear market that effectively freezes the client's income at this $71,879 level
for 12 more years. (!)

Of course, if you count inflation, then that means the
client's lifestyle is going down during that period. However, in all
but the final year of the freeze (1985) the client is taking more
income than would be allowed under the 4%-indexed formula
that Bengen has proposed.

After that, the income levels begin rising rapidly, to $87,058
in 1986, and all the way to $422,414 in 2000 and 2001, as the dis-
tribution is once again frozen by the recent market unpleasant-
ness. That's more than three times what would have been allowed
under the 4%-indexed method.

Meanwhile, the principal has grown to a relatively secure
$4,800,000.

If you reverse the sequence of stock market returns since
1970, then the client is taking a distribution of $547,799 in 2001

(frozen for the past 5 years), and the portfolio is now worth $6,800,000.

The Frozen Years

Some of you are probably still focused on those 12 years of frozen distributions, and at first Boyer was nervous about them too. "But then I started asking my clients and other retirees, at seminars, how they'd feel about tightening their belts when the market returns aren't there," he says. "And to them, it makes perfect sense. They'd much rather decrease their lifestyle a bit than risk having to ask their kids for money if the portfolio runs dry."

Boyer admits that he doesn't follow this formula exactly with his real-world clients. He, Munroe and others will always try to maintain two, three or four years of living expenses in a cash account, replenishing the money during bull market years, letting the account deplete during bear markets so the portfolio won't have to sell equities at a loss.

"For the client, having that money right there, tangible and accessible no matter what the market does, is very comforting," says Boyer.

This, of course, can bring you back down toward the 65% to 80% equity allocation that Bengen recommends, with the added bonus that if the market is down, you can simply live off of the cash, and replenish it whenever the market starts back up. That way, you are never selling stocks into a bear market.

It was much harder to create a spreadsheet that simulates this kind of distribution/allocation formula, but when I did, I was surprised to find that the numbers were very similar to Boyer's original analysis.

The two distributions (leaving out a lot of other columns on the spreadsheet) looked like this:

Year	Fully Invested Distribution	3-year Cash Cushion Distribution
1970	$60,000	$60,000
1971	$60,000	$60,000
1972	$63,621	$62,860
1973	$71,879	$69,384
1974	$71,879	$69,384
1975	$71,879	$69,384
1976	$71,879	$69,384
1977	$71,879	$69,384
1978	$71,879	$69,384
1979	$71,879	$69,384
1980	$71,879	$69,384
1981	$71,879	$69,384
1982	$71,879	$69,384
1983	$71,879	$69,384
1984	$71,879	$74,057
1985	$71,879	$74,704
1986	$87,058	$90,988
1987	$97,914	$100,679
1988	$97,914	$100,679
1989	$107,618	$108,807
1990	$135,050	$132,353
1991	$135,050	$136,680
1992	$152,038	$147,651
1993	$154,577	$149,093
1994	$160,744	$153,157
1995	$160,744	$162,402
1996	$200,905	$183,049
1997	$235,200	$209,074
1998	$299,551	$257,018
1999	$367,189	$306,126
2000	$422,414	$344,599
2001	$422,414	$344,599
Terminal Portfolio:	$4,837,469	$4,222,537

Because less money is in stocks, almost every number is slightly lower; the freeze occurs at $69,384 instead of $71,879 but it thaws two years earlier; the terminal income is $344,599 instead of $422,414, and the 2001 portfolio has grown to $4,200,000 compared to $4,800,000.

Risk Pooling Longevity

There's one more new wrinkle being talked about in the advisory world: adding immediate annuities to the retirement portfolio mix. I, personally, was a co-author of a study which used Monte Carlo analysis to study Bengen's conclusions, and then see if there was any way to alter the portfolio mix to allow for higher distributions more safely over longer periods of time. (You can find the article at http://www.journalfp.net/fpajournal.)

Monte Carlo simulations seem to produce more extreme return sequences than you can expect to see in the real world. But generally speaking, we found that after taking a 4.5% withdrawal from an aggressive portfolio like Bengen recommends for 40 years over thousands of possible market return sequences, only about 15% of the outcomes ended with the retiree going broke. That's not the ice-cold certainty that the 4%-indexed approach offers, but it sounds pretty good to me.

Is there a way to improve those odds? If 25% of the portfolio were invested in a fixed annuity, providing non-inflation-indexed income for life, then the chances of running out of money over 20, 25, 30, 35 and 40 years all went down. The odds of failure after 40 years dropped to 10.9%, and fell still further, to 7.4%, when half the portfolio was annuitized. (My guess is that if you annuitize higher percentages, the inflation effect will make the crash rate start to trend back up.)

Of course, this extra security comes at a price – if the client dies prematurely, then her money goes into the pool to pay the rest of the annuity owners, rather than to her heirs.

Accepting Longevity

It is an overstatement to say that this new "draw down investment planning service" is fully formed in the profession today; most advisors haven't even heard of it yet. The current state of the art is somewhat primitive, but is being explored vigorously in the vast laboratory of the profession.

After I sent out a column to the *Inside Information* community on drawdown planning, I asked for feedback. Weeding out messages that simply encouraged the discussion, I received a total of 273 responses from planners around the country, including two spreadsheet analyses and what looks like a promising new software program.

Taken together, these responses provide a strong first primer on the portfolio drawdown issue.

Some advisors noted that, for the first time in history, clients seem to "get" the idea that they may live longer than any previous generation. "When I started as a planner in the early 1980s and would make reference to having money last until a person was 85 (the life span I was using then), I got all kinds of eye-rolling and moans and oh I wouldn't want to live that long," says Nancy Nelson, a planner in Olympia, Washington. "I don't know who's been doing the educating, but I literally *never* hear that now."

Unfortunately, this education process is not complete. Individual investors are still entering retirement with high return assumptions, and they don't realize that volatility could bankrupt them even with above-average returns.

Frank Netti, who practices in Auburn, New York, reports that his clients are incredulous when he talks about returns below 10% a year, and have trouble understanding how a person could go bankrupt taking 8% annual distributions when annual market returns average 10%. The years those advisors have spent educating their clients about investment volatility and the importance of diversification (and the fact that less volatile returns can lead to more wealth than equally high, but volatile, returns) will have to be duplicated in this field.

Automatic Corrections

It's helpful to remember that, unlike the static spreadsheet models of the future, or the Monte Carlo simulations, real-world advisors can make annual (or more often) course corrections. And we need to recognize, somewhere in our spreadsheets, that clients tend to make these course corrections automatically.

"In a year in which the portfolio makes 30%, the beneficiaries take a dream trip or sell off a bit of their assets to replace the older car," says David Shore, who practices in Larkspur, California. "During a tough time, they tighten their belts a bit, cutting back on discretionary spending."

That means that the 4% (or 4.5%) number can be adjusted if the client is willing to cut back on expenditures during down years – which is exactly how Boyer's system worked. "In general, we're recommending a withdrawal rate of around 6%," says Bob Greenberg, who works in Costa Mesa, California, "but with the caveat that if we hit extended bear markets, they may have to limit their variable expenses like travel and gifts to the grandkids. Clients are comfortable with that," he says. "They just want to be certain that their most important expenses like food, housing and healthcare can be met without problems."

Stretching Portfolios

We saw earlier that some forward-thinking members of the planning profession have begun offering spending and budget planning services. Some advisors think that, in retirement, these new services may be the most important determinant of success.

"If there is anything that can be detrimental to retirees, it is spending more than they earn," says Vinnie Brascia, whose office is located in Newport Beach, California. "The real work lies in helping retirees be more efficient with their variable expenses, so they can stretch their retirement dollars that much further."

Unfortunately, this can be a very labor-intensive process, and there are no clear models for how to charge for it. "We probably don't get paid 'fair value' for the advice we provide in this area," Brascia confesses. "But the efforts made in this area – an area that we can control – are much more important than the efforts made in the 'withdrawal' strategy area."

Alice's Rabbit Hole

Some advisors use the Bengen estimates for years one through five of retirement, and then reassess. They've discovered that if clients can tighten their belts for the first few years of retirement, then a future course correction will almost inevitably be in a positive direction – with more safety.

This was seen clearly by the 4% distribution model that produced dozens of millions of excess dollars when left unchecked; when markets are going up more often than down, the "safe harbor" spending plans are likely to give way to something more generous unless the client is retiring into an unusually bearish scenario.

"I brace my clients for an unexpectedly tight retirement scenario," says Howard Caldwell, who practices in Brentwood, New Hampshire. "The scenario provides for withdrawing 4.5% of invested assets – and a 90% success rate in Monte Carlo and historical rate of return modeling."

"However," he adds, "I also say that there is only the obverse 10% chance that they would have to maintain that regimen throughout their entire retirement. The much higher-odds scenario is that they'll do better over time as the nest egg compounds its returns and their life expectancy shortens – allowing increased withdrawals over time. I described this," he adds, "as 'Alice's rabbit hole,' passing through a tight passage that leads to new retirement opportunities that didn't exist before."

Non-Reinvested Dividends

A number of advisors made a counterintuitive point, which is logical in light of Evensky's concern about the friction of rebalancing. They argue that one way to manage cash positions and reduce tax drag on the retirement portfolio is to avoid reinvesting the dividends and distributions thrown off by mutual funds.

Tom Sullivan, who practices in St. Paul, Minnesota, advises his peers to replenish the cash account with the dividends and capital gains distributions thrown off by his clients' mutual fund holdings. This reduces or eliminates the need to sell stock holdings (which, in turn, reduces the attendant tax consequences). "Clients understand it, and it leaves 70% to 80% of the gain [the appreciation of the fund shares themselves] reinvested in equities," he says, "which helps the only thing that creates long-term performance – staying in the market." Best of all, this eliminates all those dozens of little reinvestment transactions that are such a pain to keep track of during tax season.

Nelson, meanwhile, points out that in the real world, liquidation is easier to achieve than the one- or two-asset-class portfolios that we have been modeling. "For advisors who use a diversified approach," she says, "there should always be '*some*-thing' in the account that can be sold at a gain, or at least not be underwater."

Functional Allocation

Going further, it may be possible to drive many of the asset allocation decisions according to the client's future cash flow needs.

Come again? Thomas Murphy, who practices in Dallas, Texas, goes through a four-step process that determines a client's asset allocation without any reference to the efficient frontier:

Step 1: Calculate the necessary annual distribution amount needed.

Step 2: Keep two years worth of the necessary amount in cash or near-cash equivalents.

Step 3: Keep an additional three years of the necessary amount in bonds laddered to mature quarterly.

Step 4: Invest the remaining retirement assets in accordance with whichever allocation is most likely to achieve the necessary rate of return (usually 75% equities, 25% longer term bonds).

"Under normal circumstances, once a year we liquidate enough long-term assets to buy four new bonds to replenish the ladder," Murphy adds. Notice that this accomplishes the same thing as the 3-years-of-expenses in-cash system. "When the market is down, we don't sell equities," he says. "Clients seem to be very comfortable with the idea that they have five years worth of living expenses at hand. With our more rural clients, we explain this as the food in the kitchen, grain in the silo, crops in the field approach. They generally get it the first time."

Bill Fowler, of McKinney, Texas, offers a slightly different variation, creating a "safe money block" (made up of money market funds, CDs and laddered Treasuries), which is designed to provide for his retired clients' cash flow needs for three to five years. "As the block is consumed, I replenish the Treasury ladder as cash becomes available from the equity strategy – thus rolling the block forward indefinitely." If the market goes down, the planner can delay replenishing this block, which prevents the real killer of retirement portfolios: having to liquidate at a loss at the low end of the volatility cycle.

Bruce Heling, of Brookfield, Wisconsin, is one of the pioneers of this concept, which he calls "dynamic asset allocation." The formula is very simple: any distributions that a client will need in a year or less are invested in cash. Money that is needed two, three or four years out is invested in bonds. Money that isn't earmarked for distribution in five years or more is invested in stocks. This applies to money needed for a child's college education, or savings for a house or a vacation. When a client approaches retirement age, one year's income flows from stocks to bonds, and then another and another, and then some of the bond money is moved into cash in the year before retirement.

This is likely to become a fertile area of debate and discussion around the profession. Given the uncertainties of traditional asset allocation (who knows what future returns or correlation coefficients are going to be?), some kind of functional asset allocation could become the next accepted portfolio-building standard.

Post-Age-100 Portfolio Distributions

Others thought that being fearful of the 65-year retirement is not necessarily rational – especially when you take a hard look at the numbers. The difference between funding a retirement to age 90 and one to age 120 or even 150 is actually smaller than most planners realize.

"We typically run scenarios out to age 99 (the limit of our software package) and have found the difference between the capital needs out to 99 versus age 85 are relatively minimal," one planner told me. "For a 50 year-old person, say, with a relatively low withdrawal percentage, maybe 5% or 6%, inflated annually, the additional capital required to achieve one's objectives may be only 5 - 10% more than the lower age requirement. When you reach a point where the degree of certainty is high enough that you can feel comfortable to age 99, the additional capital required to go to 120 – or 150, for that matter – is minimal."

Creative Long-Term Care Planning

Of course, the "new retirement" concept has to be factored in here somewhere, and there is evidence that some of the leading thinkers in the profession are trying to get their arms around how to quantify the subject. A number of members of the *Inside Information* community have argued that planning for "retirement" is too simplistic, because spending levels and client circumstances change dramatically during different stages of retirement. They suggest that you start to look at retirement expenses that are incurred long before the client's appointment to leave the work force, and that we begin to look at the very back end of retirement as well.

"Second-half transition expenses, like retirement residence purchase or remodeling are incredibly important," says Eric Bruck, who practices in Century City, California. "And the biggest ticking time bomb of them all is a long-term care event for one or both spouses in the latter phase of retirement. The likelihood of this coming to pass is greater and greater with increasing longevity," he points out. "The new 'greatest risk' to one's portfolio assets is *not* the risk of outliving your money, but the risk of outliving your money in ill health."

Is there a procedural way to address this latter risk? Bruck starts by trying to define the scope of the problem. "We run a Monte Carlo simulation around one or more scenario 'lifetimes' of projected cashflows, with and without a hypothetical long-term care event plugged into the later years," he says. "The differing results become devastatingly clear. We'll get long-term care insurance quotes and plug in the appropriate premiums and coinciding benefits (inclusive of elimination periods at the time of the hypothetical event) and then rerun the Monte Carlo analysis until we achieve a scenario with a satisfactory probability of success. This becomes the client's recommended plan."

Howard Caldwell offers an out-of-the-box planning solution for special cases. "One of my clients could not independently afford long-term care insurance premiums at the 4%-Bengen spending level," he says, "but she disliked the Medicaid long-term care benefit compared to long-term care policies with home care, assisted-living, etc. Our modeling provided her a rationale to approach her grown children about some possible future help on LTC insurance premiums. Instead of retiring fully," Caldwell continues, "she would agree to continue part-time employment and pay the LTC insurance as long as she could, if they would take over later if she couldn't work and her future investment results hadn't compounded enough to pick up the premium."

Yes, the children might have done this anyway, if asked. But with a financial plan, she was able to show that with part-time work and reduced spending, she had a decent chance of producing an estate for her children (the even odds scenario), and she felt no loss of face in asking her children in advance for help *if* her health and investments both failed to keep up.

Turbo-Boosting Income

As the discussion went through another column or two, we began to realize that there were other investment planning services waiting to be born. For one thing, planners of the future will need to spend more time on deciding where the distributions are going to come from in each year.

Glenn Kenney, who practices in Citrus Heights, California, finds that most planners don't fully account for the flexibility offered by capital gains and reverse mortgages. "Generating long-term capital gains provides two strong lifetime advantages, and one huge wealth transfer advantage," he says. "Unrealized capital gains are not taxable and do not add to the Social Security tax burden. When taken, long-term gains provide a substantial reduction in the tax bite."

And, of course, with a married couple, the 100% basis step-up at the death of the first spouse provides a tax-free windfall for the survivor spouse. "In my shop, the generation of long-term capital gains is our first line of defense against outliving one's money," says Kenney. "Reverse mortgages, meanwhile, allow for the creation of tax-free income from what is the single biggest capital asset most people have, the equity in their home."

At age 70½, mandatory IRA distributions take some of the choices away, but even before that, Kenney finds it advantageous to tap the IRA money. "One of our favorite programs is to take existing tax deferred assets (IRAs and fixed annuities) and annu-itize them out for as long as they can last for income purposes," he says, "since you can't escape ordinary taxes on them anyway." The remaining investable assets are parked in an all-equity, tax-efficient portfolio where the unrealized gains are allowed to build.

"When the annuity income dries up, we start taking the highly tax advantaged unrealized gains," says Kenney. "When the death of the first spouse makes the unrealized gains tax-free to the survivor, it adds a serious turbo-boost to the estate's income-generating strength. You can get the kids to buy into this plan very easily, since the unrealized gains left in the portfolio at their surviving parent's death go income tax-free to them, too."

Precise Fudging

Interestingly, some advisors argued that we are wasting our time trying to model the future down to the penny. Instead of fancy spreadsheet work, it may be possible to introduce some very basic fudge factors into distribution planning.

"Most of my clients have a paid-for home when they retire, and I never count their home equity when I run projections," says Nelson. "That way I can say to them: if you really do run out of money at age 90 or 95, we can sell your home, invest the proceeds *very* conservatively, and you can use them to rent a unit in a retirement community."

Sometimes the fudging can be very precise. "We determine retirement needs in dollars and then add a cushion of $10,000," says Steven Cowen, of La Jolla, CA. "We calculate our clients' annual income from Social Security, fixed pensions and other income sources (rental property) and calculate the shortfall. Then we take their annuities and annuitize them on a fixed basis with a survivor option. If there are no annuities, we buy fixed annuities with a survivor option equaling the shortfall for the life of the client."

The $10,000 a year cushion can be spent if needed, or simply allowed to grow in the portfolio until the need to spend it arises.

Risk Pooling and Annuitization

The previous comment points up one of the most popular responses: the use of immediate annuities to stabilize retirement income.

Interestingly, this realization is coming primarily from practitioners who have avoided risk pooling investment products in the past, either because of their commission structure or the absence of full cost disclosure. "I hate insurance products and would never recommend them during the accumulation years," says Cowen. "But I really like their value in the retirement phase of peoples' lives."

Brascia agrees. "Frankly, I think the 'immediate annuity' concept will be critical moving forward, as it will be in many retirees best interest to spread their risk amongst a pool of other retirees," he says. "Unfortunately, I think a lot of planners will avoid the annuitization option because it takes assets under management away from the planner."

Of course, there are other ways than annuities to get guaranteed income for life. "With corporate employees, who typically have a 'lump sum or annuitization' option," Brascia continues, "I have consistently tried to get them to consider the annuitized payout for a portion of their assets."

Caldwell points out one potential drawback to the annuitization approach. "If your client is a senior with modest assets and income, you must remember that the immediate annuity will likely disqualify the senior for Medicaid long-term care. No spend down of other assets would allow qualification if there is a lifetime annuity income above the state-mandated minimums."

Quality of Old Age

In the background of the discussion, some insistent voices were pointing out that the raw longevity statistics are not necessarily as real world dangerous as they seem.

"The truth is, the life span hasn't been growing at all," says Dick Vodra, of McLean, VA. "Fewer people die early, so the survival curve is flatter than it used to be and average life expectancies have gone up because of that. Even today, essentially nobody makes it past 110, an age a few people reached a century ago," he adds. "Even if science surprises us and adds thirty years to our lives," Vodra continues, "we need to ask where the thirty years will go. Will we extend lives by adding decades to our sixties, giving people more years of relative strength and alertness, or will the years be added at the end so [people in their nineties living in] nursing homes, [and drooling], go on forever?"

"If it's the former," he says, "then people can work until they're 85. If it's the latter, God help us."

Distribution Toolkit

One common lament, from many advisors, was that they are drowning in retirement planning spreadsheets and programs, but don't have a comparable tool for distribution planning.

Others, however, managed to find some new tools – or create their own.

Bill Swerbenski (swerbo@swerbo.com), who lives and works in San Francisco, has created a program that models the risk of a portfolio running out of money under an infinite variety of circumstances (the inputs include income from a pension, from Social Security, and from an investment portfolio that can be allocated any way you want to, plus the amount of income your client will need in the first year and how the expense need should be inflated). You put in a client's numbers, your designated portfolio and your inflation expectation, push a button and the program runs a Monte Carlo analysis that gives you the chances your strategy will run out of money.

Beating the Market

Finally, there has been an ongoing lament in the *Inside Information* community that the traditional mutual fund product is somewhat outmoded. New communications technologies, and the advent of the personal computer, have made the concept of a bunch of very dissimilar people pooling their investments and getting exactly the same returns and tax treatment look somewhat quaint. How many other products have survived, virtually unchanged, since the 1920s?

But there's a better argument for creating new investment products that harness the best thinking of fund managers. It is that most fund managers have beaten the market over the past 5- and 10-year periods – even though their funds haven't.

Come again? Let me illustrate what I mean by "beating the market" with an out-of-the-box analogy. More than three decades ago, my high school track team was scheduled to compete against a rural high school. Our bus drove through fields and woods and over hills and out into the country, and about an hour after the bus rolled into an unpaved parking lot, the officials called all the sprinters over, and I lined up to run a 220-yard dash against a lanky kid who wore what appeared to be fishing boots on his feet.

I beat him by half an instant, and after the race there was no question in my mind that he was by far the better sprinter.

My contention is that fund managers are running the performance race in fishing boots. They are handicapped by the limitations of the mutual fund structure itself. Without the boots, they are beating the market.

Some will argue that the mutual fund industry in aggregate simply cannot outperform the averages, because it *is* the market, but in fact that has never been the case. The Investment Company Institute estimates that just fewer than 20% of all publicly-traded U.S. stocks are held in mutual funds. So it should be possible for a majority of the managers in the fund industry to be above-average investors.

Are they? Numerous academic studies of fund performance have basically concluded that the average mutual fund's returns trail behind its appropriate benchmark by almost exactly the fund's expense ratio. So it appears that, in aggregate, mutual fund performance is exactly average – in fact, it is below average only by the amount of fees that are charged.

As Rex Sinquefield, vice chairman and index advocate at Dimensional Fund Advisors, memorably put it: "mediocre performance doesn't come cheap."

Mitigating Circumstances

But are there circumstances that make it harder for fund managers to act on their decisions, so that their performance might not be as high as, say, your performance if you were to make the same decisions in your own investment portfolio? If the answer is yes, then we'd have evidence that the investment decisions that fund managers are making, in aggregate, are actually superior to the decisions made by other investors in the market. The more obstacles they face, the harder it is for them to implement their decisions efficiently, the more their decisions must be outperforming the average in order for their performance (minus expenses) to *be* the average.

The Size Factor

Let's start with the obvious: size. Nobody wants to talk about this in the fund world, but when your portfolio starts getting measured in ten figures ($1,000,000,000 and up), then it no longer makes a lot of sense to trade in small or microcap shares. You can't buy enough of those companies for their price movements to make much of a difference in your portfolio.

Right off the top, this can eliminate three-fourths of the possible investment options. In the case of Fidelity Magellan, whose portfolio size is measured in 12 figures, the options become even more limited. What is the effect of narrowing your effective universe by 75% or more? Nobody knows, but every reader can remember stories of a tiny fund that had terrific performance right up until it ran into a wall at half a billion or a billion under management. That strongly suggests that, for some managers at least, it is harder to turn up gems in the larger field than it was in the smaller one.

I don't know how to quantify this effect, so let's just (for now) chalk it up as somewhat heavier shoes on the feet of most fund managers as they run the race.

Directional Money Slosh

Then you have market timers – a category which, alas, includes most of the investing public. During the pre-market bubble, consumers pulled billions out of small-cap and value fund portfolios and reshuffled that money into the hot S&P 500 asset class. Then they reshuffled money into tech stocks toward the top, and then pulled out of tech stocks altogether.

In talking with fund managers and executives, I've begun to realize just how normal that is: that every portfolio manager comes into the office and looks at the computer screen to find out if he or she is a net buyer or seller of stocks that day. The decision has already been made by net fund inflows or outflows by advisors and retail investors, and the sloshing of money is nearly always in the wrong direction.

When a fund's asset class is beaten down and there are bargains everywhere, the money is inevitably moving out into some other hot asset class. The money flows back in after the asset class has gotten pricier and the performance has started to look hot. This makes it virtually impossible for fund managers to buy low and sell high – or to buy at all when their valuation models tell them to pounce. Again, the actual dollar effect of this handicap is hard to quantify, but I suspect that if somebody did it, they would find it to be considerable.

The Cost of Style Purity

And, of course, all through this process the fund has to incur trading costs above and beyond what the fund manager might have preferred. According to statistics compiled by the Investment Company Institute, the redemption rate in the fund industry has risen an average of 33% a year since the end of 1995. The cost of selling causes a drag on the performance as well.

Lately, the advisory community is demanding (for, I think, basically good reasons) that fund managers maintain style consistency or style purity. That means if they are managing a mid-cap portfolio, and a stock does really, really well, then they have to sell it when it is defined as a large-cap issue. This shows up in performance as more than just trading costs.

I remember at one of the Morningstar conferences how a fund manager who had bought Microsoft early, and reluctantly sold it when it flew out of his investment sandbox, went back and calculated what would have happened if he had held on. That one stock, he said, would have been worth more than the whole rest of the portfolio put together. In his case, the opportunity cost was enormous.

Siphoning Track Record

Finally, you have another component to trading costs, beyond the actual cost of the broker's services in buying and selling stocks – that is, your effect on a stock's price as you are trading it. *Fortune* magazine ran a cover article a while back where a nice piece of investigative reporting showed how traders have gotten in the unfortunate habit of tipping off their friends when a large buy order comes across their desks from somebody in the fund industry. The funds try to disguise their activities by placing trades through a number of brokers, and they tell me that they are constantly watching for suspicious price movements in advance of their execution. But there seems no question that others are siphoning some of the manager's track record into their own pockets.

Market Impact

Finally, you have the cost of the actual changes in supply and demand that you trigger when you unload, say, a couple thousand shares of a stock, or decide to take a big position in a company that you think is undervalued. This number has actually been quantified, to some extent, by the Barra organization in Berkeley, California. Barra looked at trades executed by the largest 150 stock mutual funds, and found that orders routinely moved the price of the stocks they were trying to buy and sell. Using a mathematical model that seems to me to slightly understate the actual effect, Barra estimated that these shifts in supply or demand clipped two percentage points off the returns of the average mutual fund. The effect was much smaller on large-cap portfolios and index funds; relatively larger on portfolios that specialize in small-cap or value securities, and was always higher when the manager was taking a large stake relative to the stock's total market cap – when, basically, the manager really liked the price to begin with.

Cumulative Impact

So start with a 2% penalty, and probably more for the portfolios that most advisors use, since the profession seems to be attracted to less efficient markets and more value-oriented securities. Next, add the effect of trading costs imposed on the portfolio from the outside. Then add the effect of somebody else deciding when you can and cannot buy securities in the market, and generally dictating the opposite of what you would normally be inclined to do based on your valuation models. The result, I think, is some mighty heavy boots on that fund manager who is still, somehow, managing to get us market returns minus the expense ratio.

The overall effect appears to be much greater than the expense ratio of the funds, and it appears that fund managers have been overcoming the rest of this effect – to the tune, in some cases, of 3% or more a year.

The conclusion I draw is that, in the aggregate, fund managers have proven themselves to be superior investors over the last five years. That helps me resolve a personal dilemma: when I talk with fund managers, they tend to be much, much smarter than I am about the investments they track, and I have trouble imagining how their extra information and all the time they spend on their craft can translate into below-average decisions.

It also helps me make sense of a growing trend in the planning market: financial planners are picking individual stocks for their clients, and many of them, after a few drinks after hours at this or that conference, tell me they are experiencing less-than-average performance. Stock picking is harder than they realized.

But if I turn this information around, another conclusion jumps out at me. Somehow, the fund industry is going to have to figure out how to take the muddy fishing boots off of their fund managers and deliver to all of us the extraordinary performance that their picks could be offering us and our clients (albeit, under different circumstances).

To do that, they are going to have to reluctantly abandon the clunky mutual fund structure itself. Funds have enjoyed a remarkably long and productive life in the American investment scene, but in the age of the Internet, fund executives are going to have to have painful discussions about how to cannibalize their highly-successful business model in order to offer customization, smaller trading orders and portfolios that are divided into many asset classes, but which allow stocks to migrate from one to another without the necessity of selling them out of one fund and buying them into another.

The New Investment Vehicle

But how, exactly, do we remove the boots and still allow the fund managers to run the same race? What will the next evolutionary stage of the mutual fund look like?

In our *Inside Information* community discussions, different pieces of the puzzle have emerged, which I think we can finally start putting together for the first time. One clear message that I've heard over and over again is that separate accounts, as presently structured, are *not* the solution. They add very little additional flexibility, are just as expensive as mutual funds, and lack the strict performance reporting standards that funds live under.

Nor are hedge funds the solution; they're way too expensive and opaque for most advisors to feel comfortable with. Yes, there are a few advisors who have clients large enough to make secure investments in that arena, but with so many new funds opening up, and untried managers taking in billions of dollars, my guess is that this is the breeding ground for the next ugly investment scandal.

If the investment vehicle is not transparent and fully disclosed, then it isn't worth your attention. The fact that the SEC doesn't regulate hedge funds just adds to the pile of objections against them.

The post-mutual-fund "New Investment Vehicle" (NIV for short) that advisors seem to have in mind would look and act very similar to the Folio concept that was introduced to our world by FOLIOfn. It would consist of an investment account that is created by the portfolio manager. This investment portfolio would exist in a trading account that is held in the name of the financial planning client and – this is very important – the same account could be holding, for the same client, other portfolios managed by other managers.

So, for example, manager X at one fund company would have small-cap expertise, and would define what stocks would be in that corner of the overall portfolio. Manager Y at another fund company might have large-cap value expertise, and define what would be in that allocated portion of the total portfolio account. But the actual securities managed by manager X and Y would reside together in the client's trading/investment account. And there might be others in there as well.

Tax Efficiency

This, of course, looks much like the core portfolio that Evensky has proposed, but with the added advantage of having active managers overlay their expertise, plus the option of transferring existing securities directly into the mix without any tax consequences.

Suppose now that you have a client who has an existing stock portfolio, and you decide to move the holdings under the management of fund/portfolio managers X and Y under the NIV system. You would transfer the client's holdings, as they exist today, into the client's investment account, contact the fund companies that employ managers X and Y, and hire them to mange the portfolio.

To keep the numbers simple, suppose manager X and manager Y would each handle 40% of the total portfolio, with the other 20% in a mixture of cash and in a protected part of the account that we'll talk about in a minute. Admittedly, this is an oversimplification. In the real world, my guess is that the planner would create detailed allocations among five to 10 different asset classes, and hire different managers for different percentages based on this overall portfolio design.

Of course, the managers would already have their existing portfolios (small-cap for X, and large-cap value for Y) in their computer. If they are planning to sell some of those holdings, then those holdings to be sold are flagged, and are not purchased for new client accounts.

The rest of the portfolio information would be sent to the custodian of the client's investment account. A computer at the custodian matches which stocks that managers X and Y have in their accounts (what they want the client to buy) against the stock positions that are already held by the client. If the client already owns some of the stocks that are going to be purchased, there is no need to take the whole portfolio to cash, re-buy those stocks, and incur those transaction costs – the stocks are already in there.

The planner, meanwhile, can go online and specify for the client's NIV account any stocks that he/she doesn't want held in that account. Suppose this particular client works for IBM and happens to hold IBM stock in his retirement plan. The planner can input a "rule" over the account that no IBM stock will be purchased for it or held in this account.

If the client happens to have socially responsible issues, and doesn't want to own Philip Morris, then the planner would input another "rule" over the portfolio. Before the client's account is reallocated, the computer checks whether any of the purchases will violate these rules – and if so, those purchases are never made, for this particular client.

Another "rule" could specify that some of the stocks the client already owns will not be sold, because (perhaps) they have significant embedded capital gains.

Asset Allocation

There is one more step that has to take place before the client's existing portfolio is reallocated. The custodian of the account will have a software program that assigns every stock, bond and mutual fund position to an asset class – or, perhaps, some multi-national corporations will be assigned fractional percentages to different asset classes and industry categories.

This would allow the planner to look at the overall portfolio mix that would result if the recommendations of manager X and Y (which are in the computer, but not yet acted on) are followed – minus, of course, the restrictions that the planner has already placed on what can be purchased. Those restrictions might have skewed the percentages that the planner wants to allocate to each asset class. In that case, the planner could "protect" some stock positions and hold them in the same account outside of the control of manager X and Y.

This is the "protected" part of the client's NIV portfolio that I mentioned earlier.

Finally, the planner pushes an "agree" button, which activates manager X and Y's engagement over the account, the rest of the stock positions are liquidated, and new stocks are purchased. The custodian would aggregate all purchases and sales within its domain, and try to match purchases and sales each day between different accounts in the same basic way that FOLIOfn does now. All the unmatched purchases and sales in all the portfolios handled under this arrangement by the custodian are then aggregated and taken to market together, in order to get the best possible trading price. After the purchase or sale has taken place, the share positions are allocated back to the individual client portfolios.

Management Issues

From here, the actual management of the NIV begins to resemble the traditional mutual fund. But there are important differences. The fund company does not handle the purchases and sales; instead, they are generated through the custodian in individual accounts. If one manager is selling and the other happens to be buying the same security, then the transactions are simply reallocated inside the account, and no trade is generated. If the client happens to be holding the security that is to be purchased in the protected part of the account, then that security is simply moved into manager X's or manager Y's part of the portfolio, without any transaction taking place.

Every week, the planner can check the percentages of each asset class in the account, and can take tax losses opportunistically as part of the rebalancing effort. If this results in a discrepancy between what the account holds and what managers X or Y are recommending, the discrepancy will show up in red on the screen whenever the account is checked. After the 30-day period, those securities can be repurchased if the planner thinks it's appropriate. There also may be mutual funds, exchanged-traded funds (ETFs), individual bonds and other securities in the protected part of the portfolio, which the planner could buy and sell to maintain target allocations.

Of course, it is unfair to calculate the manager's track record based on changes that are not under his or her control, so a separate account would be maintained by both manager X and manager Y, and the performance of this account would be tracked by the mutual fund reporting services. The custodian, meanwhile, would keep a running tally of the assets under manager X's and Y's control, and pay an asset management fee out of the portfolio itself, similar to the way the fund industry charges today.

Standards and Technology

Some may think that the New Investment Vehicle is a bizarre fantasy. But I think it's interesting to notice that every bit of the technology necessary to make this happen is here today – and most of it is at least 10 years old. There is no technological impediment at all, and yet this kind of investment service seems to be beyond the pale of our imaginations.

I invite you to stop for a moment and realize what was just said because it illustrates – with painful clarity – how little the mutual fund world is using the current technological possibilities. Or, to put it more bluntly, it shows how far behind the curve the mutual fund industry is compared with other service industries.

Does this NIV arrangement meet the standards that planners have set for all investments they recommend? Does it offer transparency, liquidity, customization, and economies of scale in trading and in leveraging the skills and analytical abilities of the fund manager and his or her information resources?

My guess is that the fund industry will object that the planner could simply replicate manager X's and Y's trades in a separate account, and effectively get the fund management for free simply by setting up a token account. But I think there's an answer to that: planners like to have somebody they can fire if the account's performance is awful. For most advisors, it's well worth the 70 to 90 basis points that the managers might charge to maintain that distance.

Similarly, front-runners might have a much harder time under this arrangement than they do currently, since the various custodians would be making lots of smaller group trades, rather than the fund company coming to market with an enormous position to unwind. And, of course, many of the trades would be matched internally at the custodial level, without ever going out to market.

There may also be problems with smaller accounts. The fund manager may want (to take an extreme example) to buy Berkshire Hathaway for all clients, but it is going to be hard to allocate precise percentages in an account that doesn't hold at least $1 million. FOLIOfn was able to solve this problem by holding fractional shares in Folio accounts; there may be a similar solution at the custodial level. Or we may have to live with close approximations.

Conclusion: The Unexplored Terrain

Investment planning in the future is going to become at once simpler and a great deal more complicated. The time-consuming chores of analyzing thousands of funds is likely to go away, but it will be replaced by a host of customized portfolio strategies, new products (e.g., NIV), and a variety of new services, including distribution planning, information filtering, functional asset allocation, and more client handholding than ever before.

Many of these new services are similar to what planners have traditionally done in the past (e.g., distribution planning is the mirror image of accumulation planning), while others will be entirely new, and may require practitioners to identify new resources.

Unfortunately, the precise shape of these services is still being worked out in the laboratory of the marketplace. Advisors who want to sprint ahead to the endpoint of these trends, and stake out terrain before the rest of the profession arrives (five to seven years in the future), should begin to join some of the discussions that are starting to define these new services.

As they become more familiar with the investment planning services of the future, they can start to achieve some measure of separation from their peers – which is one of the first principles of effective marketing.

Which takes us to the next chapter.

Interlude on *The Cutting Edge*:

The Bear Market Time Capsule

Before we go to Chapter 7, let's take a moment to recognize how extraordinary this moment in time really is. This soon-to-be-legendary 2001-2003 Bear Market is a living investment lesson.

Think about it: wouldn't it have been great if, at the height of the NASDAQ bubble, we could have opened a time capsule sent to us by the professionals who practiced through the 1973-74 bear market. The time capsule would have captured what they learned during those awful months, and what they were feeling at the time, and how the markets seemed to them as month after month of losses began to eat away at their confidence in the future.

Did they know that instead of an upturn, the markets were destined to drift for eight more years, until the dramatic upturn of 1982? Were their clients' investment horizons long enough for them to hold on? What rates of return were they projecting when the market suddenly tanked, and did they change their projections as the gloom persisted into its second year?

Today, we have that same opportunity again to learn from the markets, and pass on what we learned to investors yet to be born. We have a rare chance to extract wisdom from pain.

What should we tell the people of the future about what we're going through today? What lessons have we learned, which will be valuable to future generations of investors?

What words can we freeze into amber that will serve as a guidepost to investors as they approach, unknowing, the next 1968, 1973-74, or 2000-2001?

I posed these questions to the members of the *Inside Information* community, and they responded with more than 400 different messages – different bits of wisdom to drop into the time capsule for the people who will have forgotten, all over again, that markets inevitably come down, and that it is always, and never, different this time around.

Together, we discovered that the same market forces are having opposite effects on different planning professionals. For some advisors, the market downturn is bringing in new business and reinforcing their client relationships. For others, it is destroying client relationships, and the pipeline of new prospects has dried up.

This is not a bigger-fish-eat-the-smaller scenario, but just the opposite. Today, some of the most profitable firms in the business, which specialize in investment management, are leaking clients while struggling firms that have never strayed from traditional financial planning are picking up more and better business than they ever would have imagined.

The time capsule that was created by the *Inside Information* community for future generations of investors runs more than 50 pages, but these are its highlights.

Dear People of the Future:

We are writing to you out of one of the scariest times in world economic history, when many people are still a little bit afraid to fly and open their mail, particularly if their mail contains their latest quarterly statement. Our stocks have lost a lot of money, and economists are telling us that our stocks, on average, are still overvalued by traditional measures. Our economy is moving into a recession. Unemployment is up. Housing is down. Thirty-six months ago, the Dow was testing 12,000. Recently it tested 8,000 in the other direction.

We hope you don't have to go through this yourself, because it is not as much fun as you might think. Where you are, now, you know how all of this is going to come out. But there are some things that we can teach you from inside of this investment trough. We know what it is like to go through a traumatic market, and our lessons should not have to be relearned by every generation.

First of all, it is times like this that tell us how harmful the financial media can be. The mood of the moment is immeasurably worse because gloomy forecasts, prognoses and outlooks are broadcast every half hour and published in all the major magazines. This is the opposite of the euphoria that inflated the bubble for five straight years with ever-more-enthusiastic reports on the half-hour – which now, just thinking about them, make us collectively want to gag.

But that's not the worst of it; we're doing it to *ourselves*, using this new medium called the Internet to forward rumors and dark hints about what is to come. When I sent him a friendly message, Mark Smith told me, "I needed to hear a different voice from the apocalyptic messages that I've been receiving this week."

We have learned, after sharp market moves in both directions, that it is dangerous to pay too close attention to our herd-mentality media. Remember this, because it may be the key to your financial survival when the markets turn around again.

We have also learned that professionals matter a lot more in bear markets than in bull markets. Nancy Kister, who works with Citigroup Private Bank, puts having an advisor at the top of her list of lessons, even ahead of keeping an open mind about the markets and the world. What I like about the list is that everything focuses on the big picture, and is designed to take peoples' attention off of the short term:

1. Build a relationship with an advisor first and make sure this person understands your values and what's important to you.

2. Do some comprehensive financial planning with your advisor and set priorities as to what you want to do in life.

3. Implement a game plan that makes sense to you and act on recommendations that feel comfortable and doable.

4. Follow-up with your advisor periodically, address your concerns, and monitor your financial situation.

5. Keep an open mind. Flexibility is key as things change, your life changes and markets change as well.

I think that, in retrospect, we were most surprised to discover that most of us were expecting, on some level, a bear market to follow the tech bubble. But at the same time, none of us could have called the sequence of events that brought it on. This is crucially important for you to realize: that we, who have seen the most abrupt transition from bull to bear in a century, couldn't predict the sequence of events in a way that would have allowed us to profit from it. The most successful investors were those who didn't get caught up in the mania of the bull, or the despair of the bear.

Most of us (let us confess now) let our standards drift too far. With the benefit of hindsight, what was deemed to be "conservative" in the 1999 investment environment now looks like it was much too radical. "How many of us sector weighted towards growth during the preceding ten years?" asks Colin Smith in one of the best comments I received.

So here's the lesson: if you're feeling a strong pull away from diversification, then chances are you're going to need that diversification to protect your portfolio in the very near future.

Many advisors who contributed to our time capsule also learned the value of rebalancing. If you had rebalanced diligently during the market upsurge, instead of letting the portfolio drift toward growth and tech, you were spared the worst of the downturn. Some advisors think rebalancing will make their clients money at this part of the market too. "I have no idea if we have hit the bottom or not in this market," says Robert Thomas, "but I do know that these stocks have gone on sale."

Finally, I think we learned how easy it is to lose your long-term perspective. "For many investors, even today, "long-term" is what happened twenty minutes ago on CNBC," Smith (Colin) wrote in his time capsule message. "For many investment professionals, long-term means what is going to happen or is happening over the next quarter." The best fund managers, Smith would remind you, are looking three to five years out at a minimum.

Professionals – the sort of people who spent quality time with Morningstar's Principia database – are at their most valuable during times of economic turbulence. You people of the future can look long and hard in this chaotic market and uncertain time in history, for any messages that make as much long-term sense as the wisdom of this time capsule.

As you enter the next ugly downturn, recognize that these are the days when the cream rises to the top in every important way. During those awful times, we raise our standards and the better advice gets heard a little clearer and the people who work harder and better get a little more market share while the dilettantes and form-over-substance professionals (and organizations) are exposed. The world gets a little better in a way that it wouldn't if the downturn hadn't happened.

That, and a little wisdom from the deep inside of the bear, is our gift to you people of the future.

7 MARKETING THE CUTTING EDGE

et's start this chapter with a quick story that I think captures something important about the general subject of marketing. A planner named Lew Wallensky, who practices in the Los Angeles area, shared it with me.

"Twenty years ago, a person came into my office, and I could see immediately from his face that something was wrong," he says. "So I asked him what the problem was."

The prospective client answered: "You're the third advisor I've seen today. The others said I wasn't big or wealthy enough to work with them."

Wallensky told this man to sit down, and discovered that he was just starting a small company and had zero investible assets. He offered his best advice, and over the next two decades he played an increasingly important role in the client's business, helping him achieve and maintain balance, profitability, credit and financial health. Twenty years went by, and finally the client sold his firm for $20,000,000, giving the assets to Wallensky to manage as his retirement portfolio.

As it happens, there's another company in the Los Angeles area that's highly focused, which targets small business owners with $3,000,000 or more in assets. The principal of that firm somehow found out that Wallensky was managing the assets of this client, and wondered how his expensive marketing campaign had failed while Wallensky's zero marketing budget had landed such a big fish. "How (this person asked Wallensky) did you land a client like that?"

Now here's the punch line: this highly focused advisor was one of the people who rejected this client 20 years ago.

The point, obviously, is that the most effective marketing in any profession is done in the form of helping people, and with some degree of generosity, rather than in the brochure copy of any expensive advertising campaign. In fact, the most successful advisors in the planning profession consciously generate new business by going the extra mile for their existing clients, and receiving referral business from them in return.

I think it's clear that we have entered a place and time when advisors can no longer feel that their clients owe them referrals. As marketing consultant Dan Richards has said, "Clients have to feel like they are genuinely doing their friends a favor by introducing you to them, and be confident that their friends will thank them for the referral."

In the preceding chapters, we saw several implications of this basic truth. When you are working for hundreds and then thousands of clients, and more every year, you spread yourself too thin to offer that degree of generosity that is the new coinage to be exchanged for client referrals. But when you focus your efforts on a few, who pay you on an ongoing basis for tremendously powerful services, then you're well positioned to delight clients and gain new business.

As the profession moves forward into the uncharted waters of expanded financial planning, this interesting trend will be accelerated. Clients are likely to experience personal gains that are more meaningful and more satisfying than anything the profession has offered before. The result may well be a much higher number of referrals per client than the profession has ever experienced.

As time goes on, and you become an exemplar of a balanced, happy, satisfied life, you and your clients will begin to attract others who are envious of what you've found and accomplished.

So the rest of this chapter is about how to make it easier for people to find you and experience first-hand your generosity, and your help on their life journey.

Drip Marketing

Staying with the subject of referrals, members of the *Inside Information* community have offered some thoughts on how best to convert a referral into a client. One simple principle, often overlooked, is to follow up immediately. Indeed, one advisor confessed that she often let the names and phone numbers sit on her desk for weeks because she was too busy to call and schedule an appointment.

Others noted that many times the person being referred is not yet ready to enter into a planning relationship – which is, in their minds, a very intimate engagement that they want to step into carefully. "People are a lot more willing to talk about sex than about their finances," one advisor wrote. "So they have to have time to take a deep breath before coming in."

How do you allow that "deep breath" and still maintain contact? Jim Kirkland, who practices in the Detroit area, pioneered the simple system that has since become known as "Drip Marketing." In its simplest form, he would maintain a list of everybody who has been referred to him, who has not yet come in for an appointment, and would identify, on that list, some areas of interest that he was able to find out during a brief phone conversation. Then he and his staff would read consumer publications, and any interesting article in that area of interest would be sent to the client with a brief note – via automatically generated mailing lists. In most cases, these prospects would receive one piece of information a month.

Why is this so effective? It keeps your name in front of the person, so that whenever a crisis hits, the referred party is reminded that you're available to help. But I think more importantly, it is an act of (systematized) generosity, an effort to help that person stay on top of his or her interests.

Client Waiting Lists

If you're too busy to follow up, and yet you want the client to have a chance to take a deep breath, then you can go completely out of the box and create a waiting list for new clients. That's what Rick Volpe did for his Harleysville, Pennsylvania practice when faced with a sudden rush of interest in his firm. "I thought people would just walk away when I told them they'd have to wait six months to be a client," he says. "But I was clear that my first commitment is to my existing clients, and I want to make sure they get the full benefit of our service."

In fact, the six-month waiting period seems to have become an incentive to sign up immediately, to reserve a space in line. And waiting six months allowed people to take that deep breath and not rush into a relationship that they secretly were anxious about. Eventually, Volpe had to expand the waiting time to a year, and didn't suffer any diminution of interest.

Mission Statements

Others have noted that people respond to idealism in their practitioner. Bob Monin, who practices in Williamsville, New York, has created an elaborate package that he sends to clients, which includes letters of endorsement from current clients, and a mission statement that talks about his focus on the client's well being.

Sending the package out immediately to every referred party does two things: it tells potential clients that you're prompt and reliable, and the written materials impress them with your commitment to focus your services around their goals.

In fact, one of the strongest things you can do for your marketing efforts is create a strong mission statement, and attach it to everything you send out – the back of your business card, your stationary, and especially your brochure. Author Kevin McCarthy (*Living on Purpose*) argues that the mission statement helps clarify – in your own mind and in the minds of employees and customers – how your work makes a difference. "If you understand what you do best for people, then you can figure out how to do more of it," he says.

Too many people, he adds, create vague or wimpy statements like "to help people," which actually makes it harder to accomplish their business objectives. Better, he says, to start the mission statement with "I exist to serve by ___." and then adding two words, one ending in "ing" and the other defining something that people really desire. "I exist to serve by liberating greatness." "I exist to serve by setting people free." "I exist to serve by igniting joy." "I exist to serve by awakening worth." "I exist to serve by growing wealth."

Pamela Christensen, who we met earlier with her budgeting service, uses the following mission statement:

> *"To educate, motivate and support clients in pursuit of their financial goals by providing hope and a professional measurement of success."*

Peg and Bob Eddy, of Creative Capital Management in San Diego, have adopted a mission statement that can stand in as an anthem for the entire life planning movement:

> *"As trusted financial advisors, we empower our clients to achieve their life's dreams through proactive, integrated and fee-only wealth management services."*

Who Are You?

Meeting planners who are thinking of inviting marketing expert Pamela Yellen ("four-time presenter at the Million-Dollar Roundtable") to speak at planning conferences should remem-

ber to ask her not to deliver a 15-minute infomercial for her services and products at the end of her talk. But she did offer some
good positioning lines in a presentation at the Central Florida
FPA annual meeting in Orlando. She told the audience that she
once called a woman whose answering machine responded with
a rude message: "Who are you and why should I care?"

"I realized," Yellen said, "that this is precisely the unspoken
question in peoples' minds whenever we talk with them."

How can you respond? If you don't already have a personal
position statement, Yellen offered several possibilities:

> "I help clients maximize their wealth and mini-
> mize their taxes."

> "I show business owners how to take money out
> of their business, use it for their own personal benefit,
> and minimize the taxes they pay on it."

> "I help my clients set up a plan that will provide a
> stream of income at retirement – with no government
> limits on how much you can contribute."

> "I show my clients how to be able to send all of
> their children, or grandchildren, to the schools of their
> choice."

> "I help my clients protect their nest egg against
> bear markets, without sacrificing bull market returns."

> "I show people how to maximize their portfolio
> returns – without increasing their risk."

> "I help my clients retire as much as five to seven
> years earlier than they might have been able to if we
> had never met."

"I show people how to avoid losing everything they've worked so hard to create – including their independence and their dignity – if they need home health or nursing home care."

The Marketing Fast Track

Karen Altfest, who practices with her husband Lew in New York, believes that with a little practice, you can start constructing long-term client relationships before the person you're talking with is even a client. (The book to read is Altfest's own *Keeping Clients for Life*, published by John Wiley & Sons, 2001.)

To Altfest, marketing is really about building (and tending) relationships, and communication is the key to making this happen. The process starts with the very first phone call into the firm. Where many companies have delegated the receptionist to gather general information and schedule an appointment, Altfest consciously tries to take those calls herself.

"You can begin to develop a personal relationship from the very first phone call you get from them," she says. "How you answer this call, and how you relate to the people, even over the phone, and address their concerns and give them special attention and represent yourself, is going to determine the quality of the relationship going forward. And in many cases, even whether there will be an ongoing relationship or not."

But wait – is somebody calling for preliminary information going to get personal on that first call? Apparently, if handled properly, the answer is yes. In fact, Altfest contends that this personal connection is what the caller is really looking for. "These prospective clients say they're calling to learn about your services, your charges, your educational background, your experience," she says. "But what they're really looking for is someone to trust, someone to confide very sensitive matters to, someone who will listen to them. When prospects call me on the phone," she adds, "I'm often amazed at the things they'll disclose to a complete stranger. They're so eager to connect with someone who will listen and care."

Focus on Them, Not You

How does this happen? Instead of talking about her firm, Altfest will focus on getting the callers to talk about their experiences with their finances. "I never ask anybody what his or her assets are," she says. "I was raised to think that that would be impolite. Hello, how much money do you have? Doesn't feel good to me. But I almost always have the answer before I hang up. Instead, I say to them, are you managing your own money? That gets them talking about money. I ask them if they're using mutual funds, if they're using stocks. They start telling me. I ask them where the money is now, meaning: is it at a brokerage or are you like one of my clients who has an attic full of stock certificates that she won't part with? That starts the information flowing in a non-threatening way. And they'll tell you everything you wanted to know."

Altfest will also ask them how they did in the market over the last year. "They can't resist telling you if they were winners or losers," she says. "Ask about problems with their relatives. People love to talk about their families. If there's a lull, ask about their kids or grandkids. Even ask about the likelihood of leaving their job or maybe even their marriage."

One of Altfest's most important maxims is: Don't spend the entire time, or even half the time, talking about you, your firm, what you do – even if that was the question. "If you think callers really want to know about your services or your fees," she says, "try talking about your practice and see how quickly the conversation comes to a close. Instead, refer clients to your website for information about your firm, or offer to send them your brochure later that same day."

This, in fact, has become a mini-theme in the marketing discussions in the *Inside Information* community: the fact that most advisors tend to lead with their credentials, trying to impress the client with how much they know and how important they are considered in the profession. In discussions with clients, advisors discovered that the real message this is sending is: "This person knows so much, he could steal all my assets and I'd never know it." Or: "This person knows so much that when he looks at what a mess I've made of my financial situation, he's going to laugh at me."

Neither impression is likely to lead to a long-term client relationship.

Their Part of the Tale

So what *do* the callers want to know about you? "They're really asking, do you take my problems seriously?" says Altfest. "Will I have your full attention? Will you remember me next time I call? Do I stand out from your other clients? Are you the kind of person I want to confide in? Will you be there for me? Can I comfortably tell you things about myself that I've never told anyone? Will you keep my confidences? Listening well, being patient and available, offering a little phone sympathy, and being truly interested in the caller's story can create a bond before you ever meet in person."

Interestingly, very little of the information that Altfest is gathering in that initial conversation is captured and used in the planning process. "While on the phone, don't concentrate on typing notes into your computer," she advises. "That's a real turnoff for someone who's pouring out their heartfelt personal information and realizes you're typing, not focusing on them."

Nor does she offer any initial advice – for strategic reasons. "You never want to interrupt your callers," she says. "Sometimes when you're on a call with a new prospect it may seem to you, as it does to me, as if you've heard it all before. Yeah, yeah, I know you want to retire at 50. Your wife is a spender. You don't want to cut back on your lifestyle. Right? We've heard that. Let's get to the bottom line and start saving, whatever. That won't work," she says. "You may want to move the caller along to a conclusion. But you're going to do so at a great cost. Be patient. Try to find something you're interested in and delve further into their part of their tale."

Painless Extraction

Isn't this initial conversation getting more personal than the prospect will feel comfortable with? The best way to avoid the discomfort is to make sure the prospect is in total control of the information that is being exchanged. Altfest says this isn't as hard as it might sound. "They'll let you know if you're prying too much or if you hit a sensitive topic," she says. "Like a caller who said to me that her small son had recently died and that was why she wanted to come in. When I expressed sympathy because it sounded so moving and sad she clammed up. I felt a real chill on the line and I didn't say anything more about that. We talked about neutral things. It took her almost a year to tell me, when she was ready (I never asked) that her son had been in a pedestrian bus accident."

Ideally, this conversation will get the prospective client over several hurdles: first, the hurdle of connecting with a potential advisor, and second, the hurdle of opening up on very sensitive financial issues. "Recently, when a new client signed up," Altfest says, "she said it was because I had gotten so much personal information from her without any pain."

The Importance of Trust

Once the prospective clients come into her office, Altfest has them fill out a very brief questionnaire. "First we give them a little space to put things they know and don't have to think about and are comfortable with," she says, "like their name, address, phone. Not so much that we need that; it just lets them write something without feeling threatened."

Then the questionnaire gets down to business. It asks how they heard of Altfest's firm. "We want to know if they were referred by another client of ours or another colleague, or if they've read our name somewhere. We ask what motivated them to come, so we have a little glimmer of what we'll be discussing and what is of most concern to them. We ask what qualities they're looking for in an advisor so we know which of our skills and expertise we can stress during the meeting. And then we ask: what do you hope to get out of the meeting, so we can be sure we've covered all their issues and hit the main points before they go home that day."

Interestingly, some clients apparently come in not knowing for sure what they want from their financial advisor, so this gets them started in that thinking process. "Of all the words I've heard over the years," says Altfest, "the quality that stands out that people are looking for in an advisor is trust. That's the one that comes up most often, followed closely by synonyms for trust – reliability, honesty, and integrity. And following those," she says: "someone who's interested in me and my situation."

Conversational Marketing

Planners who have begun to offer life planning services report that the more of this service you offer, the easier it becomes to attract new clients. Even conversations with non-prospects turn up issues. Ted Roman recently talked with a

woman who could not be considered a hot planning prospect;
she was the wife of a fellow planner who happened to sit next to
him at a conference luncheon. "She asked me what I did, and I
told her that I did coaching and financial planning. She asked me
what coaching meant, and I asked her one of my questions," says
Roman: "If you could make a change in your life, and you knew
it would be successful, that you couldn't fail, what would you
do?"

The response was immediate. "She said, I'd write a book."
From there, the conversation went like this:

> "Why haven't you written a book before now?"

> "Because I'm supporting everybody else."

> "What do you mean?"

> "I mean I support my husband in his financial
> practice, and I support my family and their business,
> and my kids count on me. I am supporting everybody
> else in the things they want to do. I don't have time for
> myself."

> "If you decided to write your book, could you go
> to your husband and say, 'look, I really want to do this
> in my life, and I need some support from you. I'll sup-
> port you on the planning business, but when I need
> time to write, I will have access to it, and you will help
> me with the kids. Would he be willing to do that?'"

From there, the conversation turned to support groups and
professional writers organizations in her hometown, writers who
might be willing to mentor her – and in a half hour, Roman
reports, a significant goal in her life had taken shape – all before
the main course had been served. "She was energized and I was
too," he says. "But she may never carry through on that unless she

gets somebody to coach her or support her or mentor her," he warns. "She'll go back and get into the same muck again."

To veteran planners, this sounds an awful lot like the initial client interview – on steroids. In fact, another rule of thumb from the coaching profession is that the client should be doing 90% of the talking during these exploratory discussions. Roman admits that he has trouble keeping it to 75%, because of his financial consultant training and experience. "I always want to tell people a solution," he says. "But if people recognize that you are sincerely interested in their goals and ambitions, they'll go on and on with it."

The Personal Brochure

What about the client brochures and other information that you send to prospective clients? Are there any trends we can anticipate here?

In fact, the life planning movement appears to be making the planning relationship more personal – which suggests a more personal approach to introducing yourself and your firm. Peter Montoya, of Millennium Advertising, argues that your "brand" is really you, yourself, personally. "Has it ever happened that you've done a presentation, and in the end the person you were presenting to decided to work with you, or not, based on your personal image?" he asks rhetorically. "Everybody asks the same question: *Can I see myself doing business with this person?* If the answer is no, we look for some objective reason. But the truth is, prospects are buying into, or not buying into, your personal image."

From a marketing standpoint, what does that mean? It means that your brochure should be a clear reflection of the personal image that you want to present. You market yourself, rather than your services.

How? Montoya recommends something he calls the "personal brochure," which avoids any focus on products, designations and especially sales awards. Instead, it picks one focused benefit to working with you, which envisions a better life for the client after you start working together. And it tells a brief story about you, about how you got into the business and, perhaps, how you selected your personal mission statement. Inside the brochure somewhere is a picture of you unstiff, unposed, with your family, or if you don't have a family, with your dog. There's a display quote of the mission statement, and a caption on the picture that tells your name again, and the names of anybody else in the picture.

Montoya also warns against ever using "mug" shots in the brochure, which make the advisor look cheap and commoditized. He much prefers pictures of you walking with your spouse, talking with clients, on the beach flying a kite with the kids. "Every business relationship is personal," he says.

Conclusion: The Best of Times

Interestingly, the life cycle of the best planning firms follows a well-grooved course. You begin offering increasingly personal, increasingly client-focused advice and service, you get to a certain critical mass of clients, you start getting more referrals than you could plausibly handle, and you start thinking of ways to fend off more clients. You have more than enough.

Of course, you can't fend off everybody, and so many advisors begin culling their client list, taking on two new clients who they really enjoy working with, and then eliminating the clients who are less enjoyable. "Eliminating" how? Often by telling them that they've "graduated," that they don't need to work with you any more; they know how to do it on their own.

So the real question is "how do you get that critical mass of clients in the first place?" I think one of the best answers I've heard, from a variety of members of the *Inside Information* community, is that many advisors market at the wrong times.

Meaning what? Meaning here we are in the middle of the ugliest market downturn in a generation, when millions of people are scared, angry and confused.

Summarizing the words of 20 different remarkably similar responses, the advice of successful practitioners who are astute at marketing themselves is this: if you care about your clients, if you're good at what you do, and conscientious, and if you are really serious about this business, then this awful time right now is your best opportunity for success.

Come again? Aren't hard economic times hard on everybody? Not necessarily. In these hard economic times, there is always a flight to quality. Mediocre just doesn't cut it any more when the portfolio is down and there's anthrax in the mail.

So for some of you, this is not only a buying opportunity in the market, and a chance to keep your clients from losing even more by locking in their losses. It is a chance to get noticed for doing those things well. I suspect most of the people who read this book will benefit from this downturn if you see it for the opportunity that it is.

For you, the worst of times is the best of times.

Speaking from personal experience, I can tell you that these were not hard economic times for the members of the *Inside Information* community; it was, instead, one of those rare times in history when their knowledge and professionalism was really noticed.

And the opposite is true as well. If the planners down the street are avoiding their clients today, then today their clients are noticing more than they ever did before. If the planners on the other side of town are making frantic adjustments to their clients' portfolios, know that those clients are watching a little more carefully now than they were before.

In these difficult economic times, in the shadow of global terror, here's the best advice I'll give you all year: ask your clients to tell their friends about you.

Do it sooner rather than later, and tell them sincerely that you want to help as many people as possible get through this once-in-three-decades downturn. I think you'll be surprised at the response you get.

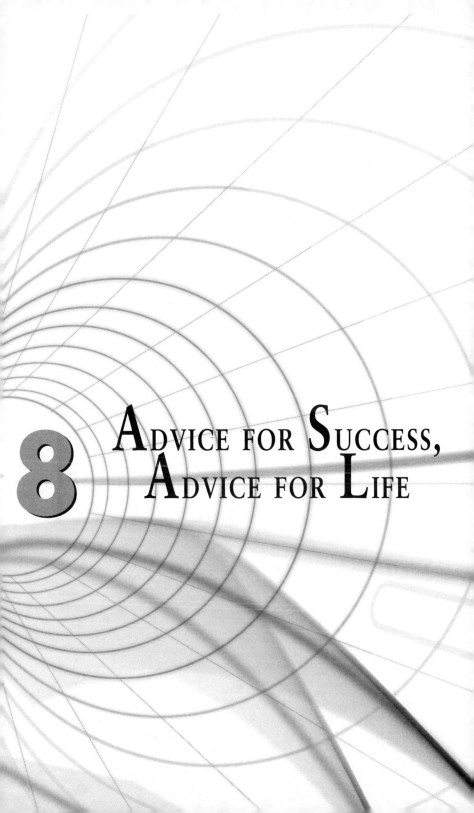

8 ADVICE FOR SUCCESS, ADVICE FOR LIFE

I think I know what you want from this book. You want the ways and means to enjoy a more successful practice, and a better life. You also want to do a better job of servicing your clients. And somewhere, somehow, you sense that you aren't getting straight answers from the trade press and the media generally.

Well, it's true. You aren't.

It's fun to bash the media for its shortcomings; I enjoy doing it myself from time to time. But the truth is, it's not the fault of the generally well-intentioned magazine publishers and newsletter editors. The people who can give you straight answers about the questions that really matter to you are your fellow practitioners – your soldiers-in-arms in this endless battle to make the world a safer place for the investment consumer.

I don't know you personally, but I can say with absolute certainty that you've learned more from a mentor in the industry than you've ever learned by reading – until now.

In my interactions with thousands of financial planners over 20 years, I've been fortunate enough to capture and relate the wisdom of what must be the wisest profession on this troubled little planet. And now, just for a moment, I'd like to give you some of the big picture lessons that these advisors have taught me, in a thousand different ways, over the course of my career. These are the themes of our professional life, the blood that runs in the veins of the *Inside Information* community, the background of all that we talk about. It is the "context" of the successful life and practice that you are now embarked on.

The Curse of Efficiency

The first big theme is to fight, hard, against the constant call for efficiency in your life and in your practice. Time and again, some commentator looks at the planning profession, with its millions of tiny individual firms, all practicing in a different way, all providing services by hand when these services could be manufactured in some home office, and declares that we are remarkably inefficient.

The big brokerage office down the street offers plans that are mass generated out of the home office, leveraging the skills of in-house CFPs, accountants and lawyers. As a result, it charges much less for these impressive-looking documents. Meanwhile, many advisors I talk to now generate financial "plans" that look more like two-page lists of goals, objectives and recommendations. Yet they are able to charge much more for these "plans" because they spend more time with the client, and because the services they provide are perceived to be more customized and individual.

My conclusion here is that maybe the planning profession doesn't really need to go overboard in its quest to get lean, leveraged and focused in order to meet the competition. In fact, I think you could argue that we need to be careful not to get too efficient.

What evidence supports this argument? A few professions have been where the planning profession is today – they listened to the experts of their day and became much more efficient. Early in the 20th century, the town banker was the trusted advisor of the community, the person people went to for advice about their finances and their lives. Then banks became more efficient. Today, a few million mergers later, trust officers have been replaced by 800 numbers, customers have to pay fees to access the ATM machine, and the terms "trusted advisor" and "bank" seldom appear in the same sentence.

Later in the 20th century, the trusted advisor was the town lawyer. Of course, this was before the law firm model took over the profession. Today you visit a lawyer only if you can't figure out a way around it.

I'm old enough to remember when the town's general practitioner doctor filled this same role: he made house calls, and, in addition to giving health advice, he was a general source of wisdom about broader life issues. Then the medical community became much more "efficient," and the personal relationship was replaced by the six-minute visit by a highly-leveraged doctor who comes in to go over the results of the tests that the nurses and nurses aides performed on you.

Each of these professions spent a wonderful decade or two in what I would call the "sweet spot" in American society, and each of them became more efficient and (for a time) vastly more profitable – with results that I would not define as positive. However, in each case, greater efficiency meant more revenues and a fatal loss of trust.

In my view, the goal is not to have the financial planning profession become more profitable, but to have it become the first profession to move into that sweet spot and refuse to budge. The profession that everybody wants is one that helps people live happier, more productive and more fulfilling lives. They will buy health services when they are sick; and they will buy legal services when they have to. They'll have a checking account and take out home loans. But these will always be peripheral to what they really want out of life.

I would argue that a planner couldn't camp out in the sweet spot in American life without embracing a kind of glorious inefficiency. If I were given the choice of working with a company that continued to offer generous client contact, or the really efficient niche advisory firm envisioned by some practice management specialists, I'd choose the first company every time.

The Road Never Before Traveled

In the same breath, these same industry commentators predict the day when "reality" will strike the financial planning profession. The default assumption seems to be that the profession will eventually "grow up" and fit itself into one of the well-defined models of other professions.

Yet Marty Moore, who practices in Charlotte, North Carolina, put his finger on one of the things that I hope we never lose, no matter how hard reality chases us: "The most disturbing part of [the industry analyses], and potentially the most damaging," he says, "is the prediction that we in the profession will soon become cutthroat competitors, unwilling to share our knowledge, our ideas and our experiences."

We assume that our willingness to share our insights and ideas with other professional colleagues will have to end, as the profession grows more competitive. However, that willingness to share, trade, exchange ideas and insights has helped the planning profession evolve faster than any comparable profession in the market. (Don't believe it? Look at the changes in the planning profession in the last ten years compared with doctors, lawyers, accountants or bankers.) The trend has been to provide more and better service, more and better advice, and to raise the profession's overall level of understanding at an astonishing rate.

This is a new path, and I don't think it has been explored before. I'd like to see us have the courage to say, "the hell with efficiency and cutthroat competition." Our professional evolution and the service we offer to our clients are both more important.

The planning profession, it seems to me, has reached a new stage of maturity and presence. Our ranks now include some larger financial services firms, and there are predictions that the future competitive landscape will force the rest of us to scrap the heart of the culture that got us here in the first place. But I wonder – if our culture is doomed to die, why are those larger competitors so interested in becoming more like us?

The High Cost of Broken Trust

As part of the *Inside Information* service, I review the contents of six consumer financial magazines, and provide links to the articles, so advisors can browse a monthly table of contents for the trade and consumer press in minutes, instead of days. It makes for a lot of reading on my part. I also read two others (for pleasure?) that cover personal finance on a fairly regular basis.

The "big story," as I write this, is the wave of corporate scandals that was touched off by the Enron mess. And as I sift through all the thousands of pages of analysis, it seems to me that the helpful investment advice that many financial magazines are delivering is that you probably shouldn't invest in Enron right now.

Behind this is a bigger picture – that over a period of years, the United States economic system has experienced a gradual, parallel, nearly total breakdown of the institutions that were created to provide accurate information to investors about the companies they invest in. Research analysts and talking heads on CNBC and CNNfn have promoted, rather than analyzed, because the "real" money wasn't in giving good information to consumers, but in winning investment banking business for their companies. These analysts were still chasing investment banking business well into the bear market, telling us to buy companies with no earnings or workable business plans long after these problems had become obvious to lay investors. With a little more vigilance, these people could have identified the accounting issues at Global Crossings and Worldcom; instead, they were too busy courting the companies' favor.

Meanwhile, accountants have long since learned that the real money is not in audits, but in consulting with their audit clients. The result is a system where companies and their consulting accountants are able to manage their earnings reports to within a penny of the estimates, and then another part of the accounting firm obediently signs off on the carefully crafted, not always truthful, and sometimes horribly misleading numbers.

In all of this, I think we've learned something very important: that there's always much more money to be made, short-term, by finding creative ways to pretend you're informing the investor/consumer when you're really serving another agenda entirely. The real money in our economic system is almost never to be found in the diligent promotion of openness, transparency and fairness.

Of course, these high, short-term returns come at a high risk. Unfairly, but perhaps inevitably, accountants in all walks of life are going to have their credibility tarnished by the various corporate scandals. Brokerage firms – who perpetrated the myth of independent analysis even after they were caught with their hands in the till – have become less credible even as they try to switch toward more consumer-friendly compensation structures. Ask Henry Blodgett (formerly of Merrill Lynch) how many investors are relying on his tech stock predictions these days.

I'd like to think that the net present value of maintaining your credibility is higher than chasing after the real money, but nobody I know has ever done a study of this. What I *do* know, however, is that public financial services companies and larger organizations seem to have a hard time breaking the habit of pretending to serve the public while continuing to serve other agendas, despite repeated scandals, negative press and eventual lawsuits.

The point for us is that organizations that follow the real money are a dime a dozen; it's a function of the business environment we live in. What is truly precious, extraordinary, and what builds long-term credibility is the profession, the firm and, most importantly, the professional who is suspicious whenever the real money shows its face, and who prefers to work for the interests of their clients and the public rather than follow their own interests exclusively.

If this describes you, I believe that individuals like you are in short supply. And I think the inevitable laws of supply and demand will reward you, and our little profession, for keeping trust when others are breaking theirs.

The Protection that Harms

But suppose we don't keep that trust – or, I should say, suppose we find that significant numbers of our profession have found a way to chase the "big money." What will the profession do then?

During the Enron scandal, and the scandals that followed, I've had a nagging feeling at the back of my mind. It was strongest while watching the C-SPAN coverage where members of Congress were questioning Arthur Andersen executives on why they felt such a compelling need to destroy those working papers before somebody at the Securities and Exchange Commission got hold of them. And then, suddenly, I realized where I had seen something eerily like this. I remembered the early days when I had just taken over as Editor of *Financial Planning* magazine in the mid-1980s, and began to read limited partnership prospectuses.

I learned several things from that exercise. First, the prospectus is not there to inform the consumer, but to wear him down with legalese and endless pointless disclosures that effectively hide the meaningful ones.

Second, I learned that you can make numbers say pretty much anything you want them to say – as in, for example, the projections at the back of these thick documents showing oil prices climbing inexorably into the stratosphere, going up every single year, totally ignoring the fact that the price of oil has historically moved in cycles for as long as there have been spot markets and warm winters. You could find the same thing with the projections on real estate properties – the rents always went up, year after year, for 20 years or more. Based on these happy assumptions, the investor always came out ahead in the end, when the properties were sold for an obscene profit, or the oil owned by the partnership was liquidated (pun intended) at ever-higher multiples of the current price at the pump.

And the third thing I learned was that you could always find an accounting firm willing to sign off on these fantastically misleading assumptions. If the numbers added up to whatever was written at the bottom of each column, then the accounting firm would, for a fee, provide a comforting letter (in the back of the prospectus) that inevitably read like an endorsement, certifying the numbers for these flagrantly misleading projections were all correct. I also remember that an uncommon number of these prospectuses were certified by Ken Leventhal & Associates, which seemed to specialize in handing out these letters to tax shelter sponsors. But virtually all of the accounting firms (referred to as the "Big Eight" back then) were represented in this interesting endorsement business.

After it was all over, and the projections didn't (to say it nicely) pan out exactly as predicted, hundreds of billions of investor dollars vaporized. The sponsors had allowed investors to think that they had vetted the projections, rather than simply having tabulated the columns. I remember wondering why nobody ever held the accounting firms responsible for putting a veneer of credibility on the most misleading part of so many misleading documents.

It was clear then – and it is clear now in the wake of the Sunbeam, Waste Management, Cendant, Enron, Global

Crossing, WorldCom, and whatever-is-next scandal – that the accounting profession has grown increasingly comfortable selling its hard won credibility to people who do not have any of their own and who need some in a hurry. No, it is not supposed to work that way, and yes, there are going to be painful corrections that will (I hope) at least temporarily restore some credibility to the broken system.

But I can't help thinking that if the leaders at the AICPA had been horrified at the accounting industry's complicity *before* the partnership debacle; or if the rank and file CPAs, who are now, unfairly, being tarred with the brush of these opportunists and credibility sellers, had just risen up and cast out of their midst everybody who exchanged credibility for cash – if, in other words, the profession had purged itself with the force of its own outrage, then we (i.e., Enron, Congress, investors, and the accounting profession) wouldn't be where we are today.

Trade and professional associations are often proud of their ability to protect their members from outside interference. I'm sure that if financial planners ever earn the kind of credibility that accountants have enjoyed, sooner or later the FPA and NAPFA will be called on to stand up for people who sold that credibility to very high bidders (as if this was a service to all members). I hope that when that day comes, we recognize that it is just the opposite – that protecting is perpetuating, and that the very best thing the profession can do for itself is make clear to the world that it will not tolerate such wolves to graze among the sheep.

The AICPA has done a tremendous disservice to its hundreds of thousands of honest, upright members by protecting the reputation of the profession when it should have been defending the profession's integrity instead; and I fear it is already down the same path again. We, however, in our still-young profession, can learn a great deal from that organization's mistake.

Conferencing to Success

How do people become successful in the financial planning business? Yes, hard work is necessary, but first you have to know how to apply that energy. Do you? Most don't. This is doubly interesting to me, because the planning profession is quietly (perhaps too quietly) evolving a process that brings hundreds of people to success and prosperity in this business. And it's so simple that anybody can do it. What is it?

The answer is simple – attending conferences.

Yes, you heard me right. You'll hear a million other answers, some of which are very technical and complicated and you would need an MBA to translate them into English, and others are useful buzz words like "emotional maturity" (which I suspect you are either born with or not). And all of them may get a few people to that same wonderful place at the top of the profession.

But this route seems to be surer and quicker than any of the others.

The trick is to get in the habit of attending professional conferences.

Why is this route such a certain road to success? The truth is, I'm not sure exactly how the mechanism works. My guess is that a few lucky advisors will get in the habit of attending when they're still struggling to get a foothold in their local market. They (like all of us) would run into some kind of business roadblock and (consciously or otherwise) mention the issue to the other practitioners they ran into at the conference.

This informal brainstorming would generate a variety of suggestions or examples of how they resolved the problem in their own practices. The people who are now on the Wealth Manager list would take this information back home – and, often as not, get around the roadblock after, often as not, putting in much more work than they expected.

Then they would go through the same process the following year, and the next, until most of the serious obstacles had been bulldozed out of the way, and they had somehow created a workable system that could be driven, however shakily, in the direction of business success. The great thing about it, these advisors tell me, is that the system continues to get smoother (or, at least, less shaky) as time goes on.

I'm going to go out on a limb here and call this process "team therapy." It is a big informal poorly organized support network for everybody who decides to attend. The point here is that most planners don't have access to it – by their own choosing.

The conferences would also give these people something that you rarely hear about in all the talk about educational sessions and exhibit hall experiences. A high percentage of the people you run into at these meetings have a lot of plain old-fashioned passion about what they do – and this passion is highly infectious. After a few conversations (and especially after a few dozen) you realize all over again why you got into this business in the first place.

At the same time, you are reinforced, over and over again, subtly and overtly, about the value of what you do for your clients – which makes you bolder about charging for your services and marketing to new prospects.

For the small business service provider, this regular infusion of passion and feedback about your value can be more important than oxygen.

Interestingly, those who become serious about attending these conferences will often take a step that brings them even more business skills and benefits: they volunteer their services with one of the professional organizations. Yes, it's time-consuming. But very few people you talk to would say they regret doing it, and most will say that they came out the other side better at what they do and more successful than when they started. Serving on this or that professional board puts them in another support group that tends to become almost like an extended family, that continues to function even after everybody has finally rolled back off the board.

It's hard to put a dollar value on something like that, but you're probably better off estimating on the high side.

Notice that every part of this formula is counterintuitive. You can become more successful more quickly by spending time away from the office attending a major professional conference, or by taking the time to read more, or by giving up weeks of your time to your professional association.

Your natural tendency, especially when your office gets busy, is to do exactly the opposite: to hole up in your office with the door closed and try to move the work off your desk. The success formula doesn't make sense, I have to admit, but you have to give at least a little credit to something that has actually worked, over and over again, in the real world.

So I invite you to the professional meeting of your choosing, and, more importantly, I invite you to join our dysfunctional little support network. Anybody with half a brain can join, and the only rule is that you have to give information as well as take it.

I guarantee you that the work will still be there on your desk waiting for you when you get back.

The Power of Integrity

One of the most interesting things I've learned from the *Inside Information* community is that "success" is not a destination that can be achieved. You struggle to get your business to the point where it makes a profit, and then, when you finally achieve consistent profitability, you struggle to get more clients. When you have more clients coming in the door than you can work with, you struggle to find more free time in your schedule, and at the same time, you search for ways to provide better and more meaningful client services.

The process never really ends.

You could say that these advisors are never satisfied, but I think a better way to describe it is that they never stop growing. You could say that they are on an endless treadmill, but a better way to say it is that they are on a journey that gets more interesting and satisfying the further they get.

So the question becomes: how can you accelerate your progress, no matter where you are in the journey? Is there any one insight that is just as important to the struggling idealist trying to make a profit, as it is to the established practitioner with a thriving business?

Until I talked with Janet Briaud, who practices in Bryan, Texas, I thought there was no one single insight that was equally important to everybody. But as we talked, I realized that the thing she focused on – her personal integrity – is something that all very successful planning practitioners have in common. I suspect you'll find a high level of what she calls "integrity" in virtually any successful person.

"Integrity" is kind of a slippery term – the sort of thing you might hear from a compliance officer or a management guru. But Janet has a very clear and very simple definition. Integrity, as she uses the term, simply means that there is always strong agreement between the things you think, say, feel and do, each and every day.

Doesn't everybody have this? No. Everywhere I go in the planning profession, I find people who would like to work one way, but actually practice another, because they have been told that they can't make a living unless they make certain compromises or accommodations.

People recommend products they don't quite believe in because there's more compensation attached. People who were happily commission-based have been told they have to take fees, even though they believe in their hearts that they should only get paid after the client has taken action.

People who would rather charge only fees still recommend commission products because they believe that's the only way they can get paid for serving nonwealthy clients.

People claim to have more expertise than they actually do, in order to attract wealthier (more lucrative) clients who they are always uncomfortable with afterwards.

People work for organizations they don't respect, or clear through firms that they have private doubts about.

I think you can see that this list could go on forever. The basic point is that the business world tempts us with compromises, and when we make those compromises, we become a little less credible to ourselves. We become a little less convincing to clients. We become a little less enthusiastic, a little less energetic, and a little less attractive to work for and with.

The successful advisors that I talk to will always, every one, tell a story of how they were told they couldn't do business the way they do. But they took a deep breath, ignored the voices that urged them to compromise, and plunged into the scary territory where they didn't know whether they'd succeed or fail.

Then they discovered something very powerful on the other side of the plunge: that because they really believed in what they were doing, people were more impressed and more comfortable with them. Their integrity – the agreement between their actions, their thoughts, their words and their spirit – was a powerful magnet that attracted clients and made for good business relationships in everything they did.

This is a powerful key to success – however you define the word. And until talking with Janet, I had never heard anybody talking about how important it is to pay conscious attention to your own integrity.

So now the question becomes: how do you get integrity? How do you get your words, actions, thoughts and spirit in increasing alignment?

I think you start by sitting down and confronting the issue directly. Take the time to make a (private) list of the things that you don't feel totally comfortable about in your business life, and the things you do that you don't totally, completely agree with.

What compromises have crept into your life and practice? One that Janet has noticed is that many planners are starting their practices without having totally mastered all the technical aspects of financial planning. For those people, she recommends a year of total immersion in books and articles on estate planning, investing, retirement planning, taxes, or any other subject you don't feel you've mastered completely.

Take courses. Go to conferences and take notes. With mastery comes confidence – which is a magnet for new business.

Some advisors will take a hard look at themselves. They'll realize that an advisor is really a natural specialist in one or two of these areas, and that he or she is really not interested in, say, insurance or tax planning/preparation. They could then increase

their confidence level in these areas by bringing in the best professional they can find from the community to work with their
clients. The result may be more respect in the community, more
confidence, and cross-referrals that build their practice to levels
they didn't imagine before. And, of course, better service for the
client.

What kind of clients are you working with? What kind of
clients would you work with if this were a perfect world?

What kind of products and services are you recommending?
Are there others that you would believe in more strongly?

Once you have the list, then comes the hard part. For each
item on the list, you gain integrity each time you take a deep
breath and make a change, even though others will always be
urging you against it.

You already know that nothing of importance comes easily
in this world, but from my talks with successful advisors, I am
beginning to realize that integrity is always rewarded. The place
on the other side of the plunge is business nirvana, and not
everybody will have the courage to reach it.

Why We Succeed and Why We Fail

A few years ago, I gave the *Inside Information* readers a
detailed review of the second FPA Retreat, which I thought (and
said) was one of the most perfectly-realized professional conferences that I've ever experienced.

But there was something I didn't say, either in the e-mail
message that they received, or the longer, more detailed report
that I sent to my subscribers. I think what I left out may have
been just as important as my coverage of the event itself.

The success of this special conference came, in good measure, from the previous Retreat in the spring of 2000, when Retreat Dean Ben Coombs tried to resurrect the meeting's original concept. At the time, I rated the 2000 Retreat good to excellent, but went on to say (correctly) that it didn't achieve its goal. However (and this is the important part) the various small failures of the 2000 Retreat allowed everybody – staff, volunteer planners and attendees – to examine what was still missing and what would be needed if the goal was ever going to become a reality.

There's a big, important lesson here, which is much too easy to ignore or forget. Whenever we (any of us) make a personal effort to reach an important or special goal, the first time we try it, we never, ever succeed. We always, every time, fall short of realizing the ideal that we have in our mind.

But that first effort, and those that come after it, are the foundation on which success is built.

I think you should stop, right here, and realize that most of the success stories you read about in the media are dangerous to your health – and misleading in the extreme. There are powerful dysfunctions in the way we think and report on events – dysfunctions, which bury this important truth and hide it from our conscious awareness. We celebrate only the times when people achieve success – and so the only time we ever become aware of a wonderful achievement is after it has happened, with little or no recognition of the long effort it took to make it happen.

This gives all of us the mistaken idea that success somehow springs up spontaneously in a few lucky people, and tends to make us impatient when we reach for our own visions, and encounter not success, but a succession of trials and errors that brings us slowly (sometimes painfully) closer to the goal we have in mind.

Because the achievement doesn't happen as quickly as we are taught to expect, many of us give up, thinking that we are on the wrong track when, in fact, we are on precisely the right one.

In every case, it is our persistence, and our willingness to put time and energy into something that doesn't succeed the first or the second or the third time, and our flexibility to change what isn't working, that transforms the vision we have in our minds into the reality of our lives.

These things – persistence, the willingness to set aside time apart from our daily tasks, and flexibility to try new things – are so unglamorous that we seldom talk about them, and few of us writers ever mention them when we are celebrating this or that achievement. Because of that, we mislead others and ourselves and cause many people to give up long before they could achieve what would have been wonderful and self-fulfilling goals.

This may be the only time you hear a writer confess that he has made the mistake of ignoring or glossing over the (boring) truth. And so I hope you will forgive me – and take this rare opportunity to engrave it on your heart in your own life.

And of course, I hope that you will pass it on to your clients, who are all struggling with the same cancerous doubt and uncertainty and conspiracy of silence about the real struggles that produce success.

The Last Words of a Friendship

We are now coming to the end of the book. Before you go away, I want to say I've enjoyed this brief time with you, and I hope you've enjoyed the experience of walking through the future at my side.

So (I ask myself), what should I say with just a few pages left? What are the most important things to communicate when time is so short?

At the end of a book, you experience the same questions that many of us will face at death.

I think the answer to these questions always comes from the heart, and it is never business-related. That, perhaps, tells us all we need to know about how to live our lives and how to set our priorities.

And so I want you to know that your world is changing, and to recognize that this is nothing new. If you look back just 15 years, you will see an entirely different profession. Back then, computerization was just beginning, and the standard financial plan was as thick as a telephone book. It was hard to track mutual fund performance, and planners explained their portfolio composition, not with asset allocation models, but by drawing investment pyramids.

Bigger changes await us in the future, and the future belongs to those who can adapt to them safely. Remember that, and keep your eyes open, and give advice only about things that you know very well, and you have most of this profession's keys to success.

There will be discussions that will outline the future, step by step, before it happens. You don't have to participate, and you certainly don't always have to agree. In fact, the best discussions we'll have next year in the *Inside Information* community will come from people who disagreed with me, and who were right.

Trust yourself to know what's right, and trust what your professional peers are saying more than the media pundits and talking heads.

Do your best for your clients, but don't forget to do good for yourself at the same time. You both deserve it.

I've learned some important lessons in the last few years, and in some cases I can even tell you where the lessons came from. Let me pass on their insights, giving credit where credit is due.

Ross Levin taught me the importance of focus. Most people waste an incredible amount of time – in front of the TV set, increasingly in front of the computer, and in more other ways than I could count here. Each of us has the same number of hours and minutes each week – you and many thousands of other planning professionals all around the country. If you take the time to determine what you really, really want to happen in your life, and redirect just a little bit of your wasted time in that direction, the difference can be enormous. It gives you an unfair advantage over everybody else.

Dick Zalack (a business coach) and Floyd Green (a remarkable planner who we met earlier) taught me that too many of us waste the limited time we have doing office chores that somebody on our staff could be doing, and we cling to these chores in the belief that nobody else could do them properly. Recognize that this is nonsense, and begin a journey of taking every task off of your desk except for spending time with clients and thinking about their situations.

A year from now, you'll be ten times as effective as you are today. Five years into this journey, your life will have become a remarkable adventure that everybody you meet will want to share.

Deena Katz taught me that it is important – even crucial – to budget a part of your time each week for nothing more than thinking about your business and your life. Make an appointment with yourself and keep it; make regular appointments with your staff, listen to their suggestions and give them the authority to change office procedures and make your business more efficient.

Don't let your weekly calendar be completely filled with chores; thinking time, time with no particular agenda so you can get your mind out of the box, is your most important work time.

George Kinder taught me that the most important thing successful people do is take the time to determine what they want to happen in their lives. This is the essence of the life planning service, but it's important for you to do it yourself first. If we in this profession are ever going to move to the next level, and help people use their financial resources to live better, more fulfilling lives, then we, ourselves, have to start living better, more fulfilling lives.

Bert Whitehead and Tracy Beckes taught me that every financial planner should have a financial planner.

Henry Montgomery taught me that financial planners should be bold enough to charge what their services are worth, because the work you do for your clients will be, over 10 or 20 or 30 years, the difference between somebody who lives a life of quiet financial desperation, and somebody who accumulates the resources to make work optional in his or her life.

Lew Wallensky once told me the story of two schoolteachers in the same high school; one hired him early in her career, and she retired a millionaire while the other teacher was still working so she could pay the bills.

Both your advice, and the work you do, are more valuable than you realize, and someday you will see it with your own eyes.

Several planners have taught me a lesson that I always seem to forget and have to relearn all over again: that if you take pride in being busy, and think that makes you important, then you will never get out of the drudgery of your office. Being really busy is not a goal, and it is does not make you important – it is a dysfunction to be cured.

A rabbi I met years ago, who was sent out to Oklahoma City to counsel and comfort the families of the victims who died in that terrible bombing incident, taught me one of the most powerful lessons you will ever hear. He said that he routinely, as part of his job, would sit with people in their last hours of life. And he said that never, ever once, did one of these people express regret for not having spent more time in the office. Give some of that wasted time back to your friends, family and loved ones, and make a place for them in your busy schedule.

As I look back on the most important lessons of life and business, I'm always surprised to see how few they are. Mastering the challenge of our lives is not really that complicated; the trick is not in the knowing, but in the remembering these important things when our desk is full of things to be done, and the doing when everything else is clamoring for your attention.

Finally, remember to respect the value of your attention. You, and all of us mortals (myself included), have only a certain amount of time in this world, which means that there is only so much of your attention to go around. Your attention is a valuable and nonrenewable resource, and it seems to me that far too many people, publications, pundits, advertising agencies, companies, billboards and gurus think they have a right to claim some of it.

I don't think you are doing a very good job of protecting your most precious commodity. You give it away far too often to people who are simply not worthy of it. I see magazine articles with screaming headlines that do nothing more than string together plausible-looking quotes and tell you things you already know, hoping to turn your attention to the advertisements on every other page. I hear speakers at local and national conferences give away a little information and a lot of promotional hype about themselves and/or their organization.

And I see well-meaning planners trying to stay on top of the news, when the news is mostly about white noise that has no long-term significance and is not worthy of their precious attention.

Once you realize the value of your attention, you start to see how many people want to steal it away from you and give you little or nothing in return. Sometimes, when I look at the world, I am amazed that so many of you are able to do as much as you do, with all the well-packaged distractions that are thrown in your way each and every day of your life.

A Last Gift

In these last few pages, I've tried to identify the things that I think are most important – about financial planning, about success, and about life. As a writer, I believe my job is to collect, from all the stray messages that surround us, those few which are relevant and important, and which have long-term significance to you and to the profession. Alas, very few of my fellow writers have this same regard for your attention.

And so this – my last piece of advice in this format – is a warning. If you want to be focused, effective and successful (however you define these terms), then you will need to stop giving away what is certainly your most precious resource, and learn to identify those who are worthy of your attention – and those who are not. As you pay attention to this issue, you will realize that some of your "friends" are taking from you far more than they give back, and that some of your clients are not honoring your advice and wisdom, which leaves you drained and frustrated. You will be surprised how few professional articles pass the "relevance" test.

And as you learn to give your attention the importance it deserves, and focus it on those people and messages that are worthy of it, you will find that the world becomes a much simpler, less cluttered and less confusing place. With this new clarity, it becomes much easier to achieve what you want, and to help others achieve what they want.

This is the gift I want to leave you with. If you honor your attention the way it deserves, then many obstacles will move out of your way.

As you learn to focus your attention, then those you decide to give it to – loved ones, friends, clients, and a few trusted information sources – will treasure it all the more.

In the course of your life, as you have thoughts, ideas, insights, questions or wisdom to share, I hope you will save my e-mail address, and send me these gifts so I can pass them on to others. My goal is to keep growing a community of ordinary people doing extraordinary things, and to help the planning profession spread this expanding recipe for success throughout the world.

I see an intensely bright future ahead. And I see you and your fellow professionals playing a significant role in making that future possible in the lives of the people you work with. Keep sharpening your saw, and the cutting edge – and the future of this remarkable profession – belongs to you.

Thank you again for your attention.

Bob Veres
bobveres@yahoo.com
http://www.bobveres.com

Index

U

V

W

Y

Z